BEST of the BEST
from
COLORADO

Selected Recipes from Colorado's
FAVORITE COOKBOOKS

BEST of the BEST
from
COLORADO

Selected Recipes from Colorado's
FAVORITE COOKBOOKS

EDITED BY

Gwen McKee

AND

Barbara Moseley

Illustrated by Tupper England

QUAIL RIDGE PRESS

Library of Congress Cataloging-in-Publication Data

Best of the Best from Colorado: selected recipes from Colorado's
favorite cookbooks / edited by Gwen McKee and Barbara Moseley;
illustrated by Tupper England.
   p. cm.
   ISBN 0-937552-84-4
   1. Cookery, American. 2. Cookery—Colorado. I. McKee, Gwen.
II. Moseley, Barbara.
TX715.B4856364 1998
641.5973--dc21
                                            98-22431
                                          CIP

QUAIL RIDGE PRESS
P. O. Box 123 • Brandon, MS 39043 • 1-800-343-1583
info@quailridge.com • www.quailridge.com

CONTENTS

Editor Gwen McKee with husband Barney, son Brian, and daughter-in-law Betsy, skiing Breckenridge.

PREFACE

Naturally blessed with beautiful mountain scenery, Colorado is one of the most picturesque states in America. In fact, "America the Beautiful," which describes the state's purple mountain majesty, was written atop one of Colorado's most famous mountains, Pikes Peak. Aside from the visual beauty, the sounds of Colorado are also awesome: quaking aspens, gurgling streams, an elk bugling, birds singing, a train whistle blowing . . . . It is common knowledge that the best skiing and hiking in the world can be found in Colorado. But what may not be quite so well known is that it is also the home of some of the best cooking and eating in the world. From farm-rich kitchens to five-star restaurants, recipes are handed down, created, spruced up, caloried down and exchanged over and again simply because they are so delicious. To be able to share these favorite Colorado recipes with you is indeed a pleasure.

If you had to give Colorado a "cuisine," it would probably be basically Southwestern—chili and beef and recipes that have been cooked on the ranch as well as the range. They like Tex-Mex and New-Mex, too; and certainly, this book attests to some of these terrific recipes like Rocky Mountain Campfire Chili, Working Barn Stew, Smoked Chicken Pesto Quesadillas, and "Way Out West" Spareribs. And Colorado's clear waters provide a bounty that certainly inspires good fish recipes. In the past agriculture dictated the fare, and still does, that being cattle, corn, wheat, oats, canteloupes, squash, pumpkins, potatoes, etc. But nowadays, dishes are derived from anything and everything—the sky's the limit, and Colorado has a very big sky! There's everything from Durango Meatballs to Pickaroon Potatoes, from Pikes Peak Spiked Apple Crisp to Spuddin' Spice Cake!

We loved discovering cookbooks from the Centennial state,

and consider ourselves privileged to have worked with new acquaintances and friends who have authored or edited or published these remarkable books that make up this collection. The Catalog of Contributing Cookbooks section beginning on page 259 lists each of the them, tells a little about them, and how you can order each book from them, which we encourage you to do. We wish also to thank the many tourist bureaus, chambers of commerce, newspapers, and persons throughout the state who graciously helped us in our research to make *Best of the Best from Colorado* truly representative of their state. Thanks also to our dependable, wonderful friend, Tupper England, whose art renderings always add to the flavor of the book.

There is a wonderful aura to Colorado that is unlike any other state. We hope this cookbook and its recipes will take you there through its beauty, its sounds, its smells . . . and its incomparable tastes.

Gwen McKee and Barbara Moseley

CONTRIBUTING COOKBOOKS

Aspen Potpourri
The Best of Friends
Beyond Oats
Cheesecake et cetera
Christine's Kitchen
Colorado Bed & Breakfast Cookbook
Colorado Boys Ranch Auxiliary Cookbook
Colorado Cache Cookbook
Colorado Collage
Colorado Columbine Delicacies
The Colorado Cookbook
Colorado Cookie Collection
Colorado Foods and More...
Colorado Potato Favorite Recipes
Cookie Exchange
Cooking with Colorado's Greatest Chefs
Country Classics
Country Classics II
Crème de Colorado Cookbook
Distinctly Delicious
Doc's Delights
The Durango Cookbook
Easy Recipes for 1, 2 or a Few
Eating Up the Santa Fe Trail
Fat Mama's Deli
The Flavor of Colorado
4-H Family Cookbook
Four Square Meals a Day
From an Adobe Oven to a Microwave Range
Goodies and Guess-Whats
Good Morning Goldie!
Grade A Recipes
Great American Beer Cookbook

CONTRIBUTING COOKBOOKS

Great Plains Cooking
Haute Off the Press
Home Cookin'
Home Cookin' Creations
How to Feed a Vegetarian
Italian Dishes et cetera
Kitchen Keepsakes
Kitchen Keepsakes by Request
Lighter Tastes of Aspen
Lowfat, Homestyle Cookbook
More Goodies and Guess-Whats
More Kitchen Keepsakes
More Than Soup Bean Cookbook
Mountain Cooking and Adventure
Mystic Mountain Memories
Nothin' but Muffins
101 Ways to Make Ramen Noodles
Palates
Pure Gold—Colorado Treasures
Quick Crockery Cooking
Raspberry Story
Recipes from Our House
Shalom on the Range
Sharing Our Best
Sharing Our Best/Muleshoe Ranch
Simply Colorado
Southwestern Foods et cetera
Special Diet Solutions
Steamboat Entertains
Taking Culinary Liberties
West of the Rockies
What's Cookin' in Melon Country
Wheat-Free Recipes and Menus

Beverages
and
Appetizers

The quiet beauty of Rocky Mountain National Park.

Hot Apricot Buttered Rum

1/4 cup packed brown sugar
2 1/2 cups water
1/2 stick unsalted butter,
  cut in bits
1/2 tablespoon cinnamon
1/4 tablespoon fresh grated
  nutmeg

3 whole cloves
1/2 cup dark rum
1/4 cup apricot flavored
  brandy
Fresh lemon juice
4 sticks cinnamon

In a saucepan, stir together brown sugar, water, butter, cinnamon, nutmeg, and cloves. Simmer for 5 minutes, stirring occasionally. Stir in rum, brandy, and lemon juice. Divide among 4 heated mugs and insert cinnamon stick. Makes 4 servings.

What's Cookin' in Melon Country

Chocolate Nog

1 quart eggnog
1 (5 1/2-ounce) can
  chocolate syrup

1/4 cup creme de cacao
1 cup whipping cream
Chocolate curls, optional

Combine eggnog, chocolate syrup, and creme de cacao; cover and chill. Before serving, beat whipping cream to soft peaks. Reserve 1/2 cup of the whipped cream for garnish. Fold the remaining whipped cream into the eggnog mixture. Pour into serving glasses. Dollop with reserved whipped cream. Garnish with chocolate curls. Makes 12 (4-ounce) servings.

Sharing Our Best

Amaretto Slush

2 cups amaretto
1 (16-ounce) can frozen
  orange juice
1 (16-ounce) can frozen
  lemonade

7 cups water
1 tablespoon instant iced tea
1/2 cup sugar
2 liter bottle 7-Up

Blend together, except 7-Up, and freeze. When ready to serve, add 7-Up.

Home Cookin'

A Punch for All Seasons

1 large package orange Jell-O	1 large can pineapple juice (not frozen)
3 cups hot water	1 large can frozen lemonade
3 cups sugar	6 cups cold water
1 large can orange juice (not frozen)	Ginger ale or 7-Up soda, to taste

Dissolve Jell-O in hot water. Stir in sugar until it dissolves. Add juices and frozen lemonade. Add cold water. Freeze in a large Tupperware bowl. To serve: Let punch defrost for an hour or two. Shave with a large spoon into punch bowl. Add ginger ale or 7-Up and stir until slushy. Makes 50 servings.

Note: A red Jell-O and cranberry juice can be substituted for orange Jell-O and pineapple juice. *Recipe from Silver Wood Bed & Breakfast, Divide.*

Colorado Columbine Delicacies

Mock Sangria

Tastes better than the real thing.

1 (40-ounce) bottle un-sweetened white grape juice, chilled	1 (33.8-ounce) bottle club soda, chilled
1 (32-ounce) bottle apple-cranberry juice, chilled	Seedless green grapes
1/2 cup lime juice, chilled	Sliced limes
	Sliced oranges

Combine juices. Just before serving, add club soda; stir and garnish. Yields 14 cups.

Per serving: Cal 47; Fat 0g; Chol 0mg; Sod 10mg.

Simply Colorado

Gluhwein

This hot spiced wine is a favorite after-skiing drink. One cup boiling water to which add a thick slice of lemon, 4 cloves, and 2 cinnamon sticks—boil 5 minutes. Then add 2 cups of any heavy red wine, (Marca Petri is good) and sugar to taste. Reheat, but do not boil.

Aspen Potpourri

Camp Fire Coffee

Here's an old-timers' recipe for camp fire coffee (yes, you actually crush up a whole egg—shell and all—into the grounds).

2 quarts cold water   **1 cup ground roasted coffee**
1 egg   **½ cup cold water**

Heat a pot of cold water to boiling. (Allow to boil only 2-3 minutes.) Place a cup of ground coffee and an egg in the middle of a piece of cheesecloth and tie the cheesecloth into a sack. Then break the egg in the sack and mix with the coffee by massaging the bag. Drop the sack into the boiling water and cook for 4 minutes. Add ½ cup cold water to settle any grounds. The coffee is absolutely superb.

Eating Up The Santa Fe Trail

Heavenly Fruit Dip

1/2 cup sugar	1 tablespoon butter or
2 tablespoons flour	margarine
1 cup pineapple juice	1 cup whipping cream,
1 egg, beaten	whipped

Combine sugar, flour, juice, egg, and butter in heavy saucepan. Cook over medium heat, stirring constantly until smooth and thick. Let cool completely. Fold in whipped cream. Serve with fresh fruit—especially good with sliced apples.

Note: Use 1/2 cup orange juice and 1/2 cup pineapple juice instead of all pineapple juice. Also use 2 cups nondairy whipped topping instead of 1 cup whipped cream.

More Goodies and Guess-Whats

Summer Pizza

Use your imagination with this one!

2 packages crescent rolls	1 teaspoon garlic salt
2 (8-ounce) packages cream cheese, room temperature	3/4 teaspoon dill
	1/4 cup chives, finely
2/3 cup mayonnaise	chopped
1 teaspoon cayenne pepper or Tabasco to taste	Toppings (see list below)
	Monterey Jack or Cheddar
1 teaspoon onion salt	cheese

Unroll crescent rolls and lay in a 13x9-inch baking dish with flat sides touching. Bake at 350° for 18-20 minutes or until golden. Combine cream cheese, mayonnaise, spices and chives. Spread onto cooled crescent rolls. Top with desired toppings; top with cheese, if desired. Cut into 2x2-inch squares and serve.

Toppings: raw vegetables such as chopped broccoli, cauliflower, mushrooms, green pepper, etc.; small canned shrimp; sliced black olives; cocktail onions; sliced cherry tomatoes.

Steamboat Entertains

Baked Brie with Caramelized Apple Topping

A perfect paring of flavors and textures.

1 large Granny Smith
apple, peeled, cored
and coarsely chopped
(about 2 cups)
½ cup pecan pieces

⅓ cup (packed) brown
sugar
2 tablespoons Kahlua
1 (about 2-pound) wheel
brie, rind left on

Mix apple with pecans, brown sugar, and Kahlua. Set aside. Place brie in shallow, oven-proof dish; top with apple mixture. Bake at 325° 10-15 minutes, or until topping is bubbly and cheese is softened. Serve with lavosh or water crackers. Makes 16-20 servings.

Palates

Colorado has two national parks, six national monuments, eleven national forests, forty state parks, and three national recreation areas, creating a vast outdoor playground for every type of recreation imaginable. More than half the state is public land.

Kahlua Pecan Brie

3 tablespoons packed
   brown sugar
¹/4 cup Kahlua or strong,
   freshly brewed coffee,
   cooled

³/4 cup pecan halves,
   toasted
1 (16-ounce) round brie
   cheese

In medium skillet, combine brown sugar and Kahlua. Heat, stirring constantly, until blended. Add pecans, simmer until hot, but not runny. Remove from heat.

Place brie on microwave-safe serving plate and spoon warm pecan mixture on top. Microwave on HIGH 1-2 minutes, or until cheese softens. Watch carefully, cheese will melt quickly. Serve with crackers and fresh fruit. Makes 8-10 servings.

Colorado Collage

Bread Pot Fondue

This is great to make ahead and heat before you need it.

1 firm, round loaf of bread
   (1¹/2 pounds, 8-10 inches in diameter)

Slice off top of bread loaf, reserving top. Hollow out inside of loaf with small paring knife, leaving ½-inch shell. Cut the removed bread into 1-inch cubes to serve later.

FILLING:

2 cups mild Cheddar
   cheese, shredded
2 (3-ounce) packages
   cream cheese, softened
1¹/2 cups sour cream
1 cup ham, cooked and
   diced
¹/2 cup chopped green onions

1 (4-ounce) can chopped
   green chilies
1 teaspoon Worcestershire
   sauce
Assorted raw vegetables
Cubed bread and crackers
   for dipping

Combine cheeses and sour cream in bowl; stir in remaining ingredients except raw vegies and dippers. Spoon filling into hollowed loaf; replace top. Wrap loaf tightly with several layers of heavy-duty aluminum foil; set on cookie sheet. Bake at 350° for 70 minutes or until filling is heated through. Remove loaf from oven and unwrap. Place on a platter and serve with fresh vegetables, cubed bread and crackers.

Country Classics II

"Twilight in the Rockies" Cocktail Kebabs

1/2 cup oil
1/2 cup soy sauce
1 tablespoon sherry
5 tablespoons brown sugar
1 teaspoon prepared
  mustard
1 garlic clove, finely minced

1 - 11/2 teaspoons red chili
  pepper, crushed
2 pounds elk, deer or beef
  steaks, sliced across the
  grain diagonally into
  paper-thin strips
  (4x1x1/4 inches)

Blend all ingredients, except steak, for marinade. In shallow pan, place meat strips and cover with marinade. Marinate steaks 20 minutes, turning to coat. Thread strips of meat on pre-soaked bamboo skewers (to prevent burning). Brush with marinade. Broil quickly on hibachi or grill over hot coals until done, approximately 5 minutes, turning and basting. Yield: 18-20 appetizers.

Colorado Foods and More. . .

Five-Layer Mexican Dip

You'll find that they won't leave this dip alone.

1 (15-ounce) can fat-free
  refried beans
1/2 cup mild salsa
1/2 ripe avocado
1/2 cup plain nonfat yogurt

2 cups lettuce, shredded
1/2 cup tomatoes, chopped
1 ounce sharp reduced-fat
  Cheddar cheese, shredded

In a small bowl, mix together beans and salsa. In a separate bowl, blend together the avocado and yogurt. In a shallow serving dish, layer ingredients beginning with the bean mixture. Top with avocado sauce, then cover with lettuce, tomato and cheese. Yields 5 cups.

Per serving: Cal 45; Fat 1g; Chol 0mg; Sod 36mg.

Simply Colorado

Guacamole Dip

4 bacon strips	1/4 teaspoon salt
2 avocados (ripe)	Pepper
1/8-inch slice onion, minced	1/4 teaspoon chili powder
Tabasco (2 dashes)	1 clove garlic, finely minced
	Mayonnaise

Fry bacon until crisp, crumble and set aside. Mash avocados, then add finely minced slice of onion, Tabasco, salt, pepper, chili powder, and garlic clove. Stir all together well, put into a small bowl and cover top completely with mayonnaise so that no air reaches avocado. Just before serving, stir mayonnaise and crumbled bacon bits into the avocado mixture. Serve with Fritos, potato chips or crackers.

The Best of Friends

Sheep Dip
(Artichoke Cheese Dip)

This recipe is the product of a number of people. My mother came up with the idea and coached the chef who added together the right ingredients. I came up with the name as a joke since my father had been a sheep rancher for 50 years. We forgot to change the name in the final printing of the menu, but it sure draws attention to our best-selling item.

1 (8-ounce) can water-packed artichoke hearts	20 ounces sour cream
6 ounces Asiago cheese or Parmesan cheese	24 ounces cream cheese
3 ounces fresh spinach, washed and patted dry	8 ounces whipping cream
1 pint half-and-half	4 bags of pita bread with each pita cut into 2-inch wedges

Blend together all ingredients (except pita bread) in food processor or blender until smooth (you will still have chunks of artichoke). Serve warm with side of toasted pita wedges. Yields one gallon of dip. *Recipe by Georgann Jouflas, owner of River City Cafe and Bar.*

West of the Rockies

Prospector's Gold Nuggets

¹/₂ cup soft butter
2 cups Cheddar cheese
  grated
¹/₂ teaspoon dry mustard
1 tablespoon canned green
  chilies, minced (or
  jalapeños)

1 teaspoon Worcestershire
  sauce
3-4 drops Tabasco
Pinch cayenne pepper
¹/₂ teaspoon onion salt
1¹/₄ cups flour

Blend together butter, cheese, mustard, chilies, Worcestershire sauce, Tabasco, cayenne, and onion salt until well-mixed. Add flour to make a stiff dough. Roll into balls. Place on ungreased cookie sheet and press lightly with tines of a fork. Bake at 350° about 15 minutes until lightly browned. Serve hot. Yield: 3½ dozen.

Colorado Foods and More. . .

Miners who went in search of Colorado gold were of many creeds, colors, and backgrounds. They brought traditions and family recipes from their native lands.

Spinach Balls

10 ounces fresh or frozen
  spinach, chopped
¹/₂ large onion, minced
2 eggs, beaten
¹/₃ cup butter, melted

¹/₄ cup Parmesan cheese
¹/₂ clove garlic, minced
¹/₂ teaspoon thyme
¹/₂ teaspoon pepper
1 cup stuffing mix, crushed

Cook spinach and squeeze dry. Mix together the spinach, onion, eggs, butter, cheese, garlic, thyme, and pepper. Add stuffing crumbs and mix thoroughly. Shape into ½-inch balls and chill for several hours to blend flavors or freeze for later use. Bake in a 350° oven for 15 minutes, or 20 minutes if frozen. Yields 8 dozen.

The Colorado Cookbook

Potato Pancake Appetizers

3 medium Colorado russet
  variety potatoes, peeled,
  grated
1 egg
2 tablespoons flour
1 teaspoon salt
¹/₄ teaspoon pepper
1 cup (1 large) carrot, grated
1¹/₂ cups (2 small) zucchini,
  grated

Olive oil
¹/₂ cup low-fat sour cream
  or plain yogurt
2 tablespoons basil, finely
  chopped plus 1
  tablespoon chives,
  chopped or 1¹/₂ teaspoons
  chili powder or curry
  powder

Preheat oven to 425°. Wrap grated potatoes in several thicknesses of paper towels; squeeze to wring out liquid. In a bowl, beat egg, flour, salt and pepper. Add grated potato, carrot, and zucchini; mix together. Oil 2 non-stick baking sheets. Portion a heaping measuring tablespoon of vegetable mixture onto baking sheets; flatten to make pancakes. Bake 8-15 minutes, until bottoms are browned. Turn and bake 5-10 minutes more. Stir together sour cream and desired herbs or seasonings. Serve pancakes warm with a dollop of herb cream. Makes about 24 appetizer pancakes.

Per serving: Cal 29; Prot .95g; Carbo 4g; Fat .90g; Chol 11mg; Sod 96mg; Dietary Fiber .51g.

Colorado Potato Favorite Recipes

Hot & Spicy Ribbon Chips

6 medium Colorado russet
  variety potatoes
Oil for frying
1 tablespoon chili powder

1 teaspoon salt
1 teaspoon garlic salt
1/4-1/2 teaspoon cayenne
  pepper

With a vegetable peeler, peel thin strips of potatoes lengthwise to make ribbons, or with a knife, cut potatoes into very thin lengthwise slices. Place in 1-quart ice water mixed with one tablespoon salt. Heat oil in a deep-fat fryer or heavy pan to 365°. Combine chili powder, salt, garlic salt, and cayenne pepper; set aside. Drain potatoes and pat dry with paper towels. Fry potatoes in batches until golden and crisp; remove to paper towels. Season with chili mixture. Makes 8-12 servings.

Per serving: Cal 91; Prot 2g; Carbo 14g; Fat 3.5g; Chol 0mg; Sod 343mg; Dietary Fiber 1.3g.

Colorado Potato Favorite Recipes

Potato Supremes

4 Colorado russet variety
  potatoes
Salt and pepper
8 teaspoons whole seed or
  grainy mustard

6 ounces brie cheese
2 tablespoons chives or
  green onion tops, finely
  chopped

Heat oven to 400°. Prick potatoes in 5 or 6 places with the tines of a fork. Bake potatoes 50-60 minutes, until tender and skins are crisp. Cut crosswise into 4 thick slices. With a melon baller or small spoon, scoop out a little potato from the center. Season with salt and pepper; spread each hollowed-out center with 1/2 teaspoon mustard. Cut up brie into 16 chunks; place one piece in each center. Sprinkle with chives. Place on baking sheet. Bake 15-20 minutes until cheese has melted and browned in spots. Serve warm. Makes 16 appetizers.

Per serving: Cal 93; Prot 3.5g; Carbo 13g; Fat 3g; Chol 10.6mg; Sod 103.6mg; Dietary Fiber 1.2g.

Colorado Potato Favorite Recipes

Crab Rangoon

1 (8-ounce) package cream cheese
1 can chopped crab meat
1 tablespoon garlic clove, mashed
1/4 teaspoon Worcestershire sauce
3 drops Tabasco sauce
1/2 teaspoon salt
1/2 teaspoon white pepper
Won ton skins

Mix together until smooth and fluffy. Put 1½ teaspoons mixture in center of won ton skin. Wet edges with water and press edges together. Deep-fry until golden brown.

Mountain Cooking and Adventure

Legendary Crab Rounds

Simple to prepare and absolutely fantastic.

1 cup mayonnaise
1/2 cup grated onion
1 cup shredded Cheddar cheese
6 drops Tabasco sauce
1/4 teaspoon curry powder
1 (6½-ounce) can crab meat, drained
2 French bread baguettes, sliced 1/2-inch thick

In medium bowl, combine mayonnaise, grated onion, Cheddar cheese, Tabasco, curry powder, and crab meat. This may be made one day in advance. To serve, place mixture on bread rounds and broil until golden brown. Serve immediately. Makes 50-55 rounds.

Crème de Colorado

Hot Mushroom Turnovers

1 (8-ounce) package cream cheese, softened
1½ cups + 2 tablespoons all-purpose flour
½ cup + 3 tablespoons butter or margarine, softened

½ pound mushrooms, minced
1 large onion, minced
¼ cup sour cream
1 teaspoon salt
¼ teaspoon thyme leaves
1 egg, beaten

In large bowl with mixer at medium speed, beat cream cheese, 1½ cups flour, and ½ cup butter until smooth; shape into ball. Wrap; refrigerate one hour. In 10-inch skillet over medium heat, in 3 tablespoons hot butter or margarine, cook mushrooms and onion until tender, stirring occasionally. Stir in sour cream, salt, thyme, and 2 tablespoons flour; set aside.

On floured surface with floured rolling pin, roll half of dough ⅛-inch thick. With floured 2¾-inch round cookie cutter, cut as many circles as possible; repeat with other half of dough. Preheat oven to 450°. Place one teaspoon of mushroom mixture on ½ of each dough circle. Brush edges of circles with egg; fold dough over filling. With fork, firmly press edges together to seal; prick tops. Place on ungreased cookie sheet; brush with remaining egg. Bake 12-14 minutes until golden. Makes about 3½ dozen.

Note: You can freeze turnovers, unbaked, then pop frozen turnovers right in the oven—just bake a bit longer.

Home Cookin'

Crab Stuffed Mushrooms

1/3 cup green pepper,
  minced
1/3 cup red bell pepper,
1/4 cup onion, minced
2 cloves garlic, minced
1/2 cup unsalted butter
1 egg, beaten

1/4 cup freshly grated
  Parmesan cheese
1/3 cup lump crab meat
1/8 teaspoon cayenne pepper
1/2 cup bread crumbs
24 firm white mushrooms

Sauté peppers, onion, and garlic in 1/4 cup butter until soft. Remove from heat and add egg, cheese, crab meat, cayenne, and bread crumbs. Remove stems from mushroom caps. Melt remaining butter and dip each cap in melted butter. Stuff with crab meat stuffing. At this point, can be refrigerated up to 3 days. Bake at 400° until lightly browned on top. Serve immediately. Makes 2 dozen.

Steamboat Entertains

Bacon Filled Cherry Tomatoes

1 pound bacon, fried
  and crumbled
1/4 cup green onions,
  chopped

2 tablespoons parsley,
  chopped
1/2 cup mayonnaise
24 cherry tomatoes

Combine ingredients except tomatoes. Cut a thin slice off top of each tomato. With a small spoon or melon baller, hollow out tomato. Fill tomatoes with bacon mixture. Make these when you are alone because your family will eat them faster than you can put them together! These were always a favorite when we catered parties. Makes 24.

Country Classics

Livestock and livestock products account for 70% of Colorado's agricultural income. Its main products are beef cattle, corn, hay, wheat, and milk.

Tortilla Pinwheels

1 (8-ounce) carton sour
  cream
1 (8-ounce) package cream
  cheese
1 (4-ounce) can chopped
  green chiles, drained
1 (4-ounce) can chopped
  black olives, drained

1 cup grated Cheddar
  cheese
1/2 cup chopped green onions
Garlic powder to taste
Seasoned salt to taste
5 (10-inch) flour tortilla
  shells

Mix all filling ingredients together. Divide and spread over tortilla shells. Roll up shells and cover tightly with plastic wrap, twisting ends. Refrigerate for several hours. Cut into slices 1/2 - 3/4 inch thick. Serve with salsa.

Doc's Delights

Smoked Chicken Pesto Quesadillas

If you really want to dazzle your friends, make this as an appetizer. The flavors meld beautifully. Be sure to make enough because it goes quickly.

8 ounces Pesto, homemade
  or good quality brand
8 (8-inch) flour tortillas
1 (8-10-ounce) smoked
  chicken breast, (or turkey),
  pulled into thin shreds

3/4 pound Provolone, or
  combine Provolone and
  mozzarella, grated
Mazola oil

Spread 3 heaping tablespoons of pesto on each tortilla. Divide the chicken breast shreds over the pesto on each tortilla. Sprinkle 1/3-1/2 cup of cheese over the chicken. Place another tortilla on top. Heat 1/8 inch of oil in a black iron frying pan and heat each side until golden brown and the cheese is melted. Serves 8-12 as an appetizer or can be used as a main course.

Lighter Tastes of Aspen

Dolmathes

(Spiced Grape Leaves)

FILLING:

2 pounds ground lamb
2 large onions, finely
   chopped or grated
1 clove garlic, minced
1/2 cup minced or chopped
   fresh parsley or 3
   tablespoons dried
1/2 cup white rice, uncooked

2 eggs
2 tablespoons minced mint
   or 1 tablespoon dried
Salt and pepper to taste
1 jar grape leaves (about
   60 grape leaves)
2-3 quarts chicken broth

Combine all ingredients except grape leaves and chicken broth. Drain and rinse grape leaves in water; separate. Measure 1 teaspoon full of filling to form a ball. Place into bottom corner of grape leaf. Fold over, fold in sides and roll up so that no meat is exposed. Place together in saucepan in even layers. Add enough broth to cover rolls, and place a small plate directly over rolls with a small jar or glass full of water to weigh them down. Cover and simmer for 1 1/2 hours. These may be served with the following Avgolemono (egg/lemon) sauce, or placed on serving plate and sprinkled with olive oil and served with plain yogurt as a dipping sauce. Easy at last minute. Makes about 60.

Note: Can use whole cabbage leaves steamed and removed from the head.

AVGOLEMONO SAUCE (EGG LEMON SAUCE):

2 1/2 cups chicken broth
4 eggs

1/3 cup lemon juice
1 tablespoon cornstarch

In a small saucepan, bring broth to a boil. In a blender, combine eggs, lemon juice, and cornstarch. Slowly add to hot broth, stirring constantly so that eggs won't curdle. Stir over low heat until thickened. Pour over meat rolls and serve hot.

Christine's Kitchen

Smoked Salmon Quesadillas

Great instead of bread with a spinach salad, or with a main course salad for a luncheon.

4 (10-inch) flour tortillas	**¹/₄ cup minced green onion**
5 ounces goat cheese,	**1¹/₂ tablespoons fresh dill or**
softened	**1¹/₂ teaspoons dried**
¹/₄ pound smoked salmon	**Capers, optional**

Spread half of each tortilla with ¼ of goat cheese. Top with ¼ salmon, onion, and dill. Sprinkle with capers, if desired. Fold tortillas in half and place on cookie sheet. Bake in preheated 500° oven for 5 minutes or until heated through and crisp. Cut in wedges to serve. Makes 10 servings.

Shalom on the Range

Spicy Black Bean and Corn Salsa

A delightfully colorful change to traditional salsa.

16 ounces cooked black	**¹/₃ cup fresh lime juice**
beans	**3 tablespoons vegetable oil**
16 ounces fresh or frozen	**1 tablespoon ground**
corn kernels	**cumin**
¹/₂ cup chopped fresh	**Salt and freshly ground**
cilantro	**black pepper**
¹/₄ cup chopped green	**¹/₂ cup chopped ripe**
onion	**tomatoes, drained**
¹/₄ cup chopped red onion	

In large bowl, combine beans, corn, cilantro, green onion, red onion, lime juice, oil, and cumin. Season with salt and pepper to taste. Cover and chill at least 2 hours or up to overnight. Just before serving, stir in tomatoes. Serve with blue and white corn chips. Makes 4-6 cups.

Colorado Collage

Baked Artichoke Hearts

1 can artichoke hearts
Melba toast rounds,
  rye or white
1/4 pound melted butter
Salt

Freshly ground pepper
Garlic powder to taste (about
  1/4 teaspoon)
Slivered almonds or sesame
seeds

Drain artichoke hearts and cut in half with shears. Place each half, cut-side-up, on a Melba round. Arrange on oven-proof dish on which they can be served. Melt butter and add salt, pepper, and garlic powder. Spoon generously over artichokes. Sprinkle with almonds or sesame seeds and bake at 350° for 10 minutes.

From an Adobe Oven to a Microwave Range

Spiced Meat Triangles

1 onion, finely chopped or
   grated
2 cloves garlic, minced
3 tablespoons olive oil
1 pound ground lamb
2 tablespoons minced or
   chopped parsley
8 ounces tomato sauce
1 cup dry wine

¹/₃ teaspoon cinnamon
¹/₂ teaspoon cumin
¹/₂ teaspoon allspice
Salt and pepper to taste
4 tablespoons grated Parmesan
   cheese
¹/₂ pound filo dough
¹/₂ pound butter, melted

Sauté onion and garlic in oil until tender. Add ground lamb
and sauté until browned; spoon excess fat from skillet. Add
remaining ingredients except for cheese, filo and butter. Cook
over medium-low heat until liquid is absorbed and mixture is
thick. Let cool. Add cheese. Unwrap filo dough and keep
moist by covering with slightly dampened towel. Using one filo
sheet at a time, brush with melted butter. Cut filo lengthwise
into 4 even strips. Fold bottom of strip over ¼ of itself and
center ³/₄ teaspoon of mixture on folded end of strip. Fold strip
end over to form a triangle shape or use two sheets of filo for
stronger triangle. Continue folding strip until you have formed
a completed triangle shape. Repeat instructions until all pieces
are formed.

Arrange triangles 1 inch apart in a buttered cookie pan.
Brush with butter and bake in preheated 350° oven until golden
and puffed (15 minutes). Makes 60 pieces. These can be made
ahead of time and refrigerated for several hours, or frozen.

Christine's Kitchen

Curried Chutney Spread

2 (8-ounce) packages cream
   cheese
¹/₂ cup Major Grey's chutney
¹/₂ teaspoon dry mustard

¹/₂ cup chopped almonds,
   toasted
1 teaspoon curry powder

Bring cream cheese to room temperature. Mix all ingredients
together well. Pack in a crock. Chill. Serve with crackers, or
use spread to stuff dates or celery. Makes 3 cups.

Colorado Cache Cookbook

Bread and Breakfast

The striking cadence and contemporary architecture of the Air Force Academy near Colorado Springs.

Focaccia

Focaccia is a cross between pizza and rustic flat bread. It's fairly easy to make and the dough is especially forgiving. At serving time, dip it in flavored olive oil or spaghetti sauce—just like the Italian restaurants!

1 teaspoon sugar	1 teaspoon dried rosemary
³/4 cup warm water (105°)	¹/4 teaspoon onion powder
1¹/2 teaspoons dry yeast	³/4 teaspoon salt
1 cup brown rice flour	2 large eggs
¹/4 cup potato starch flour	2 tablespoons olive oil
¹/4 cup tapioca flour	¹/2 teaspoon cider vinegar
1¹/2 teaspoons xanthan gum	1 tablespoon cornmeal
1 teaspoon unflavored gelatin	(optional)
powder	

TOPPING:

1 teaspoon Italian seasoning   1 tablespoon olive oil
¹/4 teaspoon salt

Dissolve sugar in warm water. Sprinkle yeast into water and stir until yeast dissolves. Set aside to foam, about 5 minutes. Combine flours, xanthan gum, gelatin powder, rosemary, onion powder, and salt in a small mixer bowl. Whisk eggs, olive oil, and vinegar into the dissolved yeast and stir the mixture into the flour. Beat dough with mixer for 2 minutes, using a spatula to keep stirring down the dough on the mixer beaters. The dough will be soft and sticky.

Transfer dough to 11x7-inch nonstick pan coated with cooking spray and cornmeal. Sprinkle with Italian seasoning, salt, and olive oil. Cover with aluminum foil and let rise in warm place for 30 minutes. Preheat oven to 400°. Bake for 15 minutes.

Per serving: Cal 200 (20% from fat); Fat 5g; Prot 6g; Carb 34g; Sod 381mg; Chol 72mg.

ALTERNATIVE TOPPINGS:

Herb: Combine ¹/2 teaspoon dried rosemary, ¹/2 teaspoon dried sage, ¹/2 teaspoon dried thyme, ¹/4 teaspoon black pepper, and 2 tablespoons Parmesan cheese.

Sun-Dried Tomato and Olive: ¹/4 cup chopped sun-dried tomatoes in oil, ¹/4 cup chopped black olives, and ¹/4 cup chopped onion sautéed until translucent in 1 teaspoon olive oil.

CONTINUED

Pesto: Purée the following in food processor just until smooth, leaving a bit of texture: 1 cup fresh basil leaves, 1 garlic clove, ½ cup pine nuts. With motor running, slowly drizzle in ¼ cup olive oil through feed tube. Add ¼ cup Parmesan cheese and a dash of freshly ground black pepper.

Wheat-Free Recipes and Menus

Potato Rolls

1 package yeast	½ cup cooking oil
½ cup lukewarm water	1 teaspoon salt
1 tablespoon sugar	½ cup sugar
¾ cup HOT water	2 eggs
¼ cup powdered milk	About 4½ cups flour
¼ cup instant mashed potato flakes	

Set yeast, ½ cup water, and one tablespoon sugar to work. Mix all other ingredients except flour. Add one cup flour. Beat hard. Add yeast and rest of flour, gradually. Knead well. Let rise until double. Place in greased pans. Let rise until almost double. Bake at 375° for 12-15 minutes. Makes about 30 rolls.

Sharing Our Best/Muleshoe Ranch

Earth Bread

1 cup oil	¼ teaspoon baking powder
3 eggs, beaten	¼ teaspoon cinnamon
2 cups sugar	1 cup zucchini, grated
2 teaspoons vanilla	finely
3 cups flour	¼ cup raw carrots, grated
1 teaspoon baking soda	½ cup banana, mashed
1 teaspoon salt	½ cup nuts, chopped

Mix the oil, eggs, sugar, and vanilla together; beat thoroughly. Add the flour and other dry ingredients, then add the vegetables and banana. Blend well until the mixture is smooth. Add the nuts.

Pour into 2 (9x5-inch) greased and floured pans. Bake for one hour at 325°. Cool for 10 minutes and turn out of pans. Cool completely on a rack. Freezes well. Excellent with honey butter spread.

HONEY BUTTER SPREAD:

1 cup honey	½ cup powdered sugar
1 cube (2 tablespoons) butter, softened	

Mix all the ingredients together with a mixer until smooth.

Great Plains Cooking

Onion Cracker Bread

This low-fat, delicious cracker bread is a great alternative to bread with a meal.

DOUGH:

1 tablespoon yeast	**1 teaspoon salt**
1¹/₃ cups water	**1 tablespoon vegetable oil**
1³/₄ tablespoons sugar	**3¹/₂ cups all-purpose flour**

Dissolve the yeast in the water. Add the remaining ingredients and knead until a smooth dough is formed—knead either by hand or in a food processor. Cover the dough and set aside to rise for 45 minutes. Preheat the oven to 450°. (Recipe prepared for high altitude cooking.) While the dough rises, prepare the topping.

TOPPING:

2 medium onions, diced	**Coarse kosher salt**
1 tablespoon vegetable oil	**1 egg white, beaten with**
1 tablespoon poppy seeds	**1 tablespoon water**
3 green onions, finely chopped	

Sauté onions in the oil until soft. Remove from heat and stir in poppy seeds and chopped green onions. In a small bowl, whisk egg white with water.

Divide dough into 3 pieces. Pat or roll into rectangles about ¹/₃-inch thick. Rest the dough for 10 minutes (to relax gluten in flour and to make dough easier to stretch). Grease 3 large cookie sheets, about 17x11 inches. If you only have one pan, just stretch and bake one at a time. Stretch each piece of dough to cover the bottom of the pans. Stretch gently with the flat palm of your hand under the dough. Don't worry about the dough being absolutely even—the irregularities are part of its charm; creating soft and crispy pieces of cracker where the dough is thick or thin.

Brush the dough with egg white. Distribute the onion-poppy seed topping evenly over dough. Sprinkle very lightly with salt. Bake until golden, about 10-15 minutes. Cool and break into pieces for serving. Serves 6-8.

Lighter Tastes of Aspen

Piña Colada Bread

1 1/2 cups shredded coconut	1 egg
2 3/4 cups flour	1 cup crushed unsweetened
2 teaspoons baking powder	pineapple
1/2 teaspoon baking soda	1/2 cup light rum
1 teaspoon salt	1 teaspoon vanilla
3/4 cup sugar	2 tablespoons vegetable oil

Spread the coconut in a single layer on an ungreased cookie sheet. Toast in a preheated 350° oven for 4-6 minutes or until golden brown. Stir often to avoid burning. Set aside to cool.

In a large bowl, combine the flour, baking powder, baking soda, salt, sugar, and 1 1/4 cups toasted coconut. Reserve the remaining 1/4 cup coconut. In a medium bowl, lightly beat the egg. Stir in pineapple, rum, vanilla, and oil. Stir this into the flour mixture, only until dry ingredients are moistened. Turn into lightly greased and floured loaf pan. Bake at 350° 50-60 minutes or until a wooden toothpick inserted in the center comes out clean. Let cool 10 minutes before turning out onto a rack over waxed paper. Drizzle Pineapple-Rum Glaze over warm bread. Sprinkle reserved coconut over bread.

PINEAPPLE-RUM GLAZE:

3 tablespoons butter	1/2 cup sugar
2 tablespoons pineapple juice	1/4 cup light rum

In a small saucepan, combine butter, pineapple juice, and sugar. Bring to a boil over moderate heat. Stir in the rum and simmer for 5 minutes, stirring constantly. Set aside to cool. Makes 1 loaf. *Recipe from The Allaire Timbers Inn, Breckenridge.*

Distinctly Delicious

At 11,000 feet, the world's highest automobile tunnel, the Eisenhower Tunnel on I-70, crosses the Continental Divide. The world's highest railroad is the Pikes Peak Cog Railway; and the Trail Ridge Road in Rocky Mountain National Park is the highest paved through-highway in the US. The Colorado Rocky Mountains constitute an area three times as large as the Swiss Alps.

60 Minute Rolls

Very good, quick roll recipe.

3¹/₂ - 4¹/₂ cups unsifted flour   **1 cup milk**
3 tablespoons sugar   **¹/₂ cup water**
1 teaspoon salt   **¹/₄ cup margarine**
2 packages dry yeast

In a large bowl, thoroughly mix 1½ cups flour, sugar, salt, and yeast. Combine milk, water, and margarine in a saucepan. Heat over low heat until liquids are very warm (120° - 130°). Margarine does not need to melt. Gradually add to dry ingredients and beat 2 minutes at medium speed of mixer, scraping bowl occasionally. Add ½ cup flour. Beat at high speed 2 minutes, again scraping bowl. Stir in enough flour to make a soft dough. Turn onto lightly floured board and knead until smooth and elastic, about 5 minutes. Place in greased bowl, turning to grease top. Cover and place bowl in pan of warm water and let rise 15 minutes.

Shape into rolls and let rise in warm place for 15 minutes. Bake at 425° about 12 minutes or until done. Makes 24 rolls.

Goodies and Guess-Whats

Caramel Bottom Dinner Rolls

1 package active dry yeast	1/4 cup shortening
1/4 cup warm water	1 teaspoon salt
1 cup milk, scalded	3 1/2 cups sifted flour
1/4 cup sugar	1 egg

Soften yeast in warm water. Combine milk, sugar, shortening, and salt; cool to lukewarm. Add half the flour and beat well. Beat in yeast and egg. Gradually add remaining flour to form soft dough, beating well. Place in greased bowl, turning once to grease surface. Cover and let rise until double. Turn out dough on lightly floured surface and shape into dinner rolls. Place rolls on top of caramel mixture. Cover and let rolls rise until double. Bake at 350° for 12-15 minutes. Cool 2-3 minutes; invert on rack; remove pan. Makes 2 dozen.

CARAMEL MIXTURE:

1/2 cup butter or margarine	1/2 cup brown sugar

Place butter and sugar in a 9x13-inch baking dish. Melt together in moderate oven or microwave.

Kitchen Keepsakes by Request

Beer Corn Bread

1 cup yellow cornmeal	2 eggs, beaten
1 cup flour	1/2 cup milk
2 teaspoons baking powder	1/2 cup beer
1/2 teaspoon baking soda	1/4 cup oil

Combine dry ingredients in large bowl. Add eggs, milk, beer, and oil; mix well. Spoon into greased 8-inch square pan. Bake at 425° for 15 minutes or until bread tests done. Yields 9 servings.

Per serving: Cal 192; T Fat 8g; 39% Cal from Fat; Prot 5g; Carbo 24g; Fiber 2g; Chol 49mg; Sod 318mg.

The Flavor of Colorado

Cornbread Spanish-Style

1 cup cornmeal	1 egg
1/4 cup sugar	1 cup milk
1 teaspoon salt	1/4 cup shortening
1 cup sifted flour	1 (16-ounce) can cream-style
3 teaspoons baking	corn
powder	1 cup cottage cheese

FILLING:

1 1/2 cups grated longhorn or	1 (4-ounce) can green chiles,
Cheddar cheese	chopped

Combine dry ingredients; add egg, milk, shortening, corn, and cottage cheese. Stir lightly. Pour half of batter in greased 9-inch square pan. Sprinkle with half the cheese and chiles. Add remaining batter; top with remaining cheese and chiles. Bake at 400° for 45 minutes.

Southwestern Foods et cetera

Cliff Palace in Mesa Verde National Park provided the Pueblo Indians with safe shelter from weather and enemies. The Ute Indians, Colorado's predominant tribe, controlled the Rocky Mountains.

Monkey Toes

2 cans cheap biscuits
1/2 cup sugar
1 teaspoon cinnamon
1/2 cup chopped nuts (optional)

1/2 stick butter or oleo
1/2 cup brown sugar
1 tablespoon vanilla

Preheat oven to 350°. Cut each biscuit into 4 pieces. Combine the white sugar and cinnamon in a plastic bag. Shake the cut-up biscuits (a few at a time) in this mixture. Put biscuit pieces in a well-greased pan (loaf, bundt or angel). Evenly add nuts, if desired. In a saucepan melt butter and brown sugar. When smooth and hot, add vanilla. Stir thoroughly and pour or spoon over the biscuit pieces. Bake 20-25 minutes or until done. Makes 5 servings.

Grade A Recipes

Dried-Cherry Buttermilk Scones

The tartness of the cherries complements the sweetness of the biscuit. If you have never tried scones, you must try these!

2 cups all-purpose flour
1/3 cup sugar
1 1/2 teaspoons baking powder
1/2 teaspoon baking soda
6 tablespoons butter, chilled

1/2 cup buttermilk
1 large egg
1 1/2 teaspoons vanilla
2/3 cup dried sour cherries

Preheat oven to 400°. In a large bowl, sift together the dry ingredients. Cut butter into 1/2-inch cubes and distribute over flour mixture. With a pastry blender, cut in the butter until the mixture resembles coarse crumbs. Stir together the buttermilk, egg, and vanilla. Add to the flour mixture. Stir in the cherries. With lightly floured hands, pat the dough into an 8-inch diameter circle on an ungreased cookie sheet. With a serrated knife, cut into 8 separate wedges. Bake 18-20 minutes, or until a cake tester inserted into the center comes out clean. Cool for 5 minutes. Serve warm. Makes 8 scones. *Recipe from Posada de Sol y Sombra, LaVeta.*

Colorado Bed & Breakfast Cookbook

Ham Quiche Biscuit Cups

1 (8-ounce) package cream
  cheese, softened
2 tablespoons milk
2 eggs
1/2 cup Swiss cheese,
  shredded

2 tablespoons chopped green
  onions
1 (10-count) can refrigerated
  flaky biscuits
1/2 cup ham, finely chopped

Preheat oven to 375°. Grease 10 muffin cups. Beat cream cheese, milk, and eggs until smooth. Stir in Swiss cheese and green onions. Separate dough into 10 biscuits. Place one biscuit in each cup. Firmly press in bottom and up sides, forming a 1/4-inch rim. Place half of ham in bottom of dough cups. Spoon about 2 tablespoons cheese and egg mixture over ham. Top with remaining ham and bake for about 25 minutes or until filling is set and edges of biscuits are golden brown. Remove from pan. Serve immediately. Serves 10. *Recipe from Meadow Creek Bed and Breakfast, Pine.*

Colorado Bed & Breakfast Cookbook

Ranch Biscuits

Biscuits that are light and high but rich in flavor. Easily put together in the morning. Pat them out on floured wax paper to toss away the mess.

2 cups unbleached flour
4 teaspoons baking powder
2 teaspoons sugar
1 teaspoon salt
1/2 teaspoon cream of tartar

1/2 cup cold butter, cut into
  1-inch cubes
2/3 cup + 2-3 tablespoons
  half-and-half

Preheat oven to 450°. Combine flour, baking powder, sugar, salt, cream of tartar in food processor bowl. Add butter and process until mixture resembles cornmeal. Transfer mixture to a bowl and stir in 2/3 cup half-and-half, adding more if dough seems dry. Mix gently and knead 5-6 times. Pat out to 1/2-inch thickness on lightly floured board and cut into round or square biscuits. Bake on parchment-lined cookie sheet for 10 minutes or until a deep golden.

Good Morning, Goldie!

Peachy Sour Cream Coffee Cake

STREUSEL TOPPING/FILLING:

2 cups pecans, chopped	**3 tablespoons sugar**
1/3 cup brown sugar	**1 teaspoon cinnamon**

Combine ingredients; set aside.

CAKE:

1/2 cup margarine	**1/2 teaspoon salt**
1 cup sugar	**1 cup sour cream**
2 eggs	**1 teaspoon vanilla**
2 cups flour	**2 cups fresh peaches, peeled**
1 1/2 teaspoons baking powder	**and sliced**
1/2 teaspoon soda	

In large mixing bowl, cream margarine and sugar until fluffy. Beat in eggs. Combine all dry ingredients; add alternately with the sour cream and vanilla to the creamed mixture. Beat until smooth. Pour half the batter into a 9-inch springform pan. Sprinkle with one cup of streusel. Top with remaining batter and 1/2 cup streusel. Bake at 350° for 30 minutes. Arrange peaches over cake; sprinkle with remaining streusel. Bake an additional 30-40 minutes or until cake tests done. Cool cake 10 minutes before removing sides of pan. Serve warm or at room temperature. Serves 10.

Country Classics

Cindy's Cream Cheese Coffee Cake

2 packages crescent rolls
2 (8-ounce) packages cream
  cheese, softened
3/4 cup sugar

1 teaspoon lemon juice
1 teaspoon vanilla
1 egg yolk, save white
Chopped almonds

Lightly grease a 9x13-inch pan. Line bottom of pan with one package of rolls. Mix cream cheese, sugar, lemon juice, vanilla, and egg yolk and pour over roll dough. Layer second package of rolls on top of cream cheese mixture. Pinch edges of rolls together. Brush slightly beaten egg white on roll dough and sprinkle with almonds. Bake at 350° for 30-40 minutes.

Kitchen Keepsakes by Request

Cinnamon Surprise

This is a light change from heavy pastries and cinnamon rolls.

2 (8-count) packages
  refrigerator crescent
  roll dough
2 tablespoons brown sugar

1 teaspoon sugar
1 teaspoon cinnamon
16 marshmallows
2 tablespoons melted butter

Separate roll dough on lightly floured surface. Mix brown sugar, sugar, and cinnamon in small bowl. Dip marshmallows one at a time in melted butter; roll in sugar mixture, coating well. Place on triangle of roll dough. Bring up edges to enclose marshmallow, sealing well. Place 2 inches apart on baking sheet. Brush lightly with remaining melted butter. Bake at 375° for 10-13 minutes or until marshmallows melt, leaving rolls with hollow, sweet-coated centers. Yields 16 servings.

Per serving: Cal 143; Prot 1.7g; Carbo 18.8g; T Fat 6.9g; Chol 3.9mg; Potas 70.1mg; Sod 249.0mg.

Beyond Oats

Colorado is tied with Hawaii for having the skinniest population. Less than 20 percent of the adults in Colorado are overweight.

Colorado Coffee Cake

4¹/₂ cups flour
1¹/₂ cups sugar
1¹/₂ cups butter or solid
  vegetable shortening
2 eggs, beaten

1¹/₂ cups sour cream
¹/₂ teaspoon salt
1 teaspoon baking powder
1 teaspoon baking soda
2 teaspoons almond extract

Preheat oven to 350°. Grease two 9- or 10-inch springform or deep round foil pans. Combine flour and sugar. Cut in butter or shortening. Reserve 2 cups of this crumb mixture. To remaining crumb mixture, add eggs, sour cream, salt, baking powder, baking soda, and almond extract. Mix well. Spread mixture over bottom and up sides of pans.

FILLING:

1 pound cream cheese,
  softened
¹/₄ teaspoon vanilla

2 eggs, beaten
¹/₄ cup sugar

Combine cream cheese, vanilla, beaten eggs, and sugar. Spread half of this mixture over the batter in each pan.

TOPPING:

1 cup raspberry preserves   1¹/₃ cups almonds, chopped

On top of the cream cheese mixture on each cake spread ¹/₂ cup of the raspberry preserves. Whirl almonds in processor until chunky. Combine with reserved crumb mixture and sprinkle over preserves on each cake. Bake cakes for 45-55 minutes until a toothpick inserted in center of cake comes out clean. Cool the cake at least ¹/₂ hour before serving. Yields 2 (10-inch) round cakes.

Hint: This recipe is better to make ahead and refrigerate.

West of the Rockies

Braided Cream Cheese Bread

1 (8-ounce) carton sour
  cream, scalded
1/2 cup sugar
1/2 cup butter or margarine,
  melted

1 teaspoon salt
2 packages dry yeast
1/2 cup warm water (105° - 115°)
2 eggs, beaten
4 cups all-purpose flour

FILLING:
2 (8-ounce) packages cream
  cheese, softened
3/4 cup sugar

1 egg, beaten
1/8 teaspoon salt
2 teaspoons vanilla extract

GLAZE:
2 cups sifted powdered
  sugar

1/4 cup milk
2 teaspoons vanilla extract

Combine scalded sour cream, sugar, butter, and salt; mix well
and let cool to lukewarm. Dissolve yeast in warm water in a
large mixing bowl; stir in sour cream mixture and eggs. Gradually stir in flour; dough will be soft. Cover tightly and chill
overnight.

Divide dough into 4 equal parts. Turn each out onto a
heavily floured surface and knead 4 or 5 times. Roll each into
a 12x18-inch rectangle. Spread 1/4 of filling over each rectangle,
leaving a 1/2-inch margin around edges. Carefully roll up
jellyroll-style, beginning at long side. Firmly pinch edge and
ends to seal. Place rolls seam-side-down on greased baking
sheets. Make 6 equally x-shaped cuts across the top of each
loaf. Cover and let rise in a warm place for one hour or until
doubled in size. Bake at 375° for 15-20 minutes. Spread loaves
with Glaze while warm.

Four Square Meals a Day

Savory Gruyère Cheesecake

This savory cheesecake is a fabulous choice for brunch or lunch. Beautiful to serve and scrumptious!

1¹/₃ cups fine toasted breadcrumbs
5 tablespoons unsalted butter, melted
24 ounces cream cheese, softened
¹/₄ cup heavy cream
¹/₂ teaspoon salt
¹/₄ teaspoon ground nutmeg
¹/₄ teaspoon cayenne pepper
4 eggs
1 cup shredded Gruyère cheese

1 (10-ounce) package frozen chopped spinach, thawed and squeezed dry
2¹/₂ tablespoons minced green onions
3 tablespoons unsalted butter
¹/₂ pound mushrooms, finely chopped
Salt and freshly ground black pepper to taste
Marinara Sauce

In small bowl, combine breadcrumbs and melted butter. Butter a 9-inch springform pan. Press crumbs onto bottom and sides of pan. Bake at 350° for 8-10 minutes; set aside to cool.

In large bowl, beat cream cheese, cream, salt, nutmeg, and cayenne pepper together until smooth. Beat in eggs, one at a time. Divide cheese mixture between 2 bowls. Stir Gruyère cheese into one. Stir spinach and green onions into the other. Pour spinach filling into cooled crust.

In medium skillet, melt 3 tablespoons butter and sauté mushrooms over medium-high heat until all moisture evaporates, stirring frequently. Season to taste with salt and pepper. Spoon mushrooms over spinach filling. Carefully pour Gruyère filling over mushrooms. Set pan on baking sheet. Bake at 325° for 1¹/₄ hours. Turn oven off and cool cheesecake for one hour with door ajar, then cool on rack until room temperature. Serve in wedges topped with warm marinara sauce. Makes 12 servings.

Crème de Colorado

Ever Luscious Apple Bread

1 cup granulated sugar
1/2 cup vegetable shortening
  or margarine
1/4 teaspoon butter flavoring
4 tablespoons sour milk or
  buttermilk
1 teaspoon baking soda

2 eggs, slightly beaten
1 teaspoon vanilla
2 cups flour
1/2 teaspoon salt
2 cups finely chopped raw
  apples
1/2 cup nuts

Cream sugar, shortening, and butter flavoring. Add soda to buttermilk, stir well and add to sugar mixture. Add beaten eggs and vanilla to mixture. Stir in flour and salt. Fold in raw apples and nuts. Turn batter into greased and floured loaf pan. Combine topping ingredients and drop dobs over top of loaf. Bake at 350° for 45-50 minutes or until loaf tests done.

TOPPING:

2 tablespoons margarine
2 tablespoons sugar
2 tablespoons flour

1/2 teaspoon cinnamon
1/2 teaspoon burnt sugar
  flavoring

Doc's Delights

Pineapple-Zucchini Bread

3 eggs
2 cups sugar
2 teaspoons vanilla
1 cup cooking oil
2 cups zucchini, peeled
  and grated
3 cups flour
1 teaspoon baking powder

1 teaspoon salt
1 teaspoon soda
1 teaspoon cinnamon
1 cup crushed pineapple,
  drained
1/2 cup raisins
1 cup chopped nuts

Beat eggs until fluffy; add sugar, vanilla, oil, and zucchini. Blend well. Add dry ingredients and mix well. Stir in pineapple, raisins, and nuts. Bake in one large greased and floured loaf pan or two small loaf pans. Bake in 325° oven for one hour.

More Goodies and Guess-Whats

Kreppel

4 eggs, well beaten
1/3 cup sugar
1 cup buttermilk
1 cup whipping cream
1/4 teaspoon salt
2 teaspoons baking powder
4 cups flour

Mix all ingredients together, adding enough flour to make a soft dough. Set in refrigerator overnight. Roll dough to pie-crust thickness. Cut into 4 to 6-inch squares. Fry in hot oil until golden brown. Sprinkle with sugar.

4-H Family Cookbook

Pork and Bean Bread

1 (16-ounce) can pork and
    beans (remove pork)
3 eggs, beaten
1 cup oil
2 cups sugar
1 cup raisins
1 cup boiling water
3 cups flour
2 teaspoons cinnamon
1/2 teaspoon baking powder
1 teaspoon baking soda
1/2 teaspoon salt
1 teaspoon vanilla
1 cup nuts

Beat pork and beans until beans are broken. Beat in eggs, oil, and sugar until smooth. Add raisins to boiling water; set aside. Add all other ingredients except nuts to bean mixture, including raisins and water. Mix until smooth. Add nuts. Pour into 3 greased and floured loaf pans. Bake at 325° for 50 minutes.

Home Cookin'

Peach Pecan Muffins

1 1/2 cups flour
1/2 cup sugar
2 teaspoons baking powder
1 teaspoon cinnamon
1/4 teaspoon salt

1/2 cup margarine, melted
1/4 cup milk
1 egg
1 cup peaches, peeled and diced

Mix dry ingredients together. Add margarine, milk, and egg; mix slightly. Stir in peaches. Fill greased or paper-lined muffin tins 3/4 full.

TOPPING:

1/2 cup pecans, chopped
1/3 cup brown sugar
1/4 cup flour

1 teaspoon cinnamon
2 tablespoons margarine, melted

Mix topping ingredients until crumbly. Top each muffin before baking. Bake at 400° for 20-25 minutes or until done. Yields 12 muffins.

Country Classics II

Walnut Streusel Muffins

Georgie's favorite! This muffin gets top honors for texture, appearance and flavor.

1 1/2 cups brown sugar, packed
3 cups all-purpose flour
3/4 cup butter or margarine
1 cup walnuts, chopped
2 teaspoons baking powder
1 teaspoon nutmeg

1 teaspoon ginger
1/2 teaspoon baking soda
1/2 teaspoon salt
1 cup buttermilk or sour milk
2 eggs, beaten

Preheat oven to 350°. Grease muffin cups. In medium bowl, combine sugar and 2 cups flour. Cut in butter to make fine crumbs. In small bowl, combine 3/4 cup of the crumbs and 1/4 cup of the walnuts; set aside. Into remaining crumb mixture, stir in remaining one cup flour, baking powder, spices, soda, salt, and remaining 3/4 cup walnuts. In another small bowl, combine buttermilk and eggs; stir into dry ingredients just to moisten. Fill muffin cups 2/3 full. Top each with a generous spoonful of reserved crumb-nut mixture. Bake at 350° for 20-25 minutes or until springy to the touch. Makes 18 muffins.

Nothin' but Muffins

Shannon's Pumpkin Date Muffins

2 cups sugar
1 cup vegetable oil
3 eggs
1 (16-ounce) can pumpkin
  (or 2 cups cooked)
3 cups all-purpose flour
1 teaspoon baking soda

$^1/_2$ teaspoon salt
$^1/_2$ teaspoon baking powder
1 teaspoon ground cinnamon
1 teaspoon ground nutmeg
1 teaspoon ground cloves
1 cup chopped pecans
1 cup chopped dates

In large mixing bowl, beat together sugar and oil. Beat in eggs until light and fluffy. Add pumpkin; mix well. Sift together dry ingredients and add to pumpkin mixture. Stir until moistened. Fold in nuts and dates. Fill greased muffin tins or line with paper cups. Bake at 325° for 20-25 minutes, or until wooden pick inserted comes out clean. Makes 2½ dozen muffins. *Recipe from Wedgewood Cottage Bed & Breakfast Inn, Colorado Springs.*

Colorado Columbine Delicacies

Saucy Blueberry Lemon Muffins

These wonderfully tart creations melt in your mouth.

$^1/_2$ cup butter or margarine
$^1/_2$ cup sugar
2 eggs
2 cups flour
3 teaspoons baking powder

$^1/_4$ teaspoon salt, optional
$^1/_3$ cup milk
1 cup blueberries, canned or
  frozen, thawed and drained
Rind of 1 lemon, grated finely

Preheat oven to 350°. Grease muffin cups. Cream butter, sugar, and eggs in a small bowl. In large bowl, combine flour, baking powder, and salt. Add creamed mixture alternately with milk, stirring only until mixed. Fold in blueberries and lemon rind. Fill muffin cups $^2/_3$ full. Bake at 350° for 25-30 minutes.

SAUCE:
$^1/_4$ cup fresh lemon juice $^1/_3$ cup sugar

Combine lemon juice and sugar in small pan and bring to boiling. Pour sauce evenly over top of baked muffins. Bakes 12 muffins.

Nothin' but Muffins

Cranberry Maple Muffins

In the summer when fresh cranberries aren't plentiful, use a can of whole cranberry sauce and reduce the sugar to ½ cup.

2 cups all-purpose flour	½ cup unsalted butter,
½ cup walnuts, chopped	softened
2 teaspoons baking powder	2 eggs
½ teaspoon baking soda	1 cup sugar
½ teaspoon salt	⅔ cup buttermilk
1½ cups cranberries, sliced	2 teaspoons maple flavoring
or chopped	

Preheat oven to 350°. Grease muffin cups. In large bowl, mix flour, walnuts, baking powder, soda, and salt. Stir in cranberries. In separate bowl, beat together butter, eggs, sugar, buttermilk, and maple flavoring. Stir into dry ingredients just until moistened. Fill muffin cups ⅓ full. Bake at 350° for 25-30 minutes. Makes 12 muffins.

Nothin' but Muffins

Cinnamon-Apple Muffins

¼ cup butter or margarine	½ teaspoon salt, if desired
2 cups sifted flour	1 egg, well-beaten
⅓ cup sugar	1 cup milk
1 tablespoon baking powder	Canned pie apples

CRUMB TOPPING:

½ cup firmly packed	⅓ cup sifted flour
brown sugar	1 teaspoon cinnamon,
½ cup butter or margarine,	or to taste
softened	

Melt ¼ cup butter and set aside. Sift together flour, sugar, baking powder, and salt; set aside. Blend egg and milk together, then add melted butter. Add this mixture all at once to dry ingredients. Place one pie apple slice in bottom of each muffin cup. Add batter. Mix together crumb topping ingredients until coarse. Top muffins. Bake at 425° for 20-25 minutes. Makes 12 muffins. *Recipe from Cinnamon Inn, Lake City.*

Pure Gold—Colorado Treasures

Raspberry Muffins

This recipe can be a bread-type or muffins; it is yummy and versatile.
Make it for a special breakfast or brunch. Make days ahead and freeze
for later.

1 1/2 cups all-purpose flour
  (or whole-wheat flour)
1/2 teaspoon baking soda
1/2 teaspoon salt, optional
1 1/2 teaspoons ground
  cinnamon
1 cup sugar

1 (12-ounce) package frozen
  unsweetened raspberries,
  thawed
2 eggs, or 4 egg whites,
  well beaten
2/3 cup vegetable oil
1/2 cup chopped pecans

TOPPING:
1/4 cup brown sugar
1 teaspoon orange or
  lemon zest

1/2 cup pecans

Preheat oven to 400°. In medium bowl, mix flour, soda, salt, cinnamon, and sugar. Make a well in the center and stir in undrained raspberries and eggs. Thoroughly mix in oil and pecans. Spoon batter into lightly vegetable-oil-sprayed muffin papers lining muffin tins. Muffin cups should be poured full. Batter is heavy and will not overflow. Sprinkle the topping evenly over the tops of muffins or bread. Bake 15-20 minutes. Cool 5 minutes before removing from pan.

If doing a loaf, bake in a 9x5-inch pan at 350° for one hour or until wooden pick inserted in center comes out clean.

Raspberry Story

Poppy Seed Coffee Cake Muffins

These muffins are absolutely delicious and freeze well.

1/4 cup poppy seeds
1 cup buttermilk
1 teaspoon almond extract
1 cup butter
1 1/2 cups sugar
4 eggs, separated

2 1/2 cups flour
1 teaspoon baking powder
1 teaspoon baking soda
1/2 cup sugar
1 teaspoon cinnamon

Preheat oven to 350°. Grease muffin cups. Combine poppy seeds, buttermilk, and almond extract; set aside. Cream butter and sugar. Add egg yolks to creamed mixture and beat. Mix buttermilk and creamed mixtures together. Sift together the flour, baking powder, and baking soda; add to buttermilk mixture just until moistened. Beat egg whites until stiff. Fold into flour mixture. Fill muffin cups 1/3 full.

Mix together 1/2 cup sugar and 1 teaspoon cinnamon; sprinkle 1/2 of mixture evenly over batter. Divide remaining batter into muffin cups. Sprinkle remaining sugar-cinnamon mixture over batter. Cut through each cup with knife to create a marbled effect. Bake at 350° for 20-25 minutes. Makes 30 muffins.

Nothin' but Muffins

Carrot Bran Muffins

Cyndi's favorite.

3 cups all-purpose flour
1 teaspoon baking soda
2 teaspoons baking powder
1/2 teaspoon salt, optional
1 tablespoon cinnamon
2 cups bran

4 eggs
1 1/2 cups vegetable oil
1 1/4 cups dark brown sugar
1/4 cup molasses
3 cups finely grated carrots
1 cup raisins or currants

Preheat oven to 350°. Grease muffin cups. Sift together flour, soda, baking powder, salt, and cinnamon. Add bran; set aside. Beat eggs; add oil, sugar, and molasses. Add carrots, flour mixture and raisins. Fill muffin cups 3/4 full. Bake at 350° for 20 minutes. Makes 24 muffins.

Note: For a different taste treat, use light brown sugar, substitute honey for 1/2 of the molasses, and add nuts.

Nothin' but Muffins

Mexican Muffins

2 English muffins	Monterey Jack cheese, grated
Guacamole	Cheddar cheese, grated
4 eggs, scrambled	

Toast the English muffin halves and butter lightly. Keep warm. On each half, put a scoop of guacamole and approximately one scrambled egg. Top with grated cheeses; broil. Serve with fresh salsa. Serves 4.

Steamboat Entertains

Marco Polos

These are a real quick whole-meal sandwich that are great for drop-in guests.

6 English muffin halves	1 tomato, sliced
1 pound thinly sliced ham	1 or 2 (10-ounce) packages
1 pound thinly sliced turkey	broccoli, cooked and
1/2 onion, sliced thin	drained

Butter each muffin half and arrange on a cookie sheet. Broil to toast. On each muffin, arrange ham slice, turkey, onion, tomato, and 1-2 stalks broccoli.

CHEESE SAUCE:

3 tablespoons butter	1-1 1/2 cups Cheddar cheese,
3 tablespoons flour	grated
2 cups milk or	1/2 teaspoon salt
half-and-half	Paprika

Melt butter in saucepan; stir in flour, then milk, stirring until thickened. Add Cheddar cheese and salt; stir until melted. Pour hot cheese sauce over warmed sandwiches (warm 10 minutes in a covered pan at 325°), then sprinkle with paprika.

Note: Sandwiches can also be heated in the microwave after the cheese sauce has been poured over them.

Kitchen Keepsakes

Best Basic Waffles

1³/₄ cups all-purpose flour   **3 eggs, separated**
2 teaspoons baking powder   **4 tablespoons melted butter**
¹/₂ teaspoon salt   **1¹/₂ cups milk**
1 tablespoon granulated sugar

Sift and resift the flour, baking powder, salt, and sugar. Beat 3 egg yolks well. Then mix in dry ingredients. Add melted butter and milk. Beat until batter is smooth. In separate mixing bowl, beat 3 egg whites until stiff peaks form. Gently fold egg whites into batter. Cook in buttered, heated waffle iron. Makes 16 waffles. Serve waffles with fresh fruit, cream cheese, fruit syrup, nuts, or with plain maple syrup and butter.

Doc's Delights

Sopapillas

4 cups flour   **3 tablespoons shortening**
3 teaspoons baking powder   **Water**
1 teaspoon salt

Sift flour, baking powder, and salt. Cut in shortening, adding enough water to make a stiff dough. Roll out dough until it is ¹/₄-inch thick. Cut into 3-inch squares and deep-fry until golden brown. Serve warm with honey. Yields 4 dozen.

From an Adobe Oven to a Microwave Range

Yeasty Belgian Waffles

Light and ethereal, these yeasty waffles are much more than breakfast fare. Try them as a base for fresh fruit topped with whipped cream or for ice cream sundaes.

3 cups unbleached flour	**1/2 cup sugar**
1 tablespoon dry yeast	**2 large eggs**
1 1/2 cups warm water	**1/2 teaspoon salt**
(110°)	**6 tablespoons melted butter**
1 1/2 cups warm Oktoberfest	**1/4 cup vegetable oil**
(110°)	**1 teaspoon vanilla extract**

Stir one cup flour with yeast. Whisk in warmed water and beer. Cover and let stand in a warm place for 15 minutes. Beat sugar, eggs, and salt until lemon colored and fluffy. In a separate bowl stir butter, oil, and vanilla. Combine the ingredients and beat 2 minutes. Cover and refrigerate from 4 hours to overnight.

Stir the batter and cook in a generously greased Belgian waffle maker until crisp and brown. Serve immediately or cool on a rack before storing in airtight container. Makes 10-12.

Great American Beer Cookbook

Crunchy Oatmeal Pecan Waffles

2 tablespoons butter, melted	**1 1/3 cups whole wheat flour**
2 tablespoons apple juice	**1/3 cup rolled oats**
3 eggs, beaten	**1/2 cup wheat germ**
2 cups skim milk	**4 teaspoons baking powder**
2 teaspoons vanilla	**1/4 cup chopped pecans**

Mix first 5 ingredients and then add remaining ingredients. Mix well. Bake in a waffle iron. Serve with honey or syrup. *Recipe from The Historic Western Hotel B&B, Ouray.*

Pure Gold—Colorado Treasures

Gingerbread Pancakes
with Nectarine Cream Sauce

1 1/3 cups flour	1 egg
1 teaspoon baking powder	1 1/4 cups milk
1/4 teaspoon salt	1/4 cup molasses
1/4 teaspoon baking soda	3 tablespoons oil
1/2 teaspoon ground ginger	Nectarine Cream Sauce
1 teaspoon cinnamon	

Combine flour, baking powder, salt, baking soda, ginger, and cinnamon. In a large bowl, beat egg with milk. Beat in molasses and then oil. Add flour mixture and stir until just combined. Batter will be slightly lumpy. Cook on a hot, greased griddle or skillet until puffed, bubbled and dry around edges. Turn and brown on other side. Makes 8 good-sized pancakes. Serves 3-4. Serve with Nectarine Cream Sauce.

NECTARINE CREAM SAUCE:

1/2 cup sugar	1 teaspoon vanilla
1/2 cup light corn syrup	1 nectarine, diced
1/2 cup whipping cream	

Combine sugar, corn syrup, and whipping cream in a 1-quart pan. Cook, stirring constantly, until sugar is dissolved. Simmer 2 minutes or until slightly thickened. Remove from heat. Stir in vanilla and nectarine. Makes approximately 2 cups.
Recipe from Double Diamond Ranch, Meredith.

Colorado Bed & Breakfast Cookbook

Wild Rice Pancakes

Yummy! I cook my wild rice the day before I plan to serve pancakes. They are well worth the pre-planning.

1 1/2 cups 2% milk,
   warmed slightly
3 eggs at room temperature
1 3/4 cups unbleached flour
3 teaspoons baking powder

1/2 teaspoon salt
1/2 teaspoon sugar
1/2 cup butter, melted
1 cup cooked and cooled
   wild rice

In a large bowl, combine milk and eggs, blending well. Mix flour, baking powder, salt, and sugar in a small bowl. Combine milk and egg mixture with the melted butter. Stir in dry ingredients, blending until smooth. Stir in wild rice.

Ladle onto medium-hot griddle and cook 2-3 minutes, until golden brown, then turn and cook 2 minutes more or until golden brown on second side. Serve with butter, warm maple syrup, and fresh raspberries or sliced strawberries. Serves 4-6.

Good Morning, Goldie!

Quick Yeast Raised Pancakes

If you like homemade bread—you will truly enjoy these fragrant pancakes.

2 cups milk
2 eggs, slightly beaten
2 tablespoons vegetable oil
2 tablespoons honey

2 cups unbleached flour
3 tablespoons dry active yeast
1 teaspoon salt

In small saucepan, heat milk, eggs, oil, and honey to 120°. Meanwhile, in large mixing bowl, mix flour, yeast, and salt. Pour liquids over flour mixture and whisk for 1-2 minutes until smooth. Set bowl in a warm spot for about 5 minutes. The batter will rise during this time. Heat griddle to medium-high and oil. Stir down batter and ladle 1/4 cup of batter onto lightly greased griddle. Cook 2-3 minutes, turn and cook 1-2 minutes longer. They should rise nicely and turn golden brown. Serve with whipped butter and warm maple or fruit syrup. Serves 4-6.

Good Morning, Goldie!

Upside-Down Apple French Toast

Prepare the night before or at least three hours in advance.

¹/₂ cup (1 stick) butter	**1¹/₂ cups milk**
1¹/₄ cups packed brown sugar	**6 eggs**
1 tablespoon water	**1 teaspoon vanilla**
3 Granny Smith apples	**Nutmeg, to taste**
Cinnamon, to taste	**Creme Topping**
¹/₂ cup raisins, optional	**Sliced almonds, for garnish**
1 loaf French bread, sliced	
1¹/₂-inches thick	

Combine butter, brown sugar, and water in saucepan. Heat on medium until bubbling, stirring frequently. Place in a 9x13-inch pan and allow to cool for 20-30 minutes. Peel, core and slice the apples. Place the slices in rows, close together (over-lapping), on top of the sauce in pan. Sprinkle with cinnamon and raisins. Place the slices of bread on top of the apples. Mix together the milk, eggs, and vanilla. Pour over bread. Sprinkle with a little nutmeg. Cover and refrigerate. Bake at 350° for approximately 60 minutes, or until golden brown and crispy on top. Serve upside-down. Spoon the sauce in the pan over the French toast. Serve with Creme Topping and garnish with almonds. Serves 6.

CREME TOPPING:

¹/₂ cup whipping cream	**¹/₄ cup sugar**
¹/₂ cup sour cream	**¹/₂ teaspoon almond extract**

Whip on high until thickened. Place 2 tablespoons of topping on top of French toast. *Recipe from The Manor, Ouray.*

Colorado Bed & Breakfast Cookbook

Rocky Mountain Blueberry French Toast

12 slices stale French bread cut into 1-inch cubes	1 cup fresh blueberries, rinsed and drained
16 ounces cream cheese, chilled and cut into 1-inch cubes	12 large eggs
	1/3 cup maple syrup
	2 cups milk

Generously grease 8 au gratin dishes. Place ½ of the bread cubes in the dishes. Scatter the cream cheese over the bread and sprinkle with one cup of the berries. Arrange the remaining bread cubes over the berries. In a large bowl combine the eggs, syrup, and milk. Mix and pour evenly over the bread-cheese mixture. Spray the undersides of 8 pieces of foil generously with a vegetable spray and cover each au gratin dish. Refrigerate overnight.

In the morning, set the dishes out to bring them to room temperature. Bake in a 350° oven, covered, for 25 minutes. Uncover and bake an additional 15 minutes or until puffed and golden. Serve with Blueberry Syrup.

BLUEBERRY SYRUP:

1 cup sugar	1 cup fresh blueberries, rinsed and drained
2 tablespoons cornstarch	
1 cup water	1 tablespoon unsalted butter

Combine the sugar, cornstarch, and water over medium-high heat. Cook for 5 minutes or until thickened. Stir occasionally. Stir in the blueberries and simmer for 10 minutes or until the blueberries burst. Add the butter. Stir until melted. Drizzle over French toast. Makes 8 servings. *Recipe from Cattail Creek Bed and Breakfast Inn, Loveland.*

Distinctly Delicious

One of Colorado's greatest treasures is its clear, pure Rocky Mountain water; used to produce one of its natural products—beer.

Stuffed French Toast

These will make your guests say, "WOW!"

1 (8-ounce) package cream
  cheese, softened
1 1/2 teaspoons vanilla
3/4 teaspoon sugar
1/2 cup chopped pecans
1 (16-ounce) loaf soft
  French bread

4 eggs, beaten
1 cup milk
1/2 teaspoon grated nutmeg
1 (12-ounce) jar apricot
  preserves
1/2 cup orange juice

Beat the cream cheese, one teaspoon of the vanilla and sugar in a small bowl until creamed. Stir in the pecans and set aside. Cut the bread into 10-12 slices, 1 1/2 inches thick. Cut a slit in each slice, creating a pocket. Fill each pocket with 1 1/2 table-spoons of the cheese mixture.

Beat the eggs, milk, the remaining 1/2 teaspoon vanilla, and the nutmeg together in a large shallow bowl. Dip the filled bread slices into the egg mixture on both sides, then cook in batches, on a lightly greased, hot griddle until both sides are golden brown. Remove to a platter and keep warm while cook-ing the remaining toast. Heat the preserves and orange juice in a small saucepan. Simmer for 3-4 minutes, or until slightly thickened. Drizzle the mixture over the French toast and serve immediately.

Mystic Mountain Memories

Strawberry or Raspberry Rhubarb Jam

4 cups chopped rhubarb
4 cups granulated sugar
1 (12-ounce) box frozen
  strawberries or raspberries

1 small box strawberry or
  raspberry Jell-O

Mix rhubarb and sugar; let stand one hour to bring out juices. Then boil 12 minutes; add strawberries or raspberries, which-ever you like. Then boil 3 more minutes. Turn off heat; add Jell-O. Stir thoroughly. (You can freeze this jam.)

Doc's Delights

Overnight Caramel French Toast

1/2 cup (1 stick) butter	6 slices thick Texas toast
1 cup firmly packed brown sugar	6 eggs
	1 1/2 cups milk
2 tablespoons light corn syrup	1 teaspoon vanilla
	Dash of salt

Melt butter in 9x13-inch glass baking dish in microwave for 1-2 minutes. Add brown sugar and corn syrup; mix well and microwave one minute more. Stir again. Lay thick bread slices on top of sugar mix. Combine eggs, milk, vanilla, and salt; whip well. Pour egg mixture over bread. Cover and refrigerate overnight. Bake uncovered at 350° for 45-60 minutes. Should be puffed and brown. When serving portions, invert so caramel is on top. Makes 8 servings. *Recipe from Meadow Creek Bed & Breakfast Inn, Pine.*

Colorado Columbine Delicacies

Fried Apples

Our Mom used to serve these with fried quail, biscuits and gravy for breakfast when we were kids. They are also excellent served with pork.

1/4 cup margarine	1/2 cup sugar
6 medium tart apples, unpeeled and sliced*	1 teaspoon cinnamon
	1/4 cup water (more if needed)

In a skillet, heat margarine; add apples, sugar, cinnamon, and water. Cover. Simmer for about 20 minutes or until apples are tender. (If apple mixture starts to thicken before apples are tender, add a little more water.)

*Jonathan apples are best for this recipe.

Country Classics

Egg Puff

8 slices white bread
2 cups ham, bacon or
  sausage, diced
2 cups sharp Cheddar cheese
6 eggs
3½ cups milk

½ teaspoon salt
½ teaspoon dry mustard
½ cup butter, melted
2 cups cornflakes, slightly
  crushed

Lay ½ of the bread in a greased 9x12-inch pan. Sprinkle the ham, bacon, or sausage and cheese over the bread and top with the remaining bread. Beat the eggs, mix in the salt, mustard, and milk. Pour over the casserole and let soak uncovered in the refrigerator overnight. Melt the butter, mix in the cornflakes and sprinkle over the casserole. Press in slightly. Bake at 350° for 45 minutes. Makes 8-12 servings.

Great Plains Cooking

Khemosabi Quiche

This is a quiche that real men will eat.

½ cup butter
2 large brown onions
8 ounces mushrooms
½ ounce dry vermouth
2 tablespoons minced
  garlic
1 cup shredded Cheddar
  cheese

1 cup shredded Monterey Jack
  cheese
2 unbaked pie shells
6 eggs
1 cup whipping cream
1 tablespoon Worcestershire
  sauce

Melt butter in skillet. Chop onions and slice mushrooms. Add wine and garlic to skillet. Add onions and mushrooms. Sauté until golden. Reserve 2 tablespoons of each cheese. Alternate layers of remaining cheeses and mushroom mixture in 9-inch pie shells until all ingredients are used. Combine eggs, cream and Worcestershire sauce in bowl; mix with wire whisk. Pour over layers in pie shells. Top with reserved cheeses. Bake at 350° for 45 minutes. Serve warm or cold. May reheat in microwave, if desired. Yields 12 servings.

Per serving: Cal 455; Prot 13.3g; Carbo 18.4g; T Fat 36.8g; Chol 212.0mg; Potas 227.0mg; Sod 463.0mg.

Beyond Oats

Company Casserole Quiche

For convenience, assemble a day ahead and refrigerate.

1 pound mushrooms,
  thinly sliced
2 tablespoons butter
8 eggs
1 pint low-fat sour cream
1 pint low-fat cottage cheese
1 cup grated Parmesan cheese
1/2 cup flour

2 teaspoons onion powder
1/2 teaspoon salt
8 drops Tabasco sauce
1 pound shredded Monterey
  Jack cheese
2 cups cooked, cubed turkey
  or chicken

In a medium skillet, sauté mushrooms in butter until tender; remove and set aside. Combine eggs, sour cream, cottage cheese, Parmesan, flour, and seasonings in a food processor (a blender can also be used, but ingredients will need to be mixed in two batches); blend until smooth. Place reserved mushrooms, shredded cheese, and turkey in 9x13-inch (3-quart) greased baking dish. Pour egg mixture over all; stir lightly to mix. (Cover and refrigerate if you do not wish to bake immediately.)

Bake, uncovered, at 350° 55-65 minutes, or until knife inserted near center comes out clean, and casserole is puffed and golden (refrigerated casseroles may take 10-15 minutes more baking time). Let stand 5 minutes before cutting. Makes 12-16 servings.

Palates

Rocky Mountain Quiche

Delightful with a fruit cup and muffin.

3 tablespoons vegetable oil
2½ cups Colorado potatoes, coarsely shredded
1 cup Swiss or Cheddar cheese, grated
¾ cup ham, chicken or sausage, cooked, diced
¼ cup chopped onion
1 cup evaporated milk
2 eggs
½ teaspoon salt
⅛ teaspoon pepper
1 tablespoon parsley flakes

In a 9-inch pie pan, stir together the oil and potatoes. Press evenly into pie crust shape. Bake at 425° for 15 minutes or until just beginning to brown. Remove from oven. Layer on cheese, meat, and onion. In a bowl, beat together milk, eggs, and seasonings. Pour egg mixture onto other ingredients. Sprinkle with parsley flakes. Return to oven and bake at 425° for 30 minutes or until lightly browned and a knife inserted into the center comes out clean. Allow to cool 5 minutes before cutting into wedges to serve. Makes 4-5 servings.

Per serving: Cal 444; Prot 23.6g; Carbo 25g; Fat 27g; Chol 166mg; Sod 856mg; Dietary Fiber 1.6g.

Colorado Potato Favorite Recipes

Bacon and Swiss Quiche

¼ pound bacon, cooked and crumbled
2 cups whipping cream
⅛ teaspoon garlic powder
⅛ teaspoon onion salt
½ teaspoon dried parsley
3 eggs
1 homemade or Pillsbury ready-made pie crust
½ cup diced Swiss cheese

Preheat oven to 375°. Separate bacon into strips, and cook about 6 minutes in microwave to remove grease. Cool and crumble bacon; set aside. Heat whipping cream, garlic powder, onion salt, and parsley in saucepan on top of stove. Remove from heat and add eggs. Beat well with wire whisk. Line quiche or pie dish with crust. Distribute cheese and bacon in pie crust. Pour cream mixture over bacon and cheese in dish. Bake for 40 minutes. Serve with fruit, and croissants or English muffins. Makes 6-8 servings. *Recipe from Engelmann Pines, Winter Park.*

Colorado Columbine Delicacies

Quiche à la Suisse

4 large eggs
1 1/2 cups cream
1/2 pound Gruyére cheese,
  grated (about 2 cups)
1 teaspoon salt
1/4 pound bacon
1/2 cup butter
2 medium onions, very
  thinly sliced

2 leeks, thinly sliced
1 teaspoon chopped chives
1 teaspoon marjoram
1 teaspoon chopped fresh
  parsley
1 (9-inch) unbaked pastry
  shell

Beat eggs with cream; add cheese and salt and set aside. Fry bacon until crisp; crumble and set aside. Melt butter in same skillet; add onions and leeks, and sauté until golden brown. Remove from heat and add chives, marjoram, parsley, and bacon. Combine with egg mixture and pour into pastry shell. Bake at 400° for about 40 minutes, or until a knife inserted in the center comes out clean. Makes 6 servings.

Colorado Cache Cookbook

Grandma BB's Pineapple Fritters

These are the greatest!

1 cup flour
1 teaspoon baking powder
1/4 teaspoon salt
2 tablespoons sugar
1/4 teaspoon cinnamon
1/4 teaspoon nutmeg

1 egg
1/3 cup milk
1 tablespoon melted fat
1 tablespoon lemon juice
1 cup shredded pineapple,
  drained

Mix and sift all dry ingredients into a small bowl. Beat egg slightly and add milk and butter. Stir the liquid mixture into the dry ingredients, beating until you have a smooth batter. Add lemon juice and drained pineapple. Drop into hot deep fryer using a teaspoon. Fry until golden brown. Remove, pat excess oil off with paper towel, and then roll in sugar or powdered sugar while hot.

Home Cookin' Creations

Jameson Inn Spinach and Ham Enchiladas

Can be prepared the night before and baked in the morning.

1 can cream of chicken
  soup
1 cup light or regular
  sour cream
Milk for sauce consistency
Onions sautéed in butter,
  to taste
1 1/2 cups grated Monterey
  Jack cheese

8-10 flour tortillas
1 can chopped green chilies
Sliced ham, to taste
10 ounces frozen spinach,
  thawed and drained
Finely chopped green
  onions

Mix soup and sour cream. Add enough milk for a sauce and keep warm on stove. Sauté onions in butter. Grate cheese. Grease 9x12-inch glass pan. Prepare individual tortillas by lining center of each with a few sautéed onions, green chilies, cheese, ham, and spinach. Roll up tortillas. Spread some sauce in baking pan, then place rolled tortillas seam-side down. Cover with remaining sauce, more cheese and chopped green onions. Bake at 350° for 25-30 minutes. Makes 8 servings. *Recipe from Jameson Inn, Golden.*

Colorado Columbine Delicacies

Breakfast Sausage Bread

2 (1-pound) loaves frozen
white bread dough,
thawed
1/2 pound mild pork sausage
1/2 pound hot pork sausage
1 1/2 cups fresh mushrooms,
sliced
1/2 cup onions, chopped
3 eggs

2 1/2 cups mozzarella cheese,
shredded
1 teaspoon dried basil
1 teaspoon dried parsley
flakes
1 teaspoon dried rosemary,
crushed
1 teaspoon garlic powder

Allow dough to rise until nearly doubled. Meanwhile, in a skillet over medium heat, cook and crumble sausage. Add mushrooms and onions. Cook and stir until sausage is browned and vegetables are tender; drain. Cool. Beat one egg, set aside. To sausage mixture, add 2 eggs, cheese and seasonings; mix well.

Roll each loaf of dough into a 16x12-inch rectangle. Spread half sausage mixture on each loaf to within one inch of edges. Roll jellyroll-style, starting at a narrow end; seal edges. Place on greased baking sheet. Bake at 350° for 25 minutes; brush with beaten egg. Bake 5-10 minutes more or until golden brown. Slice and serve warm. Yields 2 loaves.

Country Classics II

Omelets with Ramen

1 package any flavor Ramen
noodles
1 tablespoon margarine
3 eggs, beaten

1/2 cup ham, chopped
1/4 cup onion, chopped
1/4 cup green peppers,
chopped

Cook noodles and drain. Add seasoning packet. Melt margarine in skillet and add beaten eggs. Fold in other ingredients. Cook until lightly brown.

101 Ways to Make Ramen Noodles

Chile Verde Eggs

12 eggs
1/3 cup milk
1/2 teaspoon Tabasco sauce
Salt and fresh ground pepper,
  to taste
1 tablespoon butter
Chile Verde

3 ounces Cheddar cheese,
  grated
1 bunch fresh cilantro,
  chopped
1 dozen corn or flour tortillas,
  warmed

Whisk eggs, milk, Tabasco, salt and pepper until blended. Melt butter in large skillet. Pour in egg mixture, cooking until set and moist.

Heat Chile Verde thoroughly. Place eggs on serving plates and spoon 1/4 cup hot Chile Verde over. Sprinkle with 1-2 tablespoons grated cheese and cilantro to taste. Serve with warm buttered flour or corn tortillas.

CHILE VERDE:
The Ortega chiles have wonderful flavor; they seem to be hotter at times, so add to individual tastes.

1 pound pork butt, diced
  1/2-inch thick
1/2 pound ground beef or pork
2 (1-pound) cans tomatoes,
  chopped
1/2 teaspoon cumin

2 (4-ounce) cans Ortega green
  chiles
1 clove garlic, crushed
1/4 teaspoon oregano
Salt and pepper to taste

Brown diced and ground meat; add tomatoes, cumin, chiles, garlic, oregano. Bring to a boil, then reduce to simmer for 20-30 minutes. Adjust seasonings. Serves 4-6.

Good Morning, Goldie!

Morning Glory Brunch Casserole

This is an exceptional brunch dish, especially when made a day ahead . . . gives the flavors a chance to blend, and the cook an extra hour of sleep!

18 hard-boiled eggs
1 pound bacon, cooked
  and drained
1/4 cup butter
1/4 cup flour
1 cup cream
1 cup milk

1 (1-pound) jar Cheese Whiz
1/4 teaspoon thyme (crushed
  leaf)
1/4 teaspoon marjoram
1/8 teaspoon garlic powder
1/4 cup chopped parsley,
  fresh, if possible

Hard boil eggs, cool and slice thin. (An egg slicer saves a lot of time.) Prepare bacon. Make a cream sauce, adding flour to melted butter. Gradually add milk and cream, stirring constantly until thick. Add Cheese Whiz and stir until melted. Add seasonings, including half the parsley. In a buttered 9x12-inch baking dish, layer egg slices, sauce, crumbled bacon, etc., ending with sauce. Bake about 40 minutes, covered, in a 350° oven. Garnish with fresh parsley. Serve hot and bubbly. Serves 8-10.

Kitchen Keepsakes

Stacey's Western Baked Omelette

1/3 cup sliced green onions	1 medium tomato, chopped
1 tablespoon butter or margarine	6 eggs, beaten
1 1/2 cups cooked rice	1/3 cup milk
1 cup shredded Cheddar cheese	1 teaspoon Worcestershire sauce
1 can diced green chilies, drained	1/2 teaspoon salt
	Picante sauce, optional

In small skillet over medium heat, cook onions in butter until tender but not brown. Combine rice, cheese, chilies, and tomato in large bowl; add cooked onions. Combine eggs, milk, Worcestershire, and milk in small bowl. Stir into rice mixture. Pour into buttered 9-inch quiche dish or pie pan. Bake at 350° for 30-35 minutes. Serve with picante sauce, if desired. Makes 4 servings. *Recipe from The Painted Lady Bed & Breakfast Inn, Colorado Springs.*

Pure Gold—Colorado Treasures

Old Carson Inn Mexican Casserole

Tortilla chips	1/4 cup flour
2 cups Monterey Jack cheese, grated	1/2 teaspoon cumin
7 eggs	1/2 teaspoon garlic powder
1 1/2 cups milk	Salt and pepper, to taste
1 teaspoon baking powder	1 small can diced Ro-Tel tomatoes

Arrange tortilla chips on bottom and sides of shallow 2-quart dish that has been sprayed with Pam. Sprinkle cheese on top of chips. Beat together the next 7 ingredients. Pour into casserole. Spoon tomatoes on top. Bake at 350° for one hour. Garnish with sour cream. Makes 8 servings. *Recipe from Old Carson Inn, Lake City.*

Colorado Columbine Delicacies

Molly Brown

This was probably the most popular item in the restaurant I once owned. We also did a version with roast beef, turkey, and Cheddar cheese we called the Horace Tabor.

1 wide-size loaf sour-
  dough bread (unsliced)
1/3 cup mayonnaise
2 teaspoons Dijon-style
  mustard
1 teaspoon lemon juice
1 teaspoon Worcestershire
  sauce

1/4 teaspoon white pepper
6 ounces thinly sliced ham
6 ounces thinly sliced
  turkey
6 sliced Swiss cheese
Melted butter

Slice bread lengthwise; trim crust from the slices. (Save top and bottom pieces; they are great for garlic toast or croutons.) Flatten each slice with rolling pin. Combine mayonnaise, mustard, lemon juice, Worcestershire sauce, and pepper. Spread mayonnaise mixture on each slice of bread. Layer ham, turkey, and cheese on each slice. (Use amounts of ham, turkey, and cheese as needed, not necessarily the amounts mentioned.) Roll-up sandwich; secure with toothpick. Brush with melted butter and place on baking sheet. Bake in preheated oven at 375° for 12-15 minutes or until golden brown. Serves 5-6.

Mystic Mountain Memories

Tofu for Sandwiches

8 ounces hard-style
  tofu
1/4 cup mayonnaise
1 teaspoon prepared mustard
Dash garlic powder
Dash pepper
1/4 cup finely chopped
  green pepper

1 piece celery, finely
  chopped
2 teaspoons finely chopped
  onion
1/4 teaspoon soy sauce
8 slices bread

In a medium-size bowl, crumble tofu with a fork. Mix in mayonnaise. Stir in remaining ingredients, except bread. Add more mayonnaise if needed. Spread on bread; top with lettuce and top piece of bread. Makes 4 full sandwiches.

Easy Recipes for 1, 2 or a Few

Italian Hero Loaf

3¼ cups flour, divided
1 tablespoon sugar
1 teaspoon salt
1 package quick-rising yeast
1 cup hot water (125° - 130°)
1 tablespoon margarine,
  softened
8 ounces sliced cooked ham
4 ounces sliced provolone
  cheese

4 ounces sliced salami
1 (2-ounce) jar sliced
  pimientos, drained
½ cup pitted ripe olives,
  drained
1 egg white, beaten
Sesame seeds
Creamy Italian dressing
  (optional)

Set aside one cup flour. In large bowl of mixer, mix remaining flour, sugar, salt, and yeast. Stir in hot water and margarine. Mix in only enough reserved flour to make soft dough. Allow mixer to knead dough an additional 4 minutes.

On greased baking sheet, roll dough into 14x10-inch rectangle. Layer ham, provolone, and salami over center third of dough length; top with pimientos and olives. Make cuts from filling to dough edges at 1-inch intervals along sides of filling. Alternating sides, fold strips at an angle across filling; cover. Place large shallow pan on counter; half fill with boiling water. Place baking sheet over pan; let dough rise 15 minutes. Brush loaf with egg white; sprinkle with sesame seed. Bake at 400° for 25 minutes or till done. Cool slightly; serve warm with Italian dressing, if desired. Refrigerate leftovers; reheat to serve.

More Goodies and Guess-Whats

Best Chunky Sandwich Spread

1 (8-ounce) package cream
  cheese, softened
½ cup onion, chopped
½ cup green pepper,
  chopped
3 tablespoons pimiento,
  chopped and drained

3 tablespoons catsup
3 hard boiled eggs,
  chopped
1 cup pecans, finely
  chopped
¼ teaspoon salt
¼ teaspoon pepper

Combine all the ingredients together and mix well. Spoon the mixture into a covered container. Chill for one hour or longer. Makes 3 cups.

Great Plains Cooking

Six-Grain Granola

3 cups regular rolled oats
1 cup whole wheat flour
1/2 cup cornmeal
1/2 cup rye flour
1/2 cup millet meal
1/2 cup wheat germ
1/2 cup brown sugar
1/3 cup shredded coconut

1/3 cup hulled sunflower seeds
1/3 cup sesame seeds
1 1/2 teaspoons salt
1/2 cup creamy or chunky
  peanut butter
1/2 cup salad oil
1/2 cup water
1/2 teaspoon vanilla

Combine rolled oats, whole wheat flour, cornmeal, rye flour, millet, wheat germ, brown sugar, coconut, sunflower seeds, sesame seeds, and salt. In blender, combine peanut butter, oil, water, and vanilla. Add to flour mixture, mixing with hands. Crumble onto a large broiler pan evenly. Bake uncovered in a 250° oven for one hour, stirring every 20 minutes. Turn off oven; leave in closed oven until completely cooled. Store airtight. Makes 9 cups of granola. *Recipe from Hackman House B&B, Woodland Park.*

Pure Gold—Colorado Treasures

Backpack Muesli

Hearty, warm breakfast for the back country.

1 cup regular oats, uncooked
1 cup shredded whole wheat
  cereal, crushed
1/4 cup raisins
1/4 cup coconut
1/4 cup dried apples, chopped

1/4 cup nuts or seeds
2/3 cup nonfat dry milk
  powder
1 teaspoon cinnamon
3 cups water

Mix dry ingredients in a plastic bag for camping. In the evening, add 3 cups of water, cover mixture and soak all night. In the morning, heat to boiling over the fire. Add more nonfat dry milk if desired. Yields 4 servings.

Per serving: Cal 314; Fat 7.9g; Chol 2mg; Sod 88mg.

Simply Colorado

Soups

Tyrannosaurus-Rex greets visitors at the Denver Museum of Natural History.

Chuckwagon Soup

1 pound hamburger meat
1 medium onion, chopped
3 stalks celery, chopped
3 carrots, sliced
4 potatoes, peeled and cubed
  (or rice, barley or noodles)
1 (10-ounce) package frozen
  mixed vegetables (or add
  corn, peas, beans or any
  other vegetable to taste)

1 (16-ounce) can tomatoes
  (or tomato sauce)
Water to cover
4 beef bouillon cubes
1/4 teaspoon black pepper
1 1/2 teaspoons salt
1/4 teaspoon garlic powder
Cheddar cheese, grated
Flour and water mixture to
  thicken

In a large saucepan, brown the hamburger with the onion. Drain fat. Add celery, carrots, potatoes, frozen mixed vegetables and tomatoes. Add water, then seasonings. Bring to a boil, reduce heat and simmer until vegetables are tender. Ladle into bowls and top each generously with grated cheese.

As with any soup, this is better the second day as flavors have blended. This is also a good soup to make when there are little dabs of leftover vegetables to use, and it's definitely one you can make your own with dashes of your favorite seasonings. Serves 6-8.

More Kitchen Keepsakes

Southwest Ramen Vegetable Soup

1 can tomato soup
1 cup water
1 can enchilada sauce
1/2 cup corn
1/2 cup green beans
1/2 cup kidney beans
1/2 cup salsa

1/2 cup cooked chicken
chopped (optional)
1 package any flavor Ramen
noodles, crumbled
Tortilla chips and shredded
Monterey Jack cheese

Combine tomato soup, water, and enchilada sauce. Cook over medium heat until hot. Add vegetables, salsa, and chicken. Simmer for 15 minutes. Add crumbled noodles and simmer 3-5 minutes. Serve topped with chips and cheese.

101 Ways to Make Ramen Noodles

Southwestern Soup

2 chicken breasts, diced
2 quarts chicken broth (4
10-ounce cans broth,
plus 2 cups water)
1 (10-ounce) can tomatoes
and green chiles,
chopped
1 (14-ounce) can corn with
green and red peppers

1 (14-ounce) can pinto beans,
drained
1 tablespoon cilantro,
chopped
1 medium onion, finely diced
3 garlic cloves, minced
3 tablespoons ground cumin
2 tablespoons chili powder
1 package taco seasoning mix

Combine all ingredients in slow cooker. Stir. Cover and cook on low 8-10 hours. Ladle into soup bowls with sides of guacamole, black olives, tortilla, and Monterey Jack cheese. Serves 10.

Per serving: 197 calories; 3.8 fat grams.

Quick Crockery

At the ProRodeo Hall of Fame and Museum of the American Cowboy in Colorado Springs is the larger-than-life bronze statue of legendary Casey Tibbs (one of America's most celebrated rodeo cowboys) aboard the famed saddle bronc "Necktie."

Light and Healthy Bean Soup

1 (16-ounce) can seasoned tomatoes
1 (14-ounce) can chicken broth
1 cup salsa
2 cups water
1 (8-ounce) can corn
1 (16-ounce) can garbanzo beans, rinsed and drained
1 (16-ounce) can kidney beans, rinsed and drained
1 (15-ounce) can black beans, rinsed and drained
1 large onion, chopped
1 clove garlic, minced
1 medium green pepper, chopped
$1/2$ teaspoon ground thyme
$1/2$ teaspoon oregano leaves
$1/4$ teaspoon basil leaves, crushed slightly
$1/4$ cup cilantro, chopped
$1/2$ cup uncooked white rice

Put all ingredients into slow cooker. Stir. Cover and cook on low 6-8 hours. Serve with warmed tortillas or fresh, crusty bread. Serves 8-10.

Per serving: 551 calories; 5.4 fat grams.

Quick Crockery

Green Chili and Bean Soup

1 (16-ounce) package dried pinto beans
1 (3-pound) pot roast
2 cloves garlic
2 tablespoons oregano
2 tablespoons chili powder
1 (4-ounce) can green chilies, drained, chopped
1 tablespoon salt
1 medium onion, chopped
2 (28-ounce) cans tomatoes, mashed
3 cups water

Soak beans in water to cover overnight. Combine beans, pot roast, garlic, oregano, chili powder, green chilies, salt, onion, tomatoes, and water in slow cooker. Cook on medium for 6 hours. Remove roast. Discard fat and bones; shred meat. Place shredded meat in slow cooker. Cook for one hour longer.

Serve over tortillas or corn chips, topped with shredded cheese, chopped onion, chopped tomatoes, sour cream, or avocado slices. Yields 12 servings.

Per serving: Cal 306; T Fat 8g; 22% Cal from Fat; Prot 30g; Carbo 31g; Fiber 12g; Chol 64mg; Sod 864mg.

The Flavor of Colorado

Nine Bean Soup

2 cups Bean Soup Mix
2 quarts water
1 pound ham, diced
1 large onion, minced
1/4 teaspoon minced garlic
1/2 teaspoon salt

1/2 - 1 cup sliced carrots
1/4 - 1/2 cup celery, sliced
1 (16-ounce) can tomatoes
1 (10-ounce) can Ro-Tel
   tomatoes (with green
   chilies)

Wash bean mixture and soak overnight. Drain. Add 2 quarts water and ham, onion, garlic, and salt. Bring to a boil and simmer 2-3 hours or until beans are tender. Add remaining ingredients. Simmer 30 minutes.

BEAN SOUP MIX:
1 (16-ounce) package dried
   black beans
1 (16-ounce) package dried
   pinto beans
1 (16-ounce) package dried
   split peas
1 (16-ounce) package dried
   baby Lima beans
1 (16-ounce) package dried
   Northern white beans

1 (16-ounce) package dried
   barley
1 (16-ounce) package dried
   garbanzo beans
1 (16-ounce) package dried
   kidney beans
1 (16-ounce) package dried
   black-eyed peas

Mix all together in large bowl. Store. This is fun to give as a gift. Pour 2 cups of beans in a jar and give along with the recipe.

More Kitchen Keepsakes

Boulder Black Bean Soup

The perfect supper after an awesome day of skiing!

2 teaspoons olive oil
1 medium onion, chopped
3 cloves garlic, minced
1 teaspoon dried whole
  oregano
1/2 teaspoon dried thyme
1/2 teaspoon cumin
1/4 teaspoon cayenne pepper
3 cups canned black beans,
  rinsed and drained

3 cups low-sodium chicken
  broth
2 tomatoes, chopped
1/2 cup onion, chopped
  (optional)
1/2 cup reduced-fat Monterey
  Jack cheese, shredded
  (optional)

Heat oil in a large saucepan over medium heat. Sauté onion and garlic until tender (about 5 minutes). Stir in oregano, thyme, cumin, and pepper; cook one minute longer. Place half of beans in a blender and purée until smooth, adding chicken broth as needed to make a smooth purée. Add purée, remaining whole beans and broth to saucepan. Bring to a boil over medium heat then simmer uncovered for 20-30 minutes. Serve garnished with diced tomatoes and, if desired, onion and shredded cheese. Yields 8 servings.

Per serving: Cal 141; Fat 4.5mg; Chol 0mg; Sod 32mg.

Simply Colorado

Barbecued Bean Soup

2 1/2 cups pinto beans
8 cups water
2 cups carrots, chopped
1 cup onion, chopped
1 meaty ham bone
1 (16-ounce) can tomatoes

1/4 cup vinegar
2 tablespoons brown sugar
2 tablespoons Worcestershire
  sauce
2 teaspoons prepared
  mustard

Wash and soak beans. Cook with water, carrots, onion, and ham bone for 2 1/2 hours. Add the rest of ingredients and cook 1/2 hour more or till beans are tender. Remove ham bone; cut meat off of it and return meat to soup. Mash some of the beans in the blender to help thicken soup.; Makes 8-10 servings.

Per serving: Calories 442.5, prot. 24g, sugars 10.6g, fiber 24.37g, sat. Fat 3.56g, poly. Fat 1.1mg, choles. 37.5mg, sod. 384.37mg, potas. 1177mg.

More Than Soup Bean Cookbook

Cantaloupe Soup

1 ripe cantaloupe	¹/₂ cup dry sherry
2 fresh oranges	¹/₂ teaspoon allspice
¹/₂ fresh lime	

Cut cantaloupe in half and remove seeds. Remove peel and chop the cantaloupe into 1-inch pieces. Purée in a blender or food processor. Squeeze the juice from the oranges and the lime and add to the cantaloupe, along with the remainder of the ingredients. Process all of the ingredients together. Chill for an hour before serving.

Serve in bowls and garnish with any or all of the following: raspberries, blueberries, fresh sprigs of mint. Serves 4.

Lowfat, Homestyle Cookbook

Cold Buttermilk Shrimp Soup

Surprisingly good!

1 quart buttermilk	1 cucumber, peeled, seeded,
1 tablespoon dry mustard	and chopped fine (save 6
1 teaspoon sage	slices for garnish)
1 teaspoon sugar	2 tablespoons chopped chives
¹/₂ - ³/₄ pound cooked shrimp,	Garlic to taste (optional)
chopped and chilled	

Whisk together buttermilk, mustard, sage, and sugar. Add shrimp, cucumber, chives, and garlic to the whisked liquid. Chill 3 hours. Garnish each serving with ¹/₂ shrimp and 1 slice cucumber. Serves 6 cups.

Recipes from Our House

Potato Soup

2 cups diced, peeled
  raw potatoes
1/2 cup diced celery
1/4 cup diced onion
3/4 cup water

2 tablespoons salad oil
2 tablespoons flour
2 cups milk
Dash pepper
Salt to taste

In a large saucepan, bring potatoes, celery, onion, and water to a boil. Cover and simmer 10 minutes, or until veggies are tender. In another large saucepan, heat oil over low heat. Stir in flour; then gradually stir in milk. Cook until it becomes thick and smooth. Add veggies with cooking water. Cook over low heat 5 minutes. Makes 4 servings.

Easy Recipes for 1, 2 or a Few

Hearty Potato-Ham Chowder

3 cups peeled, cubed
  Colorado potatoes
1 cup water
2/3 cup onion, finely chopped
1 teaspoon dried marjoram,
  crushed
1/2 teaspoon dry mustard
2 teaspoons instant chicken
  bouillon granules

1/4 teaspoon pepper
3 cups milk
1/4 cup all-purpose flour
3/4 cup Swiss cheese, shredded
1 cup reduced-sodium ham,
  chopped
2 tablespoons parsley,
  snipped

In a large saucepan, combine the potatoes, water, onion, marjoram, mustard, bouillon granules, and pepper. Bring to boiling; reduce heat. Cover and simmer about 20 minutes or until potatoes are tender. Mash potatoes slightly; do not drain. Combine one cup of the milk and flour, whisk to blend well. Add to hot mixture along with remaining milk and cheese. Cook and stir until slightly thickened and bubbly. Cook and stir one minute more. Stir in ham and parsley; heat through. Makes 4-6 servings.

Per serving: Cal 326; Prot 16g; Carbo 41g; Fat 11g; Chol 37mg; Sod 922mg; Dietary Fiber 2g.

Colorado Potato Favorite Recipes

Cheddar Cheese Soup

3 cups water
3 chicken bouillon cubes
1 medium onion, sliced
1/2 cup diced green pepper
1/3 cup butter or margarine
1/3 cup flour

3 1/2 cups milk
4 cups (1 pound) shredded
  Cheddar cheese
1 (2-ounce) jar diced
  pimiento, drained
1/4 teaspoon hot sauce

Combine water and bouillon cubes in Dutch oven. Bring to a boil. Add vegetables; cover and simmer 12 minutes or until vegetables are tender. Melt butter in heavy saucepan. Blend in flour and cook one minute. Gradually add milk; cook over medium heat until thickened, stirring until melted. Stir cheese, pimiento, and hot sauce (if desired) into vegetable mixture. Cook over low heat. Do not boil.

Grade A Recipes

Broccoli-Cheese Soup

4 cups frozen or fresh
  broccoli
2 cans chicken broth
2 cups chopped onions
1 clove garlic or 1/8 teaspoon
  garlic powder

1/2 cup margarine
1/2 cup flour
2 cups milk
2 cups Cheddar cheese
1 teaspoon basil

Simmer until tender, broccoli, broth, and onions with garlic. Melt in saucepan margarine, flour, milk, and cheese. Mix the cheese sauce into the broccoli mixture and add basil. Heat; simmer awhile, and enjoy.

Four Square Meals a Day

Big band leader Glenn Miller is Fort Morgan High School's most famous graduate. Miller played football for the Fort Morgan Maroons and was named "Best left end in Colorado."

Cream of Zucchini Soup

This soup can be prepared the night before and served chilled for lunch or dinner the next day.

6 medium zucchini, cut in
  chunks, not peeled
1 medium onion, chopped
1 large garlic clove,
  minced

1 teaspoon salt
1/2 teaspoon pepper
1 tablespoon flour
3 (14-ounce) cans chicken
  broth

Mix all ingredients together in slow cooker. Cover and cook on high 2 hours. Remove from slow cooker and cool about 15 minutes. Put in blender and purée. Return to slow cooker and warm to serving temperature. Serves 6.

Per serving: 89 calories; 2.3 fat grams.

Quick Crockery

Mushroom and Barley Soup

1 1/2 pounds boneless beef
  chuck, cut into 3/4-inch
  cubes
1 tablespoon cooking oil
1 1/2 cups onions, chopped
1 cup carrots, diced
1 cup celery, sliced
1 pound fresh mushrooms,
  sliced
2 garlic cloves, minced
1/2 teaspoon dried thyme

1 (14 1/2-ounce) can beef broth
1 (14 1/2-ounce) can chicken
  broth
2 cups water
1/2 cup medium pearl barley
1 teaspoon salt, optional
1/2 teaspoon pepper
3 tablespoons fresh parsley,
  chopped

In a Dutch oven or soup kettle, brown meat in oil. Remove meat with a slotted spoon and set aside. Sauté onions, carrots, and celery in drippings over medium heat until tender, about 5 minutes. Add mushrooms, garlic, and thyme; cook and stir for 3 minutes. Add broths, water, barley, salt and pepper. Return meat to pan and bring to a boil. Reduce heat, cover and simmer for 1 1/2 - 2 hours or until barley and meat are tender. Add parsley. Serves 10.

Country Classics II

Cream of Corn Soup

2 strips bacon, finely chopped
2 tablespoons finely chopped
onion
2 cups frozen or fresh corn
2 tablespoons butter

2 tablespoons flour
2 cups milk
1 teaspoon salt
1/2 teaspoon pepper
2 cups light cream

Fry diced bacon until crisp; put aside and sauté onion in drippings until soft. Put corn through chopper; add to bacon and onion. Add butter and then the flour; cook slowly for 3 minutes. Add milk, salt and pepper and cook till thickened, then add cream and heat till smooth.

The Best of Friends

Midwest Corn Chowder

2 cups diced potatoes
1/2 cup chopped carrots
1/2 cup chopped celery
1/4 cup chopped onion
2 cups boiling water

1/4 cup margarine
1/4 cup flour
2 cups milk
10 ounces mellow Cheddar
16 ounces creamed corn

Simmer potatoes, carrots, celery, and onion in water 15-20 minutes, till tender. Make a cream sauce with margarine, flour, and milk. Stir shredded cheese into cream sauce until melted. Add cheese sauce and creamed corn to vegetables and their broth. Heat through but do not let this boil. Serves 6-8

Sharing Our Best

Chicken Chile Soup

2¹/₂ cups water
1 teaspoon lemon pepper
  seasoning
1 teaspoon cumin seeds
4 chicken breasts
1 garlic clove, minced
1 cup onion, chopped
2 (9-ounce) packages frozen
  white corn, thawed

2 (4-ounce) cans diced green
  chiles
1 teaspoon ground cumin
2-3 tablespoons lime juice
2 (15-ounce) cans Great
  Northern beans, undrained
²/₃ cup tortilla chips, crushed
²/₃ cup Monterey Jack cheese
  (reduced fat, if desired)

Combine all ingredients, except tortilla chips and cheese, in slow cooker. Stir. Cover and cook on low 8-10 hours. To serve, place one tablespoon each of tortilla chips and cheese in 8 soup bowls. Ladle hot soup over cheese. Serve with salsa and warm tortillas. If you have an extra few minutes, butter the tortillas and place on a cookie sheet. Bake in 400° oven for 5 minutes. Cut into wedges. Serves 8.

Per serving: 690 calories; 11.3 fat grams.

Quick Crockery

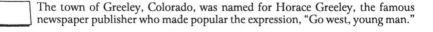

The town of Greeley, Colorado, was named for Horace Greeley, the famous newspaper publisher who made popular the expression, "Go west, young man."

Salads

Colorado's State Capitol in Denver's beautiful Civic Center Park.

Crunchy Cole Slaw

1 large head cabbage
4 green onions
1/4 cup sesame seeds

DRESSING:
1/4 cup sugar
1 cup oil
2 teaspoons salt

1/2 cup slivered almonds
2 packages Ramen noodles,
  crushed

6 tablespoons rice vinegar
1 teaspoon pepper

Chop cabbage and onions together. Spray cookie sheet with Pam and toast seeds, almonds and noodles in 350° oven till browned. Mix dressing ingredients together. Add dressing to noodle mixture at last mixture.

Home Cookin' Creations

Spring Ramen Salad

1 package chicken sesame
  Ramen noodles
1 1/2 tablespoons lemon juice
1/6 cup salad oil
1 teaspoon sugar
1/2 cup red and/or green
  seedless grapes,
  cut in half

1/4 cup red and/or green
  apples, diced
1/4 cup pineapple, diced
1 1/2 tablespoons chives or
  green onions
4 ounces smoked turkey
  breast, cut in strips
1/8 cup walnut pieces

Cook noodles and drain. Rinse with cold water. Add sesame oil (in package); refrigerate. For dressing combine lemon juice, salad oil, seasoning packet, and sugar. Combine noodles, grapes, apples, pineapple, chives, and turkey. Mix with dressing and walnuts.

101 Ways to Make Ramen Noodles

Carrot and Pineapple Slaw

²/₃ cup mayonnaise
²/₃ cup dairy sour cream
1 teaspoon grated onion
1 tablespoon lemon juice
¹/₂ teaspoon salt
1 teaspoon sugar

1 (13¹/₂-ounce) can pineapple chunks, well drained
1 cup coarsely shredded carrots
2 cups shredded cabbage
¹/₃ cup slivered toasted almonds

Blend together mayonnaise, sour cream, onion, lemon juice, salt, and sugar. Combine pineapple, carrots, cabbage, and almonds in a large bowl. Add mayonnaise mixture and toss well. Chill. Makes about 6 servings.

What's Cookin' in Melon Country

Russ's Favorite Jell-O Salad

Nice touch at buffet.

1 (3-ounce) package orange Jell-O
1 (3-ounce) package peach Jell-O
1 (3-ounce) package lemon Jell-O
1 (16-ounce) can mandarin oranges

1 (16-ounce) can sliced peaches
1 (16-ounce) can green grapes
1 (3-ounce) package instant vanilla pudding
1 (8-ounce) carton cream cheese
2 cups milk

Using a clear glass 3-quart bowl as one container, mix each flavor Jell-O individually. Use orange with mandarin, peach with peaches, lemon with grape. Drain each fruit and use the juice as part of the cold water. Refrigerate each until they are soft-set. Gently pour other 2 flavors on top of the one in the big bowl, taking care to keep the layers. An hour before serving, mix pudding according to directions and add softened cream cheese. Refrigerate until served.

Sharing Our Best/Muleshoe Ranch

Cranberry Raspberry Salad

1 (3-ounce) package raspberry
 gelatin
3/4 cup hot water
1 can whole cranberry sauce

1 (8-ounce) can crushed
 pineapple
1 cup seedless grapes
1/2 cup chopped nuts

Dissolve gelatin in hot water. Add cranberry sauce and crushed pineapple. As it begins to thicken, add grapes and nuts. Chill.

More Goodies and Guess-Whats

Pistachio Salad

1 package instant pistachio
 pudding mix
1 small can crushed
 pineapple, chilled,
 drained, reserve juice

1 small can mandarin
 oranges, chilled, drained,
 reserve juice
3/4 large carton Cool Whip,
 thawed
Mini-marshmallows to taste

Mix pudding with juices from fruit; add Cool Whip and mix well. Fold in fruit and marshmallows. Chill.

Taking Culinary Liberties

Frosted Lime-Walnut Salad

1 package lime gelatin
1 cup boiling water
1 (20-ounce) can crushed
 pineapple
1 cup small curd cottage
 cheese

1/2 cup celery, finely sliced
1 tablespoon pimiento,
 chopped
1/2 cup walnuts, chopped

Dissolve gelatin in boiling water; cool till syrupy. Stir in remaining ingredients. Turn into 8x4x4-inch loaf pan or 7x11-inch pan, rinsed in cold water; chill. When firm, unmold or leave in pan. Frost. Serves 8.

FROSTING:
1 (3-ounce) package cream
 cheese

1 tablespoon mayonnaise
1 teaspoon lemon juice

The Best of Friends

Frozen Cranberry Salad

2 (3-ounce) packages cream
cheese, softened
2 tablespoons sugar
2 tablespoons mayonnaise
1 can whole or strained
cranberry sauce

1 cup well-drained crushed
pineapple
1/2 cup finely chopped pecans,
(optional)
1 cup cream, whipped

Let cream cheese come to room temperature. Mash with fork;
add sugar, mayonnaise, cranberry sauce, pineapple, and nuts.
Mix well and add whipped cream. Mix well; pour into a lightly
buttered loaf pan and freeze for 6 hours or overnight.

Home Cookin' Creations

Gelatin and Pinto Bean Salad

1 (3-ounce) package lime
gelatin
3 tablespoons vinegar
2 cups cooked pinto beans,
drained

1 tablespoon onion, minced
1 cup green pepper,
chopped

Prepare gelatin as directed on package, using vinegar as part of
liquid. Set aside to cool. Put 1/2 of beans in 8-inch cake pan.
Sprinkle onion and green pepper over beans. Top with rest of
beans. Pour cooled gelatin over top. Chill till firm. Serve over
lettuce.

More Than Soup Bean Cookbook

Avocado, Grapefruit and Arugula Salad

4 ripe avocados, sliced
1 1/2 grapefruits, sectioned
4 handfuls of arugula, cleaned
2 tablespoons extra-virgin olive oil

2 tablespoons juice from fresh grapefruit
Freshly ground black pepper

Toss avocado, grapefruit sections, and arugula with oil and grapefruit juice. Season with pepper to taste and serve on cold plates. Serves 4. *Recipe from Chef James E. Cohen, The Wildflower, The Lodge at Vail.*

Cooking with Colorado's Greatest Chefs

Calico Corn Salad

2 (16-ounce) packages frozen corn, thawed
4 small zucchini, diced
1 large sweet red pepper, diced
2 (4-ounce) cans green chilies, chopped
5 green onions, chopped

2/3 cup olive oil
1/4 cup fresh lime juice
2 tablespoons cider vinegar
2-2 1/2 teaspoons ground cumin
1 1/2 teaspoons salt
1 teaspoon pepper
1/2 teaspoon garlic salt

In a bowl, toss corn, zucchini, red pepper, chilies, and onions. In a jar with tight-fitting lid, combine remaining ingredients; shake well. Pour over salad and stir gently. Chill for several hours or overnight. Serves 8.

Country Classics II

At the foot of the majestic Rocky Mountains, the United States Air Force Academy is the most visited military facility in the US. It is Colorado's most frequently visited man-made attraction.

Spicy Southwestern Potato Salad

1 (4-ounce) can green chiles, diced
1 hard cooked egg, finely chopped or mashed
1/4 cup dill pickle, chopped
1/4 cup onion, finely chopped
2 tablespoons mayonnaise
1 tablespoon prepared mustard
1 teaspoon prepared horseradish
1 teaspoon jalapeño sauce
1/2 cup cheese, diced (optional)
5-6 Colorado potatoes, peeled, cubed, cooked

In a mixing bowl, combine green chiles, chopped eggs, dill pickle, onion, mayonnaise, mustard, horseradish, jalapeño sauce, and cheese, if desired. Mix well. Stir in potatoes; mix well. Cover and chill several hours. Makes 6-8 servings.

Per serving: Cal 157; Prot 3.5g; Carbo 26g; Fat 5g; Chol 38mg; Sod 392mg; Dietary Fiber 2g.

Colorado Potato Favorite Recipes

Sunny Fruit Fiesta

1 whole cantaloupe, halved and seeded
1/2 whole honeydew melon, halved and seeded
1/4 cup granulated sugar
2 tablespoons fresh lemon juice
1/4 cup fresh lime juice
1 tablespoon orange liqueur, optional
1 1/2 teaspoons lime peel
1 cup fresh strawberries
1 cup seedless grapes

Using a melon baller, scoop cantaloupe and honeydew into balls (reserve melon halves). In a large bowl, combine the sugar, lemon juice, lime juice, orange liqueur, and lime peel. Stir well to dissolve sugar. Add the cantaloupe and honeydew balls, strawberries, and grapes. Toss gently to combine. Cover bowl with plastic wrap and refrigerate for at least one hour to blend flavors; stir once or twice. Spoon into melon half. Serves 6.

What's Cookin' in Melon Country

Mandarin Salad

1/2 cup sliced almonds
3 tablespoons sugar
1/2 head iceberg lettuce
1/2 head romaine lettuce
1 cup chopped celery

2 whole green onions,
  chopped
1 (11-ounce) can mandarin
  oranges, drained

DRESSING:
1/2 teaspoon salt
Dash of pepper
1/4 cup vegetable oil
1 tablespoon chopped parsley

2 tablespoons sugar
2 tablespoons vinegar
Dash of Tabasco sauce

In a small pan over medium heat, cook almonds and sugar, stirring constantly until almonds are coated and sugar dissolved. Watch carefully, as they will burn easily. Cool and store in airtight container. Mix all dressing ingredients, and chill. Mix lettuces, celery, and onions. Just before serving, add almonds, and oranges. Toss with the dressing. Makes 4-6 servings.

Colorado Cache Cookbook

Fresh Broccoli Salad

1 1/2 heads broccoli, cut
  into small florets
1 medium red onion,
  diced
1 cup raisins

8 strips bacon, cooked and
  crumbled
1 cup salted, shelled
  sunflower seeds

DRESSING:
1 cup mayonnaise
1/4 cup sugar

2 teaspoons vinegar

Combine salad ingredients in medium bowl. Mix dressing ingredients and add to broccoli mixture.

4-H Family Cookbook

The Spanish word, *colorado*, means colored red; hence the name of the Colorado River, because the river flows through canyons of red stone.

Ditch Bank Asparagus Toss

An elegant dish served on a plate with stuffed salmon.

2 pounds fresh asparagus　　**8 radishes, sliced**
8 green onions, diagonally
**　sliced**

Snap off tough ends of asparagus. Remove scales from stalks with a knife or vegetable peeler, if desired. Cut spears diagonally into 1½-inch pieces. Cook asparagus, covered, in a small amount of boiling water 6 minutes, or steam until crisp-tender; drain. Place asparagus in a large bowl, cover and chill thoroughly. Add green onions and radishes to asparagus; set aside.

DRESSING:

¼ cup white vinegar　　　**½ teaspoon basil, dried**
¼ cup olive oil　　　　　　**　(1½ teaspoons fresh)**
½ teaspoon thyme, dried　**¼ teaspoon salt**
**　(1½ teaspoons fresh)**　　**¼ teaspoon white pepper**

Combine vinegar and remaining ingredients in a small jar. Cover tightly and shake until combined. Pour dressing over vegetables. Toss gently before serving. Yields 8 servings.

Note: Asparagus grows wild in the springtime along the irrigation ditch banks in Western Colorado.

West of the Rockies

Spinach Salad

8 strips bacon	1 cup bean sprouts, drained
1 package fresh spinach	1 small can water chestnuts,
4 hard-boiled eggs, sliced	diced

Fry bacon until crisp. Drain thoroughly and crumble. Wash and drain spinach. Break into bite-size pieces. Combine ingredients and toss carefully with Tangy Dressing.

TANGY DRESSING:

1 cup salad oil	1/3 cup ketchup
1/4 cup wine vinegar	2 teaspoons Worcestershire
3/4 cup sugar	sauce
1/2 teaspoon salt	1/2 onion, quartered

Combine ingredients in blender and purée. Serves 6.

Kitchen Keepsakes

Strawberry-Spinach Salad with Honey Pecan Dressing

HONEY PECAN DRESSING:

1/3 cup light salad oil	1 teaspoon dill (optional)
3 tablespoons honey	1/3 - 1/2 cup pecans
1 tablespoon lemon juice	2 tablespoons warm water
2 teaspoons vinegar	Grated lemon rind
1 teaspoon soy sauce	2 cloves garlic

In a blender, mix all the ingredients until smooth. Chill thoroughly. This dressing can be made ahead and kept under refrigeration for about 2 weeks.

SALAD:

Spinach leaves	Fresh mushrooms
Fresh strawberries	Slices of bacon, cooked crisp

Wash and vein the spinach leaves. Place sliced, fresh strawberries and mushrooms on top. Crumble some cooked, crisp bacon on top. Arrange on a plate and spoon dressing over the top. *Recipe from The Heartstone Inn, Colorado Springs.*

Distinctly Delicious

Splendid Raspberry Spinach Salad

DRESSING:

2 tablespoons raspberry vinegar

2 tablespoons raspberry jam

1/3 cup vegetable oil

SALAD:

8 cups spinach, torn into pieces

3/4 cup chopped macadamia nuts

1 cup fresh raspberries

3 kiwis, peeled and sliced

To prepare dressing, combine vinegar and jam in blender or small bowl. Add oil in a thin stream. Put in tightly sealed container and shake to blend well. Refrigerate ahead to chill. Toss spinach, half of the nuts, half of the raspberries, and half of the kiwis with dressing on a platter or in a flat salad bowl. Top with remaining nuts, raspberries, and kiwis. Serve immediately. Serves 8.

Note: Strawberries, strawberry jam, and strawberry vinegar are equally splendid in this outstanding summer salad!

The Durango Cookbook

Chinese Chicken Salad

DRESSING:

1/2 teaspoon dry mustard
2 tablespoons sugar
2 teaspoons soy sauce

1 teaspoon sesame oil
1/4 cup salad oil
3 tablespoons rice vinegar

Combine ingredients in a tightly sealed container and shake well.

SALAD:

2 large heads iceberg lettuce
4 chicken breasts, boiled for 25-30 minutes
1 bunch celery, chopped

2 bunches green onions, chopped
1 1/2 cups toasted sliced almonds
1/4 cup sesame seeds

Shred lettuce and chicken. Add chopped celery, green onions, sesame seeds, and toasted sliced almonds. Pour dressing over and toss.

The Durango Cookbook

Charlemagne Salad with Hot Brie Dressing

1 medium head curly endive
1 medium head iceberg lettuce
1 medium head romaine lettuce
Garlic croutons, (preferably homemade)
1/2 cup olive oil
4 teaspoons minced shallots

2 teaspoons minced garlic
1/2 cup sherry wine vinegar
2 tablespoons fresh lemon juice
4 teaspoons Dijon mustard
10 ounces ripe French brie cheese (rind remains), cut into small pieces, room temperature
Freshly ground pepper

Tear lettuces into bite-size pieces. Toss with garlic croutons in large bowl. Warm olive oil in heavy large skillet over low heat for 10 minutes. Add shallots and garlic and cook until translucent, stirring occasionally, about 5 minutes. Blend in vinegar, lemon juice, and mustard. Add cheese and stir until smooth. Season with pepper. Toss hot dressing with lettuce and serve. Serves 8.

Note: Do not use high heat.

Lighter Tastes of Aspen

Herbed Vinaigrette Dressing

¹/₂ cup olive oil
¹/₂ cup water
1 ¹/₂ tablespoons red wine vinegar
1 ¹/₂ tablespoons balsamic vinegar
¹/₂ teaspoon each of cilantro, thyme, basil, and salt

¹/₄ teaspoon each of sage and ground cumin
1 teaspoon each of honey and prepared mustard
¹/₂ teaspoon garlic granules or powder
Black pepper to taste

Mix all together in a blender or food processor. Makes about 1 cup.

How to Feed a Vegetarian

Perry's Dressing

Great for tossed salad.

1 cup corn oil
¹/₂ cup red wine vinegar
2 teaspoons sugar
1 teaspoon salt
¹/₂ teaspoon pepper

¹/₂ teaspoon curry
¹/₂ teaspoon Worcestershire sauce
4 teaspoons lime juice
1 teaspoon Parmesan cheese

Mix all ingredients together. Makes 2 cups.

4-H Family Cookbook

Raspberry Wine Vinegar

2 cups fresh ripe   **2 cups white wine vinegar**
   raspberries

Pour vinegar over fruit in a large glass jar. Metal lids cause a reaction with the vinegar, so cover with plastic inside a lid or with a glass plate. Let stand for 2-3 weeks in a cool dark place. Strain well; heat, but do not boil. Pour into clean glass bottles. Close tightly. Seal. If your berries are not sweet enough, a small amount of sugar may be added.

Raspberry Story

The Royal Gorge is a 1,053-foot-deep chasm carved by the Arkansas River. Lt. Zebulon Pike had made the statement in 1806 that there was no way to cross it. But in 1929, within a six-month period, at a cost of $350,000, the world's highest suspension bridge was constructed.

Vegetables

A lovely Victorian home decorates for Christmas in the Rockies. Leadville.

Skillet Cabbage

2 slices bacon	Dash pepper
2 tablespoons brown sugar	2 cups coarsely grated
2 tablespoons vinegar	cabbage
1/4 teaspoon caraway seeds,	1 cup chopped unpeeled
optional	apples
2 tablespoons water	

In a medium skillet, cook bacon until crisp; drain, reserving one tablespoon grease in skillet. Set bacon aside; crumble. Stir in sugar, vinegar, caraway, water, and pepper; mix well. Stir in cabbage and apples. Cover; cook over low heat, stirring occasionally. For crisp cabbage, cook 15 minutes. For tender cabbage, cook 25 minutes. Stir in bacon. Makes 2 servings.

Easy Recipes for 1, 2 or a Few

Baked Cabbage Casserole

1 medium head cabbage,	1 1/2 cups boiling water
shredded	1 pound hamburger
1 medium onion, chopped	Salt and pepper to taste
1 cup uncooked rice	1 large or 2 small cans
(not instant)	tomato sauce
1 stick margarine	

Spread half of cabbage in greased casserole. Fry onion and rice until brown in margarine. Pour over cabbage; add boiling water. Brown hamburger and sprinkle over rice, add salt and pepper. Top with remaining cabbage and pour tomato sauce on top. Bake in 350° oven one hour.

Colorado Boys Ranch Auxiliary Cookbook

"Pikes Peak or Bust" was a popular slogan during the gold mining days. Though it is probably the most famous mountain in North America, Pikes Peak is only the state's 31st highest summit. It was atop this peak that Katherine Lee Bates was inspired to write "America the Beautiful."

Parmesan Fries

Most kids will love these lowfat fries!

**3-4 small baking potatoes
  (well scrubbed)**
¹/₄ cup Parmesan cheese
¹/₂ teaspoon garlic powder

¹/₈ teaspoon salt
¹/₈ teaspoon onion powder
**1 tablespoon reduced calorie
  margarine, melted**

Cut potatoes lengthwise into wedges. Cut into 30 wedges for 3 potatoes or 32 wedges for 4 potatoes. Mix together Parmesan cheese, garlic powder, salt, and onion powder in a large plastic bag. Brush melted margarine onto potatoes. Put 10-11 slices of potato into the bag at a time and shake until potatoes are coated with mixture. Place potatoes on a cookie sheet sprayed with vegetable oil cooking spray. Bake at 400° for 20-25 minutes. Serves 4.

Lowfat, Homestyle Cookbook

Scalloped Potatoes

These potatoes are great! Serve them with pinto beans and cornbread for a fabulous meal.

**6 medium potatoes, scrubbed
  and sliced**
1 medium onion, sliced

Salt and pepper
Whipping cream

Put potatoes and onions in greased casserole dish, add salt and pepper to taste. Add enough whipping cream to potatoes to barely cover. Bake at 350° for 1½ hours or until tender. Serves 6.

Country Classics

Gourmet Potatoes

1 (2-pound) bag frozen
  hash brown potatoes
2 sticks butter or margarine
Salt and pepper
1 pint sour cream

1 can cream of chicken soup
1/2 cup diced onion
2 cups shredded Cheddar
  cheese
2 cups cornflake crumbs

Thaw potatoes. Put in a 9x13-inch glass dish. Melt 1 stick butter and drizzle over potatoes. Salt and pepper to taste. Mix in separate bowl sour cream, soup, onion, and cheese. Pour over potatoes. Melt second stick of butter and mix with cornflake crumbs and sprinkle over potatoes. Bake 45 minutes at 375° and for 5 minutes at 500°.

Taking Culinary Liberties

Baked Mashed Potatoes

4 large potatoes (about
  2 pounds), peeled
  and quartered
1/4 cup milk
1/2 teaspoon salt
2 tablespoons margarine,
  melted, divided
1 egg, beaten

1 cup sour cream
1 cup small-curd cottage
  cheese
5 green onions, finely
  chopped
1/2 cup crushed butter-
  flavored crackers

Cook potatoes until tender; drain. Place in large bowl. Add milk, salt, and one tablespoon margarine. Beat until light and fluffy. Fold in egg, sour cream, cottage cheese, and onions. Place in a greased 1 1/2-quart baking dish. Combine the cracker crumbs and remaining margarine. Sprinkle over potato mixture. Bake uncovered at 350° for 20-30 minutes or until crumbs are lightly browned. Serves 4-6.

Note: This can be made ahead and refrigerated. Sprinkle crumbs on top just before baking.

Country Classics II

Tangy Mustard Potatoes

Great with hamburgers and just as good with brunch eggs.

2 medium-large baking
potatoes
3 tablespoons good mustard
2 tablespoons olive oil

3 tablespoons freshly grated
Parmesan cheese
Freshly ground pepper

Preheat oven to 425°. Peel potatoes; cut into 4 sections length-wise and then cut sections to French-fry widths (about 10 pieces per potato). In separate dish, whisk together mustard, oil, and cheese. In plastic bag, combine all ingredients to coat potatoes with mustard mixture. Spread potato pieces on a lightly greased baking sheet. Grind pepper over potatoes. Bake in preheated 425° oven for 35-40 minutes or until brown. Serves 4.

Recipes from Our House

Potatoes Montrose

6 medium potatoes
4 hard cooked eggs
1/2 cup margarine
2 cups dairy sour cream

1 1/2 teaspoons salt
1/4 teaspoon pepper
1 cup fine bread crumbs
Paprika

Peel, cook and slice potatoes. Slice eggs. Melt butter; add cream and seasonings and mix well. Put potatoes, eggs, cream mixture, and crumbs in layers in a shallow baking dish. Repeat, ending with crumbs. Sprinkle with paprika. Bake at 350° for about 30 minutes.

Mountain Cooking and Adventure

Crunchy Potatoes

6-8 medium-size potatoes **1 package onion soup mix**
1 tablespoon oil **Butter**

Scrub potatoes well. Leave peeling on, slice very thin into 2-quart casserole dish that has been greased with one tablespoon oil. Sprinkle onion soup mix over potatoes, dot with pats of butter, cover and bake in 400° oven until potatoes are soft (about 30 minutes), uncover; sprinkle with paprika and let brown.

The Best of Friends

Pickaroon Potatoes

A super accompaniment to a grilled steak after a day on the slopes.

6 large potatoes **1/2 cup whipping cream,**
2 tablespoons butter **whipped until stiff**
1/4 cup milk **1/4 cup grated Cheddar or**
Salt and pepper to taste **Parmesan cheese**
1 tablespoon hot **Paprika**
horseradish

Peel and wash potatoes and cook in salted boiling water until tender. Drain and mash with the butter and milk. Beat until light and fluffy. Season with salt and pepper, and fold in the horseradish. Pour into a buttered casserole, cover with whipped cream, sprinkle with the cheese and paprika. Bake in a pre-heated 350° oven until brown on top. Makes 6 servings.

Colorado Cache Cookbook

Prairie Schooners

4 large baked potatoes
1 (15-ounce) can ranch style
  beans
1 cup sour cream
1 stick butter, softened
Salt, pepper, and chili
  powder to taste

2 tablespoons chopped green
  pepper
2 tablespoons chopped onion
1 tablespoon butter or
  margarine
1 cup Cheddar cheese,
  grated

Slice off top ⅓ of baked potato lengthwise. Scoop out potato leaving ¼ inch around potato skin. Mash potato until free of lumps. Drain beans thoroughly, reserving juice. Mash beans. Whip sour cream, butter, mashed beans, salt, pepper, and chili powder. Add to mashed potatoes, adding enough bean juice to moisten. Spoon mixture into potato shells.

Saute green pepper and onion in margarine. Top each potato with grated cheese, onion, and green pepper. Bake at 425° about 10 minutes or until browned. Serves 4.

Kitchen Keepsakes by Request

Country Potatoes

12 red or new potatoes
  (baking potatoes can
  be substituted)
Salt and pepper to taste
2 cups sharp Cheddar cheese,
  grated

6 strips cooked bacon,
  crumbled
¼ stick butter, melted

Boil potatoes, with skins on, until done. Drain and let cool. Thinly slice the unpeeled potatoes. Butter bottom of 9x12-inch baking dish. Put one layer of potatoes, salt, pepper, half of cheese, and bacon in casserole. Dribble half of the butter over layer. Make another layer the same way. Bake, uncovered, at 350° until bubbling hot, about 15 minutes. This potato recipe is guaranteed to please! Freezes well.

More Kitchen Keepsakes

Savory Roasted New Potatoes

16 small red new potatoes,
cut into large
bite-size pieces
1 teaspoon minced fresh
garlic
1/2 teaspoon paprika (hot
variety, if available)
2 tablespoons minced fresh
rosemary
1/2 teaspoon salt
1/4 teaspoon freshly ground
black pepper
1 tablespoon Worcestershire
1/4 cup olive oil

Preheat oven to 375°. Place potatoes in large baking pan and sprinkle with garlic, paprika, rosemary, salt, and pepper. Toss to combine.

In small bowl, combine Worcestershire and olive oil and drizzle over potatoes. Toss to coat. Bake in lower half of oven, stirring occasionally, 45-55 minutes or until browned and tender. Makes 6-8 servings.

Colorado Collage

Cattlemen's Club
Twice-Baked Potatoes

5 large potatoes, scrubbed
and baked
1/3 cup half-and-half
1 cup sour cream
3 tablespoons green onions or
chives, minced
4 strips bacon, fried and
crumbled
1 cup Cheddar cheese, grated
1 1/2 - 2 teaspoons salt
1/2 teaspoon pepper
1/4 teaspoon garlic salt
1 egg, beaten
1/3 cup butter
1/2 cup mushrooms, sliced and
sautéed in butter

Bake potatoes for one hour at 350° or until tender in center. Cut in half lengthwise. Scoop out potato carefully as to not tear skins. Mash potatoes with mixer, add half-and-half and continue to beat until smooth. Add all other ingredients and mix well. Mixture should be somewhat softer than regular mashed potatoes to prevent drying out when baking again. Fill skin shells with mashed potato mixture and arrange on cookie sheet. Top each with extra grated cheese. Bake at 350° for 20 minutes. Great with steaks! Serves 8-10.

Kitchen Keepsakes

Sweet Potato Bonbons

3 pounds sweet potatoes
1/4 cup butter
1/2 cup brown sugar (packed)
1 teaspoon salt
1/2 teaspoon orange rind,
  grated

6 marshmallows, halved
1/3 cup butter, melted
4 cups cornflakes, crushed
12 pecan halves

Peel and cook sweet potatoes. Mash until light and fluffy. Beat in butter, sugar, salt, and orange rind. Divide into 12 portions. Press potatoes around each marshmallow half, being careful to keep marshmallows in center. Shape into ovals. Coat each with melted butter, roll in crushed cornflakes, top with pecan half and placc in lightly greased baking pan. Bake in hot oven, 450° for 7-8 minutes. Serves 6-8.

The Best of Friends

Southwestern Sweet Potatoes

Yes, you really do use that much tequila!

3 pounds sweet potatoes,
  peeled and shredded
1/2 cup pareve margarine or
  unsalted butter

1/4 cup lime juice
3 tablespoons sugar
2/3 cup tequila

Sauté potatoes in margarine or butter in a large skillet for 5 minutes. Add remaining ingredients and cook until al dente. Serve. Makes 8 servings.

Shalom on the Range

Luscious Yams

6 medium yams, cooked,
 peeled and halved, or
 2 (17-ounce) cans,
 well drained
1/2 cup Karo syrup
1/4 cup light cream or
 half-and-half

2 tablespoons margarine or
 butter
1/2 teaspoon ground cinnamon
1/2 cup brown sugar
1/2 teaspoon salt
Pecan pieces for top

Arrange yams in single layer in 11x7x2-inch baking dish; bake in 450° oven for 15 minutes. In heavy 1 1/2-quart saucepan, stir together remaining ingredients except pecans. Stirring constantly, bring to boil over medium heat and boil 5 minutes. Pour over yams, sprinkle pecan pieces on top, and bake for 10 minutes, basting once.

Fat Momma's Deli

Artichoke Green Bean Casserole

2 cups bread crumbs
3 toes garlic, minced
1/4 - 1 cup Parmesan cheese
1 tablespoon lemon
 juice

1 large can French-style
 green beans
2 large cans of artichoke
 hearts
Olive oil

Mix bread crumbs, garlic, cheese, and lemon juice; drain green beans and artichoke hearts; add to mixture. Add olive oil to taste (should be moist, not dry) bake at 350° for 30 minutes.

Fat Mama's Deli

Bean Casserole

1 pound hamburger
3 medium onions, diced
1 pound bacon, cooked
1 pound smoked beef sausage,
 cut into bite-size pieces
2 (31-ounce) cans pork
 and beans

1 can kidney beans, drained
1 can butter beans, drained
1 can garbanzo beans, drained
1 cup ketchup
1/2 cup brown sugar
1 tablespoon vinegar
1 tablespoon liquid smoke

Cook hamburger and drain. Sauté onions with hamburger. Cook bacon and cut up. Add bacon and remaining ingredients to hamburger and simmer together for 3 hours.

4-H Family Cookbook

Cinnamon Beans with Bacon

A new twist for an old favorite.

1 tablespoon butter
1/4 cup chopped onion
1/4 teaspoon ground
  cinnamon
1 1/4 pounds fresh green beans
1/4 cup chicken broth

1/8 teaspoon salt
Dash of freshly ground black
  pepper
2 tablespoons tomato paste
6 slices bacon, fried crisp and
  crumbled

In medium saucepan, melt butter and sauté onion with cinnamon until onion is transparent. Stir in green beans, chicken broth, salt and pepper. Heat to boiling, reduce heat and simmer 20 minutes or until beans are tender. Gently mix in tomato paste and bacon. Serve immediately. Makes 6 servings.

Crème de Colorado

Long's Peak Baked Beans

Baked beans have never tasted so good!

1/2 pound hamburger
5 sliced bacon, chopped
1 small onion, chopped
1/3 cup brown sugar
1/2 cup ketchup
2 tablespoons prepared
  mustard
1/4 teaspoon pepper
1/3 cup sugar
1/3 cup barbecue sauce

2 tablespoons molasses
1/2 teaspoon salt
1/2 teaspoon chili powder
1 (46-54-ounce) can pork and
  beans, drained
1 (15-ounce) can black-eyed
  peas, drained
1 (15-ounce) can red kidney
  beans, drained and rinsed

In a skillet, brown hamburger, bacon, and onion. Drain well. Combine remaining ingredients, except beans, and mix well. Mix in beans. Cover and bake at 350° for one hour. Best if left in refrigerator for 3-4 hours before baking.

More Kitchen Keepsakes

The Continental Divide, which separates the water of the continent, runs through the Colorado Rockies. All waters that fall to the east flow into the Atlantic Ocean and all to the west, into the Pacific Ocean.

Dove Creek "Pinto Bean Capital of the World" Beans

1 pound dried pinto beans
1 large ham bone or 2 smoked ham hocks, cracked
2 onions, chopped
3 garlic cloves, minced
2 bay leaves
1 teaspoon dried oregano leaves, crumbled
1-2 teaspoons ground cumin
1-2 tablespoons chili powder to taste

Pinch sugar
Pinch crushed red pepper flakes
Water to cover
1 (10-ounce) can Ro-Tel tomatoes with green chilies, diced
1 (16-ounce) can tomatoes with juice, broken up
1-2 canned jalapeños, to taste
Salt and pepper
1 (12-ounce) can beer

Rinse beans, discarding any bad ones, and place in large pot. Cover with water and soak overnight or bring water to a boil; boil 2 minutes; remove from heat, cover and let beans soak one hour. Discard water, rinse beans with cold water and drain.

Place beans in pot with all other ingredients. Bring to a boil, reduce heat until liquid barely simmers and simmer, partially covered for 3-4 hours, until beans are very tender. Add water and beer during cooking, as needed, to prevent sticking and scorching. Remove and discard bay leaves. Adjust seasonings while cooking, if necessary. Serves 6-10.

Colorado Foods and More. . .

Baked Avocado Halves

3 ripe but firm avocados
1 egg white
2 tablespoons mayonnaise

Salt to taste
Pimiento strips
Lettuce leaves to garnish

Peel avocados, cut in half lengthwise, and remove seeds. Enlarge cavities with a spoon, place on a lightly greased baking sheet. Beat egg white until stiff, fold in mayonnaise, and add salt. Spoon into cavities. Bake in 350° oven for 8 minutes. Slip pan under broiler until sauce is lightly browned. Decorate top with pimiento strips. Serve on lettuce leaves. Serves 6.

The Colorado Cookbook

Chili

4 large onions, chopped
1 large green pepper, seeded, chopped
3 tablespoons olive oil
1 tablespoon mustard seeds
2 tablespoons chili powder
2 teaspoons cumin seeds (optional)
2 teaspoons unsweetened cocoa
¹/₂ teaspoon ground cinnamon
3 (16-ounce) cans kidney beans, with juice
1 (6-ounce) can tomato paste
1 cup water
1 (16-ounce) can whole tomatoes
1 pound firm tofu, diced

In a large kettle, sauté onions and pepper in oil over medium-high heat until onions are golden. Add mustard seeds, and cook, stirring, for another minute. Add chili powder, cumin, cocoa, cinnamon, beans and their juice, tomato paste, and water. Pour in the liquid from the can of tomatoes, then chop tomatoes and add to the pot (or pulse the tomatoes and their liquid in a blender). Add tofu, and stir. Reduce heat and simmer for 40 minutes, stirring often.

After 20 minutes, check the consistency of your chili. If the chili is runnier than you like, simmer uncovered. If the chili is thicker than you like, add more water and simmer covered. If the chili is just right, simmer covered. In any case, stir frequently to prevent scorching. Salt to taste. Serve with relishes of grated Cheddar cheese, diced green onions, chopped tomatoes, diced green chilies, or peeled and diced cucumber. For vegans and non-dairy vegetarians, you can get a soy cheese (a non-dairy product found in the dairy section at health food stores), if you want. Serves 4-6.

How to Feed a Vegetarian

Eggplant Casserole

1 large eggplant
2 tablespoons butter
1/2 cup hot water
2 teaspoons beef stock base
1 1/2 teaspoons spaghetti
  sauce seasoning
1 cup dairy sour cream

1 tablespoon toasted onion
1/2 teaspoons salt
1/4 teaspoon pepper
1/4 cup bread crumbs
2 tablespoons grated
  Parmesan cheese

Pare eggplant and cut into cubes; melt butter in large pan and sauté eggplant for 5 minutes or until soft. Combine hot water, beef stock base, and spaghetti seasoning. Pour over eggplant; cover and simmer until eggplant is tender and liquid is absorbed. Spoon eggplant into flat baking dish.

Combine sour cream, toasted onion, salt, and pepper. Pour over eggplant; cover with crumbs and sprinkle with cheese. Bake at 350° for 20-25 minutes.

Home Cookin' Creations

Fried Eggplant

1 small eggplant
2 teaspoons salt
1 egg white
1 tablespoon water

1/4 cup flour
1/4 cup cornmeal
2 tablespoons margarine

Wash and peel eggplant. Cut into thin slices; then into strips (like French fries). Put into a bowl; cover with water to which you have stirred in 2 teaspoons salt. Soak at least one hour; drain on paper towels. In a pie pan, mix egg white and water. In another pie pan, mix flour and cornmeal. Heat margarine in a large skillet. Dip slices first into egg and water; then into flour and cornmeal, being sure to coat both sides. Fry eggplant over low heat, very slowly, turning to brown and crisp on all sides. Place on paper towels to drain. Serves 2-4.

Easy Recipes for 1, 2 or a Few

South of the Border Casserole

1 ½ pounds summer squash
(yellow or zucchini)
1 medium onion, chopped
2 tablespoons butter or
margarine
1 (4-ounce) can diced green
chilies
2 tablespoons flour
1 teaspoon salt

¼ - ½ teaspoon pepper
1 ½ cups Monterey Jack or
or mozzarella cheese
1 egg
1 cup cottage cheese
2 tablespoons parsley
½ cup Parmesan cheese

Dice squash; sauté with onion in butter until tender crisp. Fold in chilies, flour, salt and pepper. Place in 2-quart greased baking dish. Sprinkle with Monterey Jack cheese. Combine egg, cottage cheese and parsley. Layer over cheese; sprinkle with Parmesan. Bake uncovered at 400° for 25-30 minutes until heated through.

More Goodies and Guess-Whats

Squash Casserole

2 pounds fresh or 3
packages frozen squash
1 green pepper, chopped
1 small can green chilies
1 onion, chopped

2 beaten eggs
½ cup mayonnaise
½ cup grated Cheddar cheese
Salt and pepper to taste
Parmesan cheese

Place squash, green pepper, chilies, and onion in a saucepan with small amount of water. Cover and steam until tender. Drain well. Put into mixing bowl; add eggs, mayonnaise, grated cheese, salt and pepper. Mix well. Pour into buttered casserole and sprinkle top with Parmesan cheese. Bake at 325° for 45-60 minutes. Serves 6-10.

From an Adobe Oven to a Microwave Range

Denver has the nation's largest city park system, with more than 200 parks within city limits, and 20,000 acres of parks in the nearby mountains—an area larger than all of Manhattan Island.

Sautéed Squash
with Mushrooms and Onions

A good summertime vegetable dish, especially with barbecued chicken.

3 slices bacon
2-3 zucchini and/or yellow
   summer squash
1 small onion, chopped
1/2 cup fresh mushrooms,
   whole or sliced

1 tomato
1/8 teaspoon salt
Parmesan cheese

Cook bacon in skillet until crisp. Drain and remove all fat from skillet, except enough to cover bottom of pan. Cut washed squash into 1/8-inch rounds. Sauté in bacon fat along with onion and mushrooms until tender. Cut tomato into 6-8 lengthwise slices. Add tomato and crumbled bacon to squash mixture and heat well. Add salt. Turn into serving bowl and sprinkle with Parmesan cheese. Serve with extra Parmesan cheese for individual flavoring. Serves 4.

Kitchen Keepsakes

Crispy Parmesan Zucchini

Serve these as an appetizer, too.

3 large zucchini (about
   1 1/2 pounds)
1/3 cup melted butter
1/2 cup grated Parmesan cheese

Seasoned salt
Minced fresh herb like
   marjoram of basil
   (optional)

Preheat broiler. Cut zucchini into 1/4-inch thick diagonal slices. Dip one cut surface of each slice into melted butter, then cheese, coating well. Place zucchini slices, cheese-side up, on greased pan(s) with shallow sides. Sprinkle with seasoned salt and herb, if desired. Broil 4-6 inches from heat until crisp and golden, about 6-8 minutes. Serve immediately. Makes 6-8 servings.

Palates

Zucchini Casserole

This has been a family favorite casserole for years. The recipe has been duplicated and shared with numerous friends. Enjoy!

3 cups cooked sliced
zucchini squash
1/2 cup sour cream
1 can cream of chicken
soup
1 (2-ounce) jar chopped
pimento

1 small onion, finely chopped
1/2 cup margarine
1 (6-ounce) package corn-
bread stuffing mix

Combine zucchini, sour cream, soup, and pimento in bowl; mix well. Sauté onion in margarine in skillet until soft. Add both packages from stuffing mix; mix well. Alternate layers of zucchini mixture and stuffing in 1½-quart casserole, ending with stuffing. Bake at 350° for 30 minutes or until hot and bubbly. Yields 8 servings.

Per serving: Cal 268; Prot 5.0g; Carbo 23.6g; T Fat 17.5g; Chol 9.4mg; Potas 255.0mg; Sod 809.0mg.

Beyond Oats

Red Peppers and Yellow Squash

2 pounds yellow squash,
washed and sliced
1/4-inch thick
2 sweet red peppers, washed
and cut into pieces
about 1 x 1 inch
2 tomatoes, washed and
sliced 1/4-inch thick
6 scallions, washed and
sliced 1/4-inch thick
(include tops)

1 clove garlic, peeled and
crushed
1/2 teaspoon crushed dill seed
1/2 teaspoon crushed
coriander seed
1 teaspoon salt
1/8 teaspoon fresh ground
black pepper
3 tablespoons butter or
margarine

Place all vegetables in a 9x13x2-inch baking pan; sprinkle with seasonings; dot with butter. Toss all together lightly. Cover pan with aluminum foil and let stand at room temperature about 3 hours. Bake at 350° for about one hour.

Southwestern Foods et cetera

Stuffed Peppers

4 large red or green
  peppers
1 tablespoon olive oil
1 medium onion, chopped
2 stalks celery, diced
1 1/2 teaspoons cumin
1 1/2 teaspoons chili powder

1 1/2 teaspoons basil
1 teaspoon oregano
1 (15-ounce) can kidney beans
2 cups cooked brown rice
2 tablespoons tamari sauce
Cayenne pepper
1 (15-ounce) can tomato sauce

Preheat oven to 350°. Wash peppers, cut in half lengthwise, and remove seeds. Place cut-side-down in a single layer on a vegetable steamer over boiling water. Cover and steam until just starting to get soft, about 10 minutes. You may have to do this in two batches.

Heat olive oil in skillet. Add onions, celery, cumin, chili powder, basil, and oregano. Sauté until the onions are almost soft. Remove from heat. Drain and rinse kidney beans. Add the beans and rice to the onions, and mix. Add the tamari sauce, and for extra zest, add a bit of cayenne pepper to taste. Mix again.

Fill each pepper with rice mixture, and place in a lightly oiled 7x11-inch baking pan. When all peppers are stuffed and in the dish, pour the can of tomato sauce over the top. Cover with aluminum foil, and bake at 350° for 30 minutes. Serves 4.

How to Feed a Vegetarian

Peperonata

2 tablespoons butter or
  margarine
1/4 cup olive oil
1 pound onions, sliced
  1/8-inch thick (about
  4 cups)
2 pounds green and red
  peppers, peeled,* seeded,
  and cut in 1-inch strips
  (about 6 cups)

2 pounds tomatoes, peeled,
  seeded and coarsely
  chopped (about 3 cups)
1 teaspoon red wine
  vinegar
1 teaspoon salt
Freshly ground pepper

In a heavy 12-inch skillet, melt butter with olive oil over moderate heat. Add onions and cook them, turning frequently, for 10 minutes, or until they are soft and lightly browned. Stir in peppers. Reduce the heat, cover, and cook for 10 minutes.

Add tomatoes, vinegar, salt, and a few grindings of black pepper; cover the pan and cook for another 5 minutes. Then cook the vegetables uncovered over high heat, stirring gently, until almost all the liquid has boiled away. Serve the peperonata as a hot vegetable dish, preceding or along with the main course, or refrigerate and serve cold as part of an antipasto or as an accompaniment to cold roast meats or fowl.

*To peel peppers easily, place on cookie sheet and broil for about 5 minutes until skins turn black. Put peppers in a paper bag for about 15 minutes. Peel.

Italian Dishes et cetera

Denver is a sports capital, with all four Major League sports as well as two professional soccer teams and a professional women's basketball team, two of the world's largest rodeos, an international golf tournament, plus horse, dog, and stock car racing,

Corn and Cheese Pie

3 large eggs
1 (8.5-ounce) can cream corn
1 (8-ounce) can whole corn, drained
1 stick margarine, melted
1/2 cup cornmeal
1 cup sour cream

4 ounces Monterey Jack cheese, shredded
4 ounces sharp Cheddar cheese, shredded
2 tablespoons chopped green chilies
1/2 teaspoon salt
1/4 teaspoon Worcestershire sauce

Beat eggs and add rest of ingredients. Pour into a lightly greased 9-inch pie pan. Bake at 350° for 45-55 minutes or until firm and browned. Let rest 10 minutes before serving. Can be stored in refrigerator for 3 days or 3 months in freezer. If frozen, thaw and reheat at 350° for 20 minutes. Serves 6.

Kitchen Keepsakes by Request

Grilled Stuffed Onions

1 1/2 cups herb seasoned stuffing mix
1 cup Cheddar cheese, shredded
1 teaspoon poultry seasoning

1/3 cup butter or margarine, melted
1/3 cup hot water
6 medium sweet onions
Vegetable cooking spray
Fresh oregano (optional)

Combine first 5 ingredients, stirring until well blended and set aside. Cut each onion into 3 horizontal slices. Spread 2 tablespoons stuffing mixture between slices and reassemble onions. Place each onion on a 12-inch square piece of heavy-duty aluminum foil coated with cooking spray. Bring opposite corners together and twist to seal. Cook, covered with grill lid, over medium hot coals (350°-400°) 25 minutes or until tender. Garnish with fresh oregano, if desired. Makes 6 servings.

Note: Onions may be baked, unwrapped, in a lightly greased, covered, 11x7x1/2-inch baking dish at 350° for one hour or until tender.

What's Cookin' in Melon Country

Spinach-Cream Cheese Enchiladas

This is a really nice dish for entertaining. The sauce can be made a day ahead and the enchiladas can be filled ahead of time. When your guests arrive, pour the sauce over the filled tortillas, top with cheese and bake.

SAUCE:

3 tablespoons oil
3 cloves garlic, minced
2 teaspoons dried Mexican oregano
1 tablespoon dried ground red chile peppers

3 tablespoons unbleached flour
1 (6-ounce) can tomato paste
4 cups water
1 teaspoon salt or to taste
1 tablespoon apple cider vinegar

In oil, sauté garlic over low heat for 3 minutes. Add oregano, dried ground chiles, and flour, and stir until oil is absorbed. Stir in tomato paste, water, salt, and vinegar, and continue stirring until smooth. Bring to a boil; reduce heat and cook over medium heat until thickened.

FILLING:

1 (8-ounce) package cream cheese (room temperature)
1 (10-ounce) package frozen chopped spinach, thawed and squeezed dry
4 scallions, diced

1/2 cup roasted, peeled, and chopped green chile peppers
2 tablespoons lemon juice
12 (8-inch) flour tortillas
1/2 cup grated Monterey Jack cheese

Mix cream cheese, spinach, scallions, green chile peppers, and lemon juice.

Preheat oven to 350°. Grease a 9x13-inch baking pan. Fill each tortilla with 2 tablespoons filling and roll up. Place in baking pan. Reserving one cup sauce for serving at table, pour remaining sauce over filled tortillas. Top with grated cheese. Bake 20 minutes or until sauce is bubbling. Serve with reserved enchilada sauce. Makes 12 enchiladas. Serves 6.

The Durango Cookbook

Broccoli and Cheese Casserole

¹/₂ cup chopped celery
¹/₂ cup chopped green onions
2 tablespoons margarine
2 cups cooked rice

1 package cooked broccoli
¹/₂ roll jalapeño cheese
1 can mushroom soup

Sauté celery and onions in margarine; add remaining ingredients and mix all together. Bake in covered dish at 325° for 30 minutes.

Fat Mama's Deli

Broccoli with Dill Cheese Sauce

4 cups broccoli flowerets   ¹/₂ cup water

CHEESE SAUCE:
1 cup low-fat buttermilk
¹/₄ cup Parmesan cheese,
  grated

1 teaspoon Dijon mustard
2 teaspoons cornstarch
1 teaspoon dried dill weed

Place broccoli flowerets and water in a microwave safe dish. Cover dish with plastic wrap and microwave on HIGH power for 8-10 minutes or until tender. Meanwhile, combine buttermilk, Parmesan cheese, Dijon mustard and cornstarch in a small saucepan. Using a wire whisk, stir constantly until sauce boils. Cook over low heat for 2 minutes. Stir in dill weed and serve over drained broccoli. Yields 4 servings.

Simply Colorado

Apricot-Glazed Carrots

Good with poultry or pork.

**2 pounds carrots, cut on
diagonal**
**3 tablespoons butter or
margarine**
1/3 cup apricot preserves
1/4 teaspoon ground nutmeg

1/4 teaspoon salt
**1/2 - 1 teaspoon freshly grated
orange peel**
2 teaspoons fresh lemon juice
Parsley, for garnish

Cook scraped and cut carrots in salted water until just tender, about 20 minutes. Drain. Melt butter and stir in preserves until blended. Add nutmeg, salt, orange peel, and lemon juice. Toss carrots with apricot mixture until well coated. Garnish with parsley and serve at once. Makes 4-6 servings.

Colorado Cache Cookbook

Oriental Carrots

This is an easy, make-ahead recipe.

1 can tomato soup
1/2 cup oil
1 cup (scant) sugar
1/2 cup vinegar
1 teaspoon (scant) salt
1/4 teaspoon pepper

1 teaspoon prepared mustard
5 cups sliced cooked carrots
**1 medium onion, finely
chopped**
**1 green bell pepper, finely
chopped**

Combine tomato soup, oil, sugar, vinegar, salt, pepper, and mustard in saucepan. Simmer until sugar is dissolved, stirring constantly. Combine carrots, onion, and green pepper in bowl; mix well. Pour tomato soup mixture over vegetables. Marinate, covered, overnight in refrigerator. May serve cold or hot. Yields 6 servings.

Per serving: Cal 397; Prot 2.6g; Carbo 57.6g; T Fat 19.3g; Chol 0.0mg; Potas 498.0mg; Sod 797.0mg.

Beyond Oats

Beet Jelly

This is different and delicious, also very colorful. Fun to have everyone guess what the ingredients are. Everyone wants this recipe!

4 cups strained beet juice*　　**6 cups sugar**
1/2 cup fresh lemon juice　　　**1 small package raspberry**
1 package Sure-Jell　　　　　　**Jell-O**

Mix beet juice, lemon juice, and Sure-Jell in medium saucepan. Bring to a full boil. Add sugar and gelatin and boil hard for 10 minutes. Ladle into prepared jelly glasses and cover with 1/8 inch melted paraffin.

*To get beef juice, scrub fresh beets and cover with boiling water. Boil until beets are tender. Remove beets and use the water they have been cooked in. Save beets to eat later. (You can have your beets and eat them, too!)

Mystic Mountain Memories

Pasta, Rice, Etc.

Denver's 16th Street Mall is a mile-long pedestrian plaza through the heart of downtown.

Steamboat Alfredo

Try this Alfredo—Steamboat style!

10 ounces medium-size
  shrimp, peeled and
  deveined
10 ounces sea scallops
1/4 cup butter
2 tablespoons cream sherry
1/2 cup heavy cream

1 egg, beaten well
2 cloves garlic, minced
Salt and pepper to taste
Parsley
3/4 cup grated Romano and
  Parmesan cheese
1 pound fettuccine, cooked

Sauté seafood in butter 3-6 minutes until scallops turn white. Add sherry and simmer for about one minute. Add cream and bring to a slow boil, stirring constantly. Add egg, garlic, salt, pepper, and a bit of fresh parsley. Stir in cheese until smooth. Add cooked fettuccine and toss well. Garnish with lemon wedges and fresh parsley. Serves 4.

Steamboat Entertains

Rice Pepita

1 cup raw white rice
2 cups beef broth

1/2 cup pumpkin seeds, salted

Cook rice in broth until tender. Toss cooked rice with pumpkin seeds. Serves 6-8.

The Colorado Cookbook

Sesame Tofu

1 cake hard-style tofu,
  thinly sliced
2 tablespoons whole wheat
  flour

1 tablespoon sesame seeds
1-2 tablespoons butter or
  margarine

Place tofu slices on paper towels and allow to stand for 15 minutes to reduce moisture. On flat plate combine whole wheat flour and sesame seeds. Dredge tofu in flour mixture, covering both sides of slice. In a large skillet, melt the butter or margarine and then add the tofu. Fry for 2 minutes on each side or until the tofu is golden brown.

4-H Family Cookbook

Crested Butte Chili Cheese Supreme

2 tablespoons vegetable oil
1 medium green pepper, chopped
1 clove garlic, minced
1 (15.5-ounce) can kidney beans, drained
1 (16-ounce) can tomatoes, with juice, coarsely chopped
1 (15-ounce) can tomato sauce
1 tablespoon chili powder, or to taste

1 (15-ounce) carton ricotta cheese
2 cups (8 ounces) Monterey Jack cheese, shredded
1 (4-ounce) can chopped green chilies, drained
1 bunch green onions, finely chopped
3 eggs, beaten
1 (8-ounce) bag tortilla chips
2 cups (8 ounces) mild or medium Cheddar cheese, shredded

Heat oil in skillet over medium-high heat. Sauté green pepper and garlic until tender. Add kidney beans. Set aside.

In saucepan, combine tomatoes, tomato sauce, and chili powder. Bring to a boil, then reduce heat and simmer, uncovered, for 15 minutes. Add to kidney bean mixture. Combine ricotta and Monterey Jack cheeses, chiles, onions, and eggs.

Spread ¼ of cheese mixture evenly in greased 9x13-inch glass baking dish. Arrange ¼ chips over cheese. Spread ¼ tomato mixture over chips. Repeat layer 3 more times. Cover with foil and bake at 325° for 30-40 minutes. Remove foil and top with Cheddar cheese. Bake 10-15 minutes more. Let stand 5 minutes before serving. Yields 10-12 servings.

West of the Rockies

Italian Stuffed Shells

12 ounces jumbo pasta shells
8 ounces part-skim mozzarella cheese, shredded
12 ounces herb-seasoned spaghetti sauce
1 (10-ounce) package chopped spinach, thawed and drained
8 ounces cooked skinless chicken breasts, chopped

Bring 3 quarts of water to a boil. Cook pasta shells for 18-20 minutes, stirring frequently. Spray a 9x13x2-inch baking dish with vegetable oil cooking spray. Place shells in dish. Mix together ½ of the mozzarella, ½ of the spaghetti sauce, the spinach, and the chicken in a bowl. Stuff mixture into the shells and cover with the remainder of the sauce. Sprinkle with the remainder of the mozzarella. Bake at 350° for 15-20 minutes, or until the cheese is bubbly and slightly browned.

Lowfat, Homestyle Cookbook

Warm Ziti Pasta

1 (14½-ounce) can diced tomatoes
3 tablespoons olive oil
1½ tablespoons balsamic vinegar
1 clove garlic, minced
½ cup marinated sun-dried tomatoes, drained and chopped
⅓ cup chopped Greek olives
½ cup chopped red bell pepper
⅓ cup chopped fresh basil or 2 teaspoons dried basil
½ teaspoon freshly ground pepper
1½ cups Italian 6-cheese blend or ¼ cup each shredded mozzarella, Provolone, Parmesan, Romano, fontina and asiago
8 ounces ziti pasta, cooked according to package directions

Combine all ingredients except pasta in a large bowl and toss well. Add pasta and toss again. Heat briefly in microwave, but do not melt cheese. Makes 8 servings.

Shalom on the Range

Spaghetti Pie

8 ounces spaghetti
3 tablespoons butter
2 eggs, lightly beaten
1/3 cup grated Parmesan
   cheese
1 1/2 pounds ground beef
1 small onion, chopped
1 small green pepper,
   chopped
1 (8-ounce) can tomatoes,
   chopped

1 (6-ounce) can tomato paste
1 1/2 teaspoons oregano
1 1/2 tablespoons brown sugar
1/4 teaspoon salt
2 cloves garlic, minced
1 cup cottage cheese, well
   drained
1 cup shredded mozzarella
   cheese

Cook the spaghetti until just tender. Drain and stir butter, eggs, and Parmesan cheese into spaghetti. Press the spaghetti mixture into a buttered 10-inch pie plate as a crust.

In a skillet, cook ground beef, onion, and green pepper until meat is done. Drain off excess fat. Stir in the next 6 ingredients and simmer for 30 minutes. Spread cottage cheese over the spaghetti crust. Pour in meat-tomato mixture. Cover with foil and bake in a 350° oven for 45 minutes. Uncover and top with mozzarella cheese. Bake 7-8 minutes more, until cheese has melted. Serves 8.

Mystic Mountain Memories

Make Ahead Macaroni Frankfurter Bake

Very, very good!

6 slices bacon
5 frankfurters
3/4 cup sliced celery
1/2 cup chopped onion
2 tablespoons bacon fat
1 tablespoon flour
1/2 teaspoon salt

1/2 teaspoon pepper
1 (10 1/2-ounce) can cream of
celery soup
1 can evaporated milk
3 cups hot cooked macaroni
1/2 cup grated Cheddar cheese

Fry bacon crisp; reserve 2 tablespoons fat. Slice 3 frankfurt-ers. Sauté sliced frankfurters, celery, and onion in bacon fat. Stir in flour, salt, and pepper. Add soup and milk. Cook 10 minutes until slightly thickened, stirring constantly. Crumble bacon; add to sauce. Alternate layers of macaroni and cream sauce mixture in a 1 1/2-quart casserole. Split 2 frankfurters lengthwise. Place on top of casserole. Top with cheese. Bake in moderate oven for 20-25 minutes. Makes 6-8 servings.

Goodies and Guess-Whats

Tomato Pasta with Sausage and Shrimp

Excellent . . . a man pleaser.

**24-29 large raw shrimp
  in shell**
**1/2 pound penne round
  pasta**
**1 pound hot Italian bulk
  sausage, chopped**
**4-6 medium garlic cloves,
  minced**

1 shallot, minced
**1/2 teaspoon dried thyme
  leaves**
**1 (16-ounce) can chopped
  tomatoes, with juice**
1/3 cup heavy cream
2 bay leaves
Salt and pepper to taste

Peel shrimp; cut in halves lengthwise, leaving end intact to keep together. Cook penne. Brown sausage and drain, saving one tablespoon grease to sauté garlic, shallot, and thyme in. Sauté, then add tomatoes with juice, cream, and bay leaves. Add sausage. Gently simmer 10 minutes. Add shrimp and cook on low just until shrimp curls. Season with salt and pepper. Sprinkle liberally with Parmesan and freshly ground pepper. May be made ahead, warming and adding shrimp just before serving. Serves 6.

Recipes from Our House

Chili Relleno Casserole

Great do-ahead party dish.

**1 (27-ounce) can whole
  green chilies**
3 eggs
2 tablespoons flour
Small can Pet milk

1 small can tomato sauce
1 tablespoon sugar
**1 pound grated Cheddar
  cheese**
1 pound grated Jack cheese

Split chilies, remove seeds and black spots. Blend eggs, flour, and milk. In separate bowl blend tomato sauce and sugar. Place layer of bite-size chilies, flattened on bottom of 9x13-inch baking dish. Use 1/2 of each kind of cheese, then another layer of chilies followed by cheeses again. Pour egg mixture over chili/cheese layers. Bake 30 minutes uncovered at 350°. Remove and pour tomato sauce mixture over top and bake 15 minutes more. Serves 8.

Sharing Our Best

Gourmet Grits Casserole

Grits aren't just for breakfast. This is fabulous for brunch or a side dish with grilled meats.

6 cups water
1¹/₂ cups uncooked grits
1 pound longhorn Cheddar, shredded
1 (4-ounce) can diced green chiles, drained
3 eggs, beaten
¹/₄ cup butter, softened

1 tablespoon savory salt
2-3 cloves garlic, minced
Dash Tabasco sauce
Dash Worcestershire sauce
Dash paprika
Salt and pepper to taste
1 cup crushed cornflakes
¹/₄ cup melted butter

Cook grits in boiling water according to package directions. Stir in remaining ingredients except cornflakes and melted butter; mix well. Pour into greased 9x13-inch baking dish. Combine cornflakes and butter; sprinkle over casserole. Top with additional paprika, if desired. Bake at 250° 1½ - 2 hours, or until set. Makes 10-12 servings.

Note: Casserole can be prepared a day ahead, covered and refrigerated. Additional baking time may be needed.

Palates

Poultry

The world's highest suspension bridge and a spectacular aerial tramway cross the Royal Gorge near Canon City.

Chicken and Cola

Try chicken wings with this recipe as an appetizer. It's a perfect alternative to your favorite hot wings recipe.

1 fryer, cut into pieces
1 teaspoon salt

¹/₂ cup catsup
1 (12-ounce) can cola

Rinse chicken and remove skin, if desired. Place in slow cooker. Mix salt, catsup, and cola together and pour over chicken. Cover and cook on low 6-8 hours. Serves 6.

Per serving: 332 calories; 12.0 fat grams.

Quick Crockery

Lo Mein Ramen

1 tablespoon oil
1 tablespoon soy sauce
1 package chicken Ramen
noodles
1 pound chicken breast strips

¹/₂ cup onions, sliced
¹/₂ cup green peppers,
chopped
¹/₄ cup carrots

In skillet mix oil, soy sauce, and ¹/₂ seasoning packet. Add chicken, brown. Boil noodles and drain. Add vegetables to chicken, cook until tender. Add noodles separately and cook on medium for 5 minutes, stirring constantly.

101 Ways to Make Ramen Noodles

Hot Chicken Salad

2 cups diced chicken
1¹/₂ cups celery, diced
1 teaspoon grated onion
1 teaspoon salt
¹/₄ teaspoon white pepper
¹/₂ teaspoon monosodium
glutamate

1 teaspoon lemon juice
1¹/₂ cups mayonnaise
¹/₃ cup chopped pecans
¹/₂ cup grated Cheddar cheese
1 cup finely crushed potato
chips

Combine all ingredients, except pecans, cheese, and potato chips, and allow to marinate overnight. Add nuts and top with cheese and potato chips. Bake for 25 minutes at 350°. Serve hot.

Mountain Cooking and Adventure

Chinese Chicken Skillet

1 tablespoon oil or
   margarine
1 (4-piece) package
   chicken breasts
1 teaspoon salt
1/4 cup cooking sherry
2 tablespoons soy sauce
1 can chicken broth

1 (1-pound) package frozen
   Chinese-style vegetables
Some chopped onion and/or
   fresh gingerroot, if
   desired
1 cup sliced fresh mushrooms
2 cups cooked rice

Melt margarine in electric skillet; add the chicken, cut in chunks.
Add salt, sherry, and soy sauce; commence cooking. Add broth
and vegetables, also onion, ginger. Cover and cook until chicken
and veggies are almost done. Add mushrooms and cook another 10 minutes or so. Add either more broth or water as
needed. Stir in rice and serve.

Sharing Our Best/Muleshoe Ranch

Twelve-Boy Curry

6 tablespoons butter
1 cup minced onion
1 cup chopped celery
4-5 cloves garlic, minced
1/2 cup flour
1-2 tablespoons curry powder,
   or to taste
1 teaspoon dry mustard

1/2 teaspoon salt
1/4 teaspoon pepper
1 teaspoon paprika
Dash of cayenne pepper
1 1/4 cups strong beef stock
1 cup light cream
3 tablespoons catsup
1 (3-pound) chicken, stewed,
   cut into bite-size pieces

Melt butter in a large skillet. Add onion, celery, and garlic, and cook over medium heat until onion is limp. Combine all of the dry ingredients and add to the onion mixture, stirring over low heat until blended. Slowly add beef stock and cream, and stir until smooth. Add catsup. Cook for 2 minutes, then add chicken and heat to boiling point. Let stand one hour, then reheat. Serve over hot buttered rice with any, or better yet, all of the condiments. Makes 6 servings.

CONDIMENTS:

Chopped hard cooked eggs
Chopped onion
Shredded coconut
Chopped salted peanuts
Sweet pickle relish
Chutney

Chopped green pepper
Chopped green or ripe olives
Orange marmalade
Chopped, cooked crisp bacon
Raisins
Crushed pineapple

Note: This curry is best if made a day ahead and reheated.

Colorado Cache Cookbook

Chicken Breasts with Asparagus

1 tablespoon cooking oil
4 chicken breasts, skinned,
  boned, and halved
1 can cream of asparagus
  soup
1/3 cup milk

1/2 teaspoon pepper
3/4 pound asparagus spears,
  cut up or 1 (10-ounce)
  package frozen
  asparagus cuts

In skillet, over medium heat in hot oil, cook chicken 10 minutes. Remove and set aside. Spoon off fat. In skillet, combine soup, milk, and pepper. Stir in asparagus. Heat to boiling. Return chicken to skillet. Cover and cook over low heat for 10 minutes or until chicken is no longer pink and asparagus is tender-crisp, stirring often.

Home Cookin' Creations

Poached Breast of Chicken with Citrus-Garlic Sauce

CITRUS-GARLIC SAUCE:

2 1/2 cups chicken stock
10 garlic cloves, sliced
1 tablespoon chopped fresh
  dill

3 tablespoons orange juice
  concentrate
4 grapefruit segments,
  membranes removed

Place all ingredients in large sauté pan, bring to a boil, reduce heat to low, and simmer for 10 minutes.

POACHED BREAST OF CHICKEN:

4 (4 to 5-ounce) boneless,
  skinless chicken breasts

1 red bell pepper, julienned
  for garnish

Place chicken breasts in sauté pan with sauce, and poach (covered) on one side for 4-5 minutes. Turn chicken over and poach (covered) for an additional 3 minutes or until done. Remove chicken breasts and keep warm. Increase heat to high and cook sauce 4 minutes or until it thickens. Strain, reserve sauce. Place chicken on individual plates, top with sauce, and garnish with bell peppers. Serves 4. *Recipe from Chef Stephen Reynolds, C Lazy U Ranch, Granby.*

Cooking with Colorado's Greatest Chefs

Marinated Chicken Breasts in Pepper Sauce

The combination of chicken and red and yellow peppers is as much fun for the eye as it is for the palate.

MARINADE:

1/2 cup olive oil	1 tablespoon crushed
1/4 cup minced fresh basil	red pepper flakes
3 tablespoons fresh lemon	2 teaspoons minced garlic
juice	2 pounds boneless
	chicken breasts

In shallow dish, mix all ingredients except chicken breasts. Add chicken, turning to coat. Cover and refrigerate overnight.

5 tablespoons unsalted	2 cups heavy cream
butter, divided	1 cup sliced mushrooms
1 medium red bell pepper,	1/2 teaspoon salt
cut into julienne strips	3/4 cup freshly grated
1 medium yellow bell pepper,	Parmesan cheese
cut into julienne strips	1/4 cup minced fresh basil
1/2 cup dry white wine	12 ounces spinach fettucine,
1/2 cup chicken broth	cooked al dente and drained

In large skillet, melt 3 tablespoons butter and sauté peppers for 2 minutes. Remove peppers; reserve. Stir in wine and chicken broth. Increase heat to high and boil until sauce is reduced to 2 tablespoons, about 5 minutes. Add cream and cook until sauce is reduced by half, about 4 minutes. In another skillet, sauté mushrooms in 2 tablespoons butter over medium-high heat until slightly browned. Add peppers, cream sauce and salt. (At this point pepper sauce can be refrigerated for up to 24 hours.)

Drain chicken, discarding marinade. Broil chicken 4 inches from heat, turning once, cooking until tender and juices run clear. (Chicken may also be grilled.) Discard skin and cut chicken into 1/2-inch strips.

Stir Parmesan and 1/4 cup basil into heated pepper sauce. On heated serving platter, arrange chicken attractively on top of warm fettucine, and pour sauce over top to cover. Serve immediately. Makes 6-8 main dish servings.

Crème de Colorado

Chicken Cordon Bleu

Breaded chicken rolls may be stored in refrigerator or freezer until you are ready to cook them.

1 pound chicken breast filets	1/2 cup Italian bread crumbs
4 ounces thinly sliced ham	3 tablespoons butter
4 ounces thinly sliced Swiss cheese	1 (12-ounce) jar home-style chicken gravy
1 egg, beaten	1 cup white wine
	1 1/2 cups sliced mushrooms
	1 tablespoon parsley flakes

Rinse chicken and pat dry. Flatten to 3/8-inch thickness. Layer ham and cheese on chicken. Roll up chicken to enclose ham and cheese; secure with toothpicks. Dip in beaten egg; coat with bread crumbs. Brown in butter in skillet over low heat. Place in deep baking dish. Top with chicken gravy, wine, and mushrooms. Sprinkle with parsley flakes. Bake, covered with foil, at 350° for 45 minutes or until tender. Yields 4 servings.

Per Serving: Cal 602; Prot 45.0g; Carbo 16.5g; T Fat 34.8g; Chol 210.0mg; Potas 591.0mg; Sod 1147.0mg.

Beyond Oats

Spicy Gazebo Springs Chicken

1 pound boneless chicken breasts, skinned	2 tablespoons cornstarch
2 tablespoons corn oil	1/2 cup dry sherry
1/4 cup slivered orange peel	1 cup chicken broth
1 clove garlic, minced	1/3 cup soy sauce
3/4 teaspoon ground ginger	1/3 cup orange marmalade
	3/4 teaspoon dried crushed red pepper

Thinly slice chicken. In a wok or large skillet, heat corn oil over medium-high heat. Add chicken, a few slices at a time. Stir-fry 3 minutes or until browned. Return all chicken to wok. Add orange peel, garlic, and ginger. Stir-fry one minute. Stir together remaining ingredients in a small bowl. Stir into chicken. Stirring constantly, bring to a boil over medium heat and boil several minutes. Serve over rice or pasta. Serves 4.

Steamboat Entertains

Chicken à l'Orange

A healthy recipe.

3 pounds chicken breasts
  or parts
1/2 cup flour
2 teaspoons grated orange
  rind
1 teaspoon paprika
3/4 teaspoon black pepper
1 tablespoon vegetable oil

1/2 cup water
1 1/2 cups orange juice
1/4 cup chopped pecans
2 tablespoons light brown
  sugar
3/4 teaspoon cinnamon
1/4 teaspoon ginger
Orange slices for garnish

Remove skin from chicken. In a paper or plastic bag, combine flour, orange rind, paprika, and 1/2 teaspoon of the black pepper. Set aside 2 tablespoons of the mixture. Add a few pieces of chicken to the bag at a time. Coat well, shaking off excess flour.

In a large skillet, heat oil until moderately hot. Add chicken. Brown on all sides. Add water. Bring to boil. Reduce heat and simmer, covered, until chicken is tender, about 30 minutes.

Remove chicken to a serving platter; keep warm. Stir 2 reserved tablespoons flour mixture into chicken drippings. Add orange juice, pecans, brown sugar, cinnamon, ginger, and remaining 1/4 teaspoon black pepper. Cook over moderate heat, stirring until thickened. Spoon sauce over chicken. Garnish with orange slices. Serves 4.

Mystic Mountain Memories

Drunken Chicken

Easy and delicious. Boneless chicken breasts are ideal for today's over-scheduled cook.

4 whole chicken breasts, halved, boned and skinned
Salt and freshly ground black pepper to taste
1 cup all-purpose flour
2 tablespoons olive oil
2 tablespoons butter
1 large onion, finely chopped

2 tablespoons freshly minced parsley
1 (16-ounce) can tomato wedges
1/2 teaspoon ground cinnamon
1/4 teaspoon ground cloves
1/4 cup packed light brown sugar
1 cup dry sherry or vermouth
1/2 cup golden raisins
1/2 cup slivered almonds

Season chicken with salt and pepper and dredge with flour. In large skillet, brown chicken in oil and butter. Place browned chicken in shallow 3-quart casserole. In same pan, cook onions until transparent. Add parsley, tomatoes with liquid, cinnamon, cloves, brown sugar, sherry, and raisins and simmer uncovered for 15-20 minutes, stirring occasionally. Pour over chicken and sprinkle with almonds. Bake at 375° for 30 minutes. Makes 6 servings.

Crème de Colorado

Baked Pineapple Chicken

1 (20-ounce) can pineapple slices
1 clove garlic, crushed
2 teaspoons cornstarch
2 teaspoons Worcestershire

2 teaspoons Dijon mustard
1 teaspoon rosemary
6 chicken breasts halves, boned
1 lemon, sliced thinly

Drain pineapple; reserve juice. Combine juice, garlic, cornstarch, Worcestershire, mustard, and rosemary. Place chicken in shallow baking pan or broiler-proof dish skin-side-up. Broil chicken until browned. Stir sauce and pour over chicken. Add pineapple and lemon slices. Bake at 400° for 40 minutes. Serve with rice.

Colorado Boys Ranch Auxiliary Cookbook

Honey Pecan Chicken

HONEY CREAM SAUCE:

2 tablespoons butter
1 tablespoon minced
  shallots
1 cup fresh orange juice
1/4 cup bourbon

1 cup whipping cream
2 tablespoons honey
1 tablespoon cider vinegar
Salt and pepper to taste

Heat butter in medium saucepan; add shallots, and cook over low heat 3-4 minutes or until tender but not brown. Add orange juice and bourbon, increase heat, and continue cooking until liquid is reduced to 1/2 cup. Add cream and reduce until slightly thickened. Add honey and vinegar and season with salt and pepper.

PECAN CHICKEN:

1/4 cup all-purpose flour
1 teaspoon minced fresh
  thyme
1/4 cup finely chopped pecans

Salt and pepper to taste
6 boneless, skinless chicken
  breast halves
Olive oil for sautéing

Mix flour, thyme, pecans, and salt and pepper. Dredge chicken breasts in flour mixture. Heat a small amount of oil in a large sauté pan; add chicken, and sauté until golden brown. Pour sauce onto each plate and place chicken breast in center. Serve additional sauce separately. Serves 6. *Recipe by Chef Clyde R. Nelson, The Home Ranch, Clark.*

Cooking with Colorado's Greatest Chefs

Perfectly Roasted Chicken

Simple ingredients give this flawless chicken an intense malty essence that is divine.

1 (3 to 4-pound) chicken, cleaned of fat, skin on, rinsed, and patted dry
Juice of 1 lemon
1 1/2 teaspoons kosher salt (to taste)
1 teaspoon freshly crushed black pepper
1 large clove garlic
1 tablespoon dried sage or thyme (for fresh sage use 1 teaspoon)
4 tablespoons butter or margarine, softened
Cooking twine
1 1/2 cups Vienna or Marzen-style beer

Rub chicken inside and out with lemon juice. Sprinkle inside with half the salt and pepper. With side of a cleaver, mash garlic and remaining salt to form a paste and mix with sage and butter. Carefully lift skin on each side of the chicken breast and push some of the mixture under. Rub the remaining mixture over the outside.

Truss (using cooking twine, tie the legs together, turn and tie wings together) and place chicken breast-side down on well-greased rack in a shallow pan. Pour beer into pan and place in 425° oven for 40 minutes, basting every 10 minutes with beer and pan drippings. Turn breast-side up and roast 25 minutes, basting every 8 minutes. Continue roasting and basting until meat thermometer inserted into the thickest part of the thigh registers 160°. The juices should run clear when you puncture the skin at the thigh joint. Remove from pan and place on heated platter. Cover with foil and allow to rest 10 minutes before carving. Serve with pan juices or make into gravy. Or save pan juices to simmer with the carcass for a delicious soup. Serves 4.

Variation: You can use the same recipe and cooking method for a small fresh turkey.

Great American Beer Cookbook

Copper Mountain's Copper Creek Golf Club is billed as the highest 18-hole course in the US.

Chicken Provençal

Definitely a family favorite!

¼ cup Italian-style bread
  crumbs
2 tablespoons Parmesan cheese
2 skinless, boneless chicken
  breasts, cut in half
1 tablespoon cornstarch

1 (14-ounce) can Italian-style
  tomatoes (with onion and
  and green pepper), chopped
1 cup mushrooms, sliced and
  sautéed, optional

Mix together bread crumbs and Parmesan cheese. Spread mixture on a plate. Roll chicken breasts in mixture until coated. Spray a large skillet with vegetable oil cooking spray and heat to medium. Cook chicken for 5 minutes, then turn and cook another 5 minutes, or until thoroughly cooked. Remove chicken from skillet and keep warm.

Mix together cornstarch and tomatoes in skillet; cook on medium heat and stir constantly for about 4 minutes. Place chicken breasts on individual plates and spoon over tomato mixture. Top with sautéed mushrooms, if desired. Serve with a green salad and a side dish of pasta. Serves 4.

Lowfat, Homestyle Cookbook

Chicken Divan

1 small chicken	1 can evaporated milk
2 packages frozen broccoli spears	1 can mushroom soup or of chicken soup
6 ounces Cheddar cheese	1 can onion rings

Preheat oven to 350°. Boil chicken until tender. Debone. Place shredded chicken in bottom of 9x13-inch pan. Cook and drain broccoli spears. Place over chicken in pan. Shred cheese and sprinkle over broccoli and chicken. Mix together evaporated milk and mushroom soup. Pour over everything. Bake in pre-heated oven, uncovered, for 25 minutes. Put onion rings on top and bake for 5 more minutes.

Four Square Meals a Day

Colorado Chicken Casserole

4 large chicken breasts	1 (7-ounce) bottle green taco sauce
4-6 chicken thighs	
1 (10-ounce) cans cream of mushroom soup	2 (7-ounce) cans chopped green chilies
2 (10-ounce) cans cream of chicken soup	15 corn tortillas, quartered
1 onion, grated	16 ounces longhorn cheese, shredded

Rinse chicken. Place in saucepan with water to cover. Cook until very tender. Drain, reserving broth. Remove skin and bones; discard. Cut chicken into cubes. Mix next 5 ingredients in bowl. Alternate layers of tortillas, chicken and soup mixture in greased 9x13-inch baking dish until all are used. Top with cheese. Bake at 325° for 1½ - 2 hours, adding some of reserved broth if mixture becomes dry. Yields 10 servings.

Per serving: Cal 512; T Fat 28g; 47% Cal from Fat; Prot 36g; Carbo 33g; Fiber 4g; Chol 111mg; Sod 1452mg.

The Flavor of Colorado

Durango lies in the heart of the Four Corners region; the only place in the United States where four states meet.

Chicken and Bean Enchiladas

3 cups plain yogurt
1 cup chicken, cooked and diced
1 (4-ounce) can chopped green chilies
1/2 cup onion, chopped
2 cups refried beans
1 (8-ounce) can tomato sauce
1 teaspoon chili powder
1 package tortillas
1 1/2 cups sharp cheese, grated

Spread 1/2 cup yogurt in 9x13-inch baking dish. Mix 1/2 cup yogurt, chicken, drained green chilies, onion, beans, tomato sauce, and chili powder. Spread each tortilla with 1/4 cup mixture, roll, and place seam-side down. Top with the remaining yogurt and cheese. Bake at 400° for 20 minutes, until cheese melts.

Microwave Option: Place in glass baking dish. Cover with plastic wrap. Cook on HIGH for 8 minutes. Makes 6 servings.

Per serving: Calories 276, prot. 26.8g, sugars 11.6g, fiber 9.3g, sat. Fat 5.5g, poly. Fat 1.3mg, choles. 45.8mg, sod. 956.6mg, potas. 969.3mg.

More Than Soup Bean Cookbook

Creamy Chicken Enchiladas

1 (10-ounce) can tomatoes
1 (10-ounce) can green
  chilies
1 cup dairy sour cream
1/2 teaspoon salt
1/2 teaspoon ground
  coriander
1 (3-ounce) package cream
  cheese, softened

3/4 teaspoon chili powder
2 cups chopped, cooked
  chicken
1/4 cup finely chopped green
  onions
Cooking oil
12 corn tortillas
1 cup (4 ounces) shredded
  Cheddar cheese

Reserve 1/4 cup tomatoes and green chilies. In blender container, combine remaining tomatoes and chilies, sour cream, salt, and coriander; cover and blend until smooth. Set aside. Combine reserved tomatoes and chilies, cream cheese, and chili powder. Stir in chicken and onions.

In skillet, heat a small amount of cooking oil. Dip tortillas, one at a time, into hot oil; fry just until limp, approximately 5 seconds per side. Drain well. Spread cream cheese and chicken mixture on tortillas; roll up. Place, seam-side-down, in a 9x13-inch baking dish. Cover with foil; bake in a 350° oven for 30 minutes. In saucepan, heat sour cream mixture just until hot. Do not boil. Pour over tortillas; sprinkle with cheese. Return to oven to melt cheese, 2-3 minutes. Makes 6 servings.

Mountain Cooking and Adventure

Ramen Fajitas

1 package any flavor Ramen
  noodles
1 skinned chicken breast,
  cut in strips

1 tablespoon oil
1 cup onions, sliced
1 cup salsa
1/2 cup sour cream

Cook noodles and drain. Brown chicken in skillet in oil. Add onions and salsa; cook over medium heat until onions are tender. Serve over noodles and top with sour cream.

101 Ways to Make Ramen Noodles

Chicken Rellenos

6 boneless chicken breast
halves (about 1¹/₂ pounds)
1¹/₂ cups shredded Monterey
Jack cheese (6 ounces)
3 tablespoons diced green
chilies
3 tablespoons sliced
pimentos
30 Ritz crackers, coarsely
crushed (about 1¹/₂ cups
crumbs)

¹/₂ teaspoon chili powder
¹/₄ teaspoon ground cumin
2 tablespoons all-purpose
flour
1 egg, beaten
3 tablespoons margarine,
melted
1 (16-ounce) jar salsa (mild,
medium, or hot) or
your own homemade

Pound each chicken breast to ¹/₄-inch thickness; top each with ¹/₄ cup cheese. Combine chilies and pimentos; sprinkle one tablespoon chile mixture over cheese. Roll up chicken from short edge; secure with toothpicks. Mix cracker crumbs, chili powder, and cumin. Coat chicken rolls with flour; dip in egg, then roll in crumb mixture. Place chicken rolls in 12x8-inch baking dish. Drizzle margarine over chicken. Bake at 350° for 35-40 minutes or until done. Remove toothpicks; serve with salsa. Makes 6 servings.

Doc's Delights

Chicken Chalupas

2 chicken breasts, cooked,
boned, and diced
2 cans cream of chicken
soup
1 can chopped green chilies
1 pint sour cream

4 green onions, chopped
1 can chopped black olives
2 cups Monterey Jack cheese,
shredded
Corn tortillas

Mix all ingredients except cheese and tortillas. Put a small amount of mixture in center of corn tortilla. Roll up and place in oiled pan, seam-side-down. Pour remainder of ingredients on top of rolled tortillas. Top with cheese. Cover with foil. Bake at 350° for one hour.

Home Cookin' Creations

Chicken Salad Burritos

1 cup cooked, chopped
  chicken
1/2 cup chopped celery
1/4 cup chopped onion
2 tablespoons sliced black
  olives

1/2 cup grated cheese
1/4 cup mayonnaise
2 tablespoons salsa
2-3 (6-inch) flour tortillas

In a medium bowl, mix chicken, celery, onion, olives, and cheese. Stir in mayonnaise and salsa. Spoon evenly down center of tortillas. Fold tortillas; place seam-side down on greased 9-inch pan. Bake at 350° for 20 minutes.

Option: Put tortillas in glass pan; heat in microwave on HIGH 2 minutes, or until hot.

Easy Recipes for 1, 2 or a Few

Working Barn Stew

A filling, zesty family stew.

2 tablespoons olive oil
4 boneless, skinless chicken
   breast halves, (about
   1 pound), cut into
   1-inch pieces
1 cup chopped onion
1/2 medium green bell
   pepper, chopped
1/2 medium yellow bell
   pepper, chopped
1 teaspoon chopped garlic

2 (14 1/2-ounce) cans stewed
   tomatoes
1 (15-ounce) can pinto beans,
   drained and rinsed
3/4 cup medium picante sauce
1 tablespoon chili powder
1 tablespoon ground cumin
1/2 cup shredded Cheddar
   cheese
6 tablespoons sour cream

In large stockpot, heat olive oil over medium heat. Add chicken, onion, bell peppers, and garlic, and cook until chicken is no longer pink. Add tomatoes, beans, picante sauce, chili powder, and cumin. Reduce heat to low and simmer 25 minutes or up to 2 hours. Place in individual serving bowls and top with cheese and sour cream. Makes 6 servings.

Colorado Collage

Cranberry Glazed Roast Turkey

Try this recipe with Cornish game hens for a special dinner.

1 (4-pound) turkey roast
1 (16-ounce) can whole or
   jellied cranberry sauce
1/4 cup butter or margarine
1 teaspoon Worcestershire
   sauce

1/4 cup orange juice
2 teaspoons orange rind,
   grated
1/8 teaspoon poultry
   seasoning
2 teaspoons brown sugar

Place turkey roast in slow cooker. Mix together cranberry sauce, butter, Worcestershire sauce, orange juice, orange rind, poultry seasoning, and brown sugar. Pour over turkey. Cover and cook on low 8-10 hours. Baste turkey with cranberry glaze before removing turkey to warm platter to slice. Offer cranberry sauce on the side for those who want extra. Serves 6.

Per serving: 553 calories; 14.4 fat grams.

Quick Crockery

Rice Dressing for Turkey

A great stuffing for people with wheat or corn allergies.

3 cups uncooked rice
7 pork sausage links,
   sliced
1 1/2 cups onion slices
8 ounces mushrooms,
   sliced
1 1/2 cups pecans

1 cup chopped celery and
   leaves
3 tablespoons chopped
   parsley
3 tablespoons simple syrup
Salt and pepper to taste

Cook rice using package directions. Sauté sausage, onions, mushrooms, pecans, and celery in skillet. Combine rice, sautéed mixture, parsley, simple syrup, salt and pepper in bowl; mix well. Stuff turkey using wrapper directions. Yields 12 servings.

Per serving: Cal 308: T Fat 13g: 37% Cal from Fat; Prot 6g; Carbo 43g; Fiber 2g; Chol 6mg; Sod 111mg.

The Flavor of Colorado

Hot Turkey Sandwiches

1 cup chopped cooked
   turkey breast
1/4 cup mayonnaise
1 teaspoon soy sauce
2 tablespoons thinly sliced
   water chestnuts
2 tablespoons grated carrot

2 tablespoons thinly sliced
   green pepper
1 tablespoon sesame seeds
1 tablespoon finely chopped
   onion
2 sandwich buns

In a medium bowl, mix all ingredients for filling. Make sandwiches; place each on a piece of foil. Wrap foil around bun; place on cookie sheet. Bake at 350° for 15 minutes. Serves 2.

Easy Recipes for 1, 2 or a Few

Denver is the largest city in a 600-mile radius—an area almost the size of Europe. The capitol city also has the nation's largest airport, and the world's largest brewery (Coors). In addition, Denver is the most educated city in the nation, with more high school and college graduates per capita than anywhere else.

Miners' Turkey Burgers with Black Bean Salsa

3 tablespoons olive oil,
  divided
1/2 small red onion, minced
1 carrot, finely chopped
1 stalk celery, finely chopped
1 pound ground turkey
1 slice white bread, crumbled

1 (4-ounce) can chopped mild
  green chilies, drained
1/2 teaspoon salt
4 (8-inch) flour tortillas,
  hamburger buns or
  pita breads
1 head Boston lettuce

Heat one tablespoon oil in a large skillet over medium heat. Sauté onion, reserving one tablespoon onion. Add one tablespoon oil to skillet; add carrot and celery. Sauté until very tender, about 10 minutes. Remove from heat and place in a mixing bowl. Add turkey, bread crumbs, chilies, and salt. Combine well and shape into 4 (3/4-inch) thick patties. Heat one tablespoon oil in same skillet over medium heat. Cook patties about 10 minutes or until thoroughly cooked and lightly browned on both sides.

To serve, heat tortillas, buns or pita breads. Top with lettuce leaves and turkey patty. Spoon salsa over patties. Makes 4 servings.

BLACK BEAN SALSA:
2 tablespoons lime juice
1/4 teaspoon coarsely ground
  pepper
1 tablespoon olive oil
1/2 teaspoon salt
1 large tomato, seeded
  and diced

1 avocado, diced
1 (15-ounce) can black beans,
  rinsed and drained
1 (8 3/4-ounce) can whole
  kernel corn, drained

Mix lime juice, pepper, oil, and salt. Stir in tomato, avocado, black beans, corn, and reserved onion.

Shalom on the Range

Seafood

Rock climbing above Horsetooth Reservoir.

Chilean Sea Bass Sonora

MARINADE:

1 (46-ounce) can pineapple
  juice
1/2 cup soy sauce
1/2 cup sherry
8 (7-ounce) Chilean sea
  bass fillets

1 tablespoon ground ginger
1 1/2 teaspoons mace
1/2 cup canola oil
2 teaspoons sesame oil

Mix all marinade ingredients and allow to stand for one hour before using.

SALSA DIABLO NARANJA:

1 1/2 cups orange marmalade
3/4 cup crushed pineapple
3/4 cup apple jelly
1/4 cup white cream
  horseradish

1 tablespoon dry mustard
1 tablespoon cracked black
  pepper
1 jalapeño, finely minced

Mix all ingredients for salsa in a large mixing bowl on medium speed until well blended. Allow to stand one hour before use.

Marinate the sea bass at least 6 hours. Grill fish over medium heat on a covered grill, basting with the Salsa Diablo as it cooks. Serve as soon as fish flakes easily, or cooked to taste. Excellent with Spanish rice and grilled leeks. Serves 8.

Recipe by Bob Starkekow—Silverheels Southwest Grill, Silverthorne, Colorado.

Haute Off The Press

Northwest Colorado Springs is home to the Garden of the Gods, a 1,365-acre park where fantastic red sandstone formations resemble human figures and animals, with massive spires twisting and spiraling up from the hills. The mile-long Cave of the Winds was discovered there in 1881 by two young brothers on a church picnic; until then this rare geological formation had been hidden for more than 200 million years deep within the Williams Canyon limestone.

Broiled Swordfish with Marmalade-Ginger Glaze

4 (8-ounce) 1¹/₂-inch thick
   swordfish steaks
Soy sauce
Sesame oil
Pepper
12 tablespoons strained
   fresh orange juice
12 tablespoons fresh lemon
   juice

4 tablespoons orange
   marmalade
4 teaspoons minced fresh
   ginger
¹/₂ cup vegetable oil
4 orange slices, twisted

Brush fish with soy sauce and sesame oil on both sides. Season with pepper. Let stand. Boil orange juice, lemon juice, marmalade, and ginger in small saucepan until reduced to 8 tablespoons, stirring occasionally, about 6 minutes. Cool slightly. Whisk in vegetable oil.

Preheat broiler. Arrange fish in foil-lined broiler pan. Brush with half of glaze; cook 3 minutes. Turn. Brush with rest of glaze and keep cooking about 4-5 minutes. Transfer to plates. Garnish with orange slices.

The Durango Cookbook

Grilled Teriyaki Fish

Has fish become humdrum? Try this rather exotic-flavored marinade next time you grill seafood. The combination of soy sauce, porter, and seasonings elevates plain seafood to uncommon heights.

MARINADE:

¹/₄ cup honey, warmed
¹/₃ cup light soy sauce or
3 tablespoons tamari sauce
¹/₃ cup porter, stout, or
smoked beer, or
substitute liquid smoke
for smoked beer
2 tablespoons olive oil or
other vegetable oil
¹/₂ teaspoon liquid smoke
(optional)

1 tablespoon dark sesame oil
2 cloves garlic, finely minced
and crushed
¹/₈ teaspoon hot red chili
flakes, ground (optional)
1 teaspoon ground ginger or
¹/₂ teaspoon fresh ginger,
chopped
Freshly ground black pepper,
to taste
1 tablespoon sugar

Whisk together the ingredients and let stand at room temperature one hour.

4 pounds mahi-mahi or
other firm fish or
large, shelled shrimp
or sea scallops

²/₃ cup flour

Brush Marinade over fish and refrigerate for 2 hours before grilling. Sprinkle the fish with flour, and grill, basting often with marinade. Large shelled shrimp or sea scallops may be used in place of the fish. Cook fish 10 minutes per inch of thickness. Cook shrimp until they turn pink and scallops until they are no longer translucent. Serves 8.

Great American Beer Cookbook

Salmon with Cilantro Sauce

Moist, flavorful and easy.

1 (12-ounce) salmon fillet, cut into 4 equal-size portions	1 tablespoon olive oil
	1/2 teaspoon ground cumin
	1/4 teaspoon salt
1/4 cup lime juice	1/8 teaspoon pepper
3 tablespoons chopped fresh cilantro	3-6 drops Tabasco sauce

Preheat oven to 500°. Prepare 4 (12x12-inch) squares aluminum foil, sprayed with nonstick spray. Place a piece of salmon on each foil square. Combine remaining ingredients; drizzle evenly over fish. Tightly seal foil into packets. Place baking sheet in oven 2 minutes to preheat. Put packets on hot baking sheet. Bake 8 minutes, or until fish is opaque and flakes easily with a fork. Makes 4 servings.

Palates

Glazed Salmon

4 salmon steaks or fillets	2 tablespoons lemon juice
1/4 cup butter	Salt and pepper to taste
1/4 cup brown sugar, firmly packed	Crushed red pepper flakes (optional)

In small saucepan, combine all ingredients except salmon, and melt. Marinate salmon in glaze for one hour. Arrange salmon on lightly greased broiler pan. Brush with glaze. Broil 5 to 6 inches from heat, 8-10 minutes on each side or until fish flakes easily, brushing occasionally with remaining glaze. Place salmon on serving platter and spoon over any leftover glaze. Serve with lemon wedges. This dish is also great when cooked on a grill. Serves 4.

Steamboat Entertains

Grilled Salmon with Hoisin and Ginger Butter Sauce with Tomato, Basil Fettuccine

**2 (6-ounce) boneless
salmon fillets
Olive oil**

**Salt and pepper
2 ounces oriental hoisin
sauce**

Coat the salmon fillets with olive oil, hoisin sauce, salt and pepper. Make the Ginger Butter.

GINGER BUTTER SAUCE:

**3 shallots, minced
1 cup white wine***
1/2 cup white wine vinegar*
1/4 - 1/2 cup heavy cream

**1/4 pound unsalted butter,
cold
Salt and pepper to taste
1/4 cup pickled ginger**

In a small saucepan, reduce the shallots, wine and vinegar. When syrupy, add the heavy cream. Mound in the cold butter. Add salt and pepper to taste and the ginger. Grill the salmon fillets; do not overcook. Meanwhile make the sauce for the fettuccine.

PASTA:

**3 shallots, minced
3 cloves garlic, minced
2 vine-ripened tomatoes,
diced
1 tablespoon olive oil
Julienned fresh basil**

**Salt and pepper
Homemade fettuccine or a
good quality dried
fettuccine
Reggiano Parmesan, grated**

Sauté shallots, garlic, and tomatoes in olive oil. Add the basil (save some for garnish), salt and pepper. Cook the pasta in boiling, salted water until tender. Drain and toss into the sauté pan with other ingredients. Serve immediately and garnish with Parmesan and fresh basil. Serve the sauce either on top or underneath the fish, with fettuccine on the side.

If you're watching your fat intake, avoid the sauce; the fish is delicious coated with olive oil, hoisin sauce, salt and pepper and grilled. Serves 2.

*Use good quality wine and wine vinegar.

Lighter Tastes of Aspen

Grilled Salmon with Warm Pineapple Sauce

A delicious and healthful dish with very little cholesterol.

2 tablespoons fresh lemon or lime juice
2 teaspoons minced garlic
1/2 teaspoon freshly ground black pepper
6 (6-ounce) salmon fillets
2 tablespoons butter
2 tablespoons minced shallots

2 teaspoons seeded, minced jalapeño peppers
3 tablespoons peeled, minced fresh ginger root
1 1/4 cups fresh orange juice
1/2 teaspoon curry powder
2 cups fresh chopped pineapple
2 tablespoons chopped fresh mint

In shallow glass dish, combine lemon juice, garlic, and pepper. Add salmon and marinate, at room temperature, 30 minutes. Preheat grill to medium-high. In medium skillet, heat butter over medium heat. Add shallots, jalapeño, and ginger and cook 2 minutes. Add orange juice and curry powder and cook until reduced by half, about 10 minutes. Add pineapple and mint, reduce heat to low, and cook until thoroughly heated. Grill salmon 4-5 minutes per side. Place salmon on individual servings plates and spoon warm pineapple sauce on top. Makes 6 servings.

Colorado Collage

Salmon Cakes

2 shallots, finely minced
2 ribs celery, finely chopped
Butter
1 tablespoon parsley,
  minced
Pinch of cayenne
1 cup plain bread crumbs
1/4 teaspoon Worcestershire
  chopped

1/8 teaspoon salt
1/8 teaspoon pepper
1 cup mayonnaise
1/4 teaspoon paprika
1 1/2 tablespoons capers,
  sauce
1 pound cooked salmon,
  chilled

Soften shallots and celery in a little butter. Cool. Add all ingredients except salmon together. Gently flake salmon into mixture with a fork. Chill for at least one hour. Form into desired cake size and sauté in a non-stick pan with minimal oil. Drain on paper towels and serve with a Dijon hollandaise sauce. Makes 10 small cakes. *Recipe by Holly Mervis—La Petite Maison, Colorado Springs, Colorado.*

Haute Off The Press

Cheese-Topped Orange Roughy

An amiable blending of Parmesan cheese and fish—soon to be a favorite.

2 pounds orange roughy (sole, cod
  or snapper can be substituted)

TOPPING:
1/3 cup light mayonnaise
1/3 cup Parmesan cheese,
  grated
1/4 cup green onion, sliced

1/2 teaspoon lemon juice
1/4 - 1/2 teaspoon garlic powder
Hot sauce to taste

Preheat oven to 350°. Place fish in a shallow glass casserole coated with cooking spray; bake 8 minutes or until fish flakes easily when tested with a fork. Meanwhile, mix topping ingredients. Spread Topping evenly over cooked fish fillets. Broil 6 inches from heat for 5 minutes or until topping is lightly browned. Yields 6 servings.

Per serving: Cal 134; Fat 4.5g; Chol 53mg; Sod 211mg.

Simply Colorado

Shrimp Chow Mein

1 pound medium shrimp, raw (20-24 count per pound)	2 cups fresh snow peas
2 tablespoons cornstarch	1/4 cup onions, chopped
1/4 cup low sodium soy sauce	6-7 mushrooms, sliced
1 cup low sodium, lowfat chicken broth	1 clove garlic, minced
	2 cups mung bean sprouts
	1 (8-ounce) can water chestnuts
2 tablespoons safflower oil	Chow mein noodles or cooked rice

Remove shells from shrimp. Put cornstarch in a medium-size bowl, then gradually stir in soy sauce until cornstarch is dissolved. Add chicken broth to the soy sauce and cornstarch. Heat one tablespoon of the oil in a large non-stick skillet. Stir-fry shrimp until cooked through. Remove shrimp from skillet. Heat the other tablespoon of oil and stir-fry the peapods, onions, mushrooms, and garlic, then remove from pan . Add bean sprouts and water chestnuts, and stir-fry approximately one minute. Return shrimp and other stir-fried vegetables to skillet.

Add sauce mixture to skillet and cook until thickened, stirring continuously. Serve immediately over chow mein noodles or rice. Serves 4.

Lowfat, Homestyle Cookbook

Grilled Trout Fillets with Tomato Butter

This is the fisherman's way to eat fish!

Trout fillets (or any other firm-fleshed white fish fillets)

Lemon pepper
Melted butter

For the best flavor, soak several handfuls of mesquite wood chips in water. Prepare a moderately hot charcoal fire. When the coals are covered with light ash, remove the chips from the water and spread over the coals. Start cooking the fish immediately.

Place one-inch thick fillets, brushed with mixture of lemon pepper and butter, on the grill. Cook for 5-8 minutes on each side, basting often, until fish flakes. Serve immediately with Tomato Butter.

TOMATO BUTTER:

¹/₄ pound unsalted butter
2 tablespoons tomato paste

¹/₂ teaspoon salt
¹/₄ teaspoon sugar

Cream all ingredients in a food processor until light and fluffy. Chill, and serve with trout fillets.

More Kitchen Keepsakes

Crab Stuffed Trout

1 can crab meat
1 cup bread crumbs
1 small onion, chopped
12 medium trout, washed
  (preferably boned)
Salt and pepper to taste

6 slices of bacon, diced and
  fried
Parsley
Avocado wedges
Lemon wedges

Pick over crab meat and toss with bread crumbs and onion. Put in trout. Salt and pepper to taste. Put bacon on trout and wrap in foil. Cook over slow heat on grill or in 350° oven for 25-30 minutes. Garnish with parsley, avocado, and lemon wedges. Serves 6-10.

From an Adobe Oven to a Microwave Range

Deviled Crab

1/4 cup melted butter
3 tablespoons flour
2 tablespoons mustard
1 1/2 teaspoons paprika
1/8 teaspoon nutmeg
1/8 teaspoon cayenne pepper
1/8 teaspoon black pepper
1 cup milk

2 cups flaked crab meat
3 hard-boiled eggs, chopped
Salt to taste
1 tablespoon lemon juice
8 crab shells
1/2 cup cracker crumbs
2 tablespoons melted butter
2 tablespoons chopped
  parsley

Combine 1/4 cup melted butter and next 6 ingredients in saucepan; mix well. Add milk; mix well. Cook over medium heat until mixture thickens, stirring constantly. Remove from heat. Add crab meat, eggs, salt, and lemon juice; mix well.

Spoon into crab shells. Sprinkle with mixture of cracker crumbs and 2 tablespoons melted butter. Bake at 350° for 10 minutes or until brown. Garnish with chopped parsley. Yields 8 servings.

Per serving: Cal 195; T Fat 13g; 61% Cal from Fat; Prot 11g; Carbo 8g; Fiber <1g; Chol 143mg; Sod 320mg.

The Flavor of Colorado

Crab Soufflé

4¹/₂ tablespoons unsalted butter

Grated Parmesan cheese, enough to dust soufflé dishes

3¹/₂ tablespoons all-purpose flour

1¹/₂ cups milk

¹/₃ cup white wine

6 egg yolks

1 tablespoon Dijon mustard

1 cup flaked crabmeat

1 cup grated Swiss cheese

¹/₂ teaspoon each minced fresh chervil, tarragon, and chives

Salt and pepper to taste

Pinch of nutmeg

12 egg whites

Pinch of cream of tartar

12 crab claws and 6 tablespoons clarified butter butter for garnish (optional)

Preheat oven to 375°. Butter inside of 6 individual soufflé dishes with one tablespoon of the butter. Sprinkle lightly with Parmesan cheese. Melt remaining 3½ tablespoons of butter in saucepan, stir in flour, and cook 3-4 minutes. Whisk in milk and wine and cook, stirring constantly, until thick. Remove from heat. Add egg yolks, one at a time, mixing well after each addition. Stir in remaining ingredients, except egg whites and cream of tartar, and set aside. (The recipe can be made ahead to this point and refrigerated. Bring to room temperature before continuing.)

Beat egg whites, adding cream of tartar, until stiff peaks form. Gently fold into milk-and-egg-yolk mixture. Pour into prepared dishes and bake for approximately 20-25 minutes. Center should be slightly runny, edges firm. As an optional garnish, steam crab claws and garnish each serving with 2 claws and a small ramekin of clarified butter. Serves 6. *Recipe from Chef Dennis J. Shakan, Tall Timber, Durango.*

Cooking with Colorado's Greatest Chefs

Denver gets more hours of sunshine per year than either Miami or San Diego. Colorado boasts 255 days of sunshine yearly.

Crab Quiche

3 eggs, slightly beaten
1 cup sour cream
1/2 teaspoon Worcestershire
  sauce
3/4 teaspoon salt
1 cup Swiss cheese, grated

1 (6 1/2-ounce) can crab,
  drained
1 (3-ounce) can French fried
  onions
1 (9-inch) baked pie shell

Combine eggs, sour cream, Worcestershire sauce, and salt. Add cheese, crab, and onions. Pour into crust. Bake at 300° for 55-60 minutes or until a knife is tested clean.

The Best of Friends

Crab Fettuccini

1 1/2 sticks butter or
  margarine
1 teaspoon garlic powder
1 1/2 pounds crab meat or
  artificial crab meat

2 packages frozen chopped
  asparagus
1 (1-pound) box fettuccini
  noodles
1 1/2 cups whipping cream

Melt butter, add garlic powder, crab, asparagus; mix well until heated. While fish is cooking, cook fettuccini noodles per instructions. Drain noodles well. Combine all together. Add container of whipping cream. Salt and pepper if needed. Keep on low heat until ready to serve.

Sharing Our Best

Hot Crab Open Faces

7¹/₂ ounces flaked crab meat,
  fresh or canned
¹/₄ cup mayonnaise
3 ounces cream cheese
1 egg yolk
1 teaspoon onion, finely
  chopped

¹/₄ teaspoon prepared
  mustard
¹/₈ teaspoon salt
6 English muffin halves
Hard boiled eggs, tomatoes
  or avocados (optional)

Mix the crab meat, mayonnaise, cream cheese, egg yolk, onion, mustard, and salt together in a bowl. Spread the mixture on the muffin halves. Arrange the halves on a broiler pan and broil 2-3 minutes, until the top is golden brown. Garnish with sliced hard boiled eggs, tomatoes or avocados, depending upon whether it is being served for brunch or lunch. Makes 6 servings. *Recipe from Abriendo Inn, Pueblo.*

Distinctly Delicious

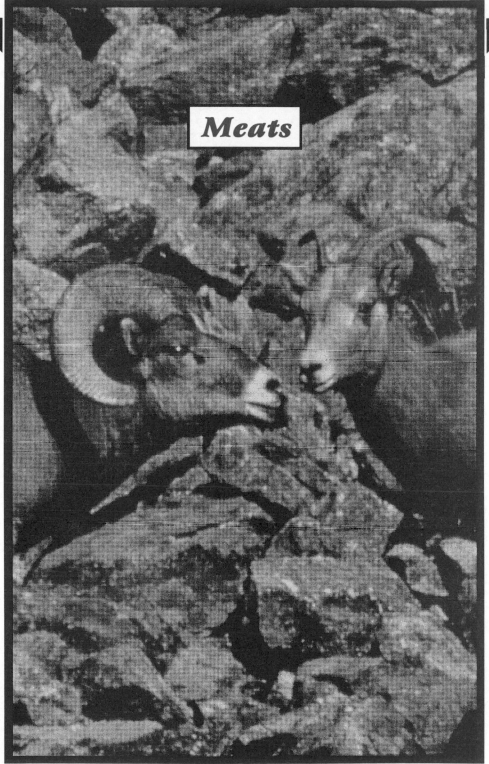

Meats

Rocky Mountain bighorn sheep.

Gourmet Tenderloin with Wine Sauce

The height of luxury, but so easy to prepare.

2 (4-ounce) lobster tails
1 (6-pound) beef tenderloin
1 tablespoon melted butter
1 1/2 teaspoons lemon juice
6 slices bacon, partially
  cooked
1/2 cup butter

1/2 cup chopped green onion
1/2 cup dry white wine
1 clove garlic, crushed
1/4 pound mushrooms, fluted,
  if desired
Watercress

Place lobster in just enough boiling, salted water to cover; return to boiling. Reduce heat; simmer 5 minutes. Remove lobster meat from tails; cut in half lengthwise. While lobster cooks, butterfly tenderloin by cutting lengthwise through center of meat to within 1/2 inch of the opposite edge.

Open butterflied tenderloin; place pieces of lobster end-to-end down center of meat. Mix melted butter and lemon juice; drizzle over lobster. Close tenderloin around lobster; tie securely with kitchen twine every inch or so. Roast on a rack in a shallow pan at 425° about 20 minutes for rare beef, or longer to desired doneness. Top with bacon; roast 5 minutes longer, or until bacon is crisp.

Meanwhile, cook green onion in butter in a saucepan over low heat until tender. Blend in wine and garlic; heat, stirring often. Keep warm. Place sliced meat on heated serving platter. Garnish with mushrooms and watercress. Pass wine sauce. Makes 8-10 servings.

Palates

Stuffed Tuscany Tenderloin

This easy-to-make stuffing creates a flavorful dish to celebrate a special occasion.

2 tablespoons vegetable oil
1 medium onion, peeled and minced
1/2 pound fresh spinach, rinsed, stemmed, and chopped
1/2 teaspoon salt
1/2 teaspoon freshly ground black pepper
1/4 cup freshly grated Parmesan cheese

1/4 cup finely chopped oil-packed sun-dried tomatoes
1 (3-4-pound) beef tenderloin, cut from center of tenderloin
1 beef bouillon cube
1/4 cup dry sherry
1 1/2 cups water
Fresh parsley sprigs for garnish

In large skillet, heat oil over medium heat. Add onion and cook until tender and golden, stirring occasionally. Add spinach, salt, and pepper. Cook just until spinach wilts, stirring constantly, about one minute. Remove from heat and stir in Parmesan and sun-dried tomatoes.

Preheat oven to 425°. Make a lengthwise cut along center of tenderloin, cutting almost in half, but not all the way through. Lay open, spread with spinach mixture, and fold to enclose filling. Tie securely with string. Place, cut-side up, on rack in roasting pan. Cover stuffing with foil to prevent drying out. Cook 45-50 minutes, or until meat thermometer registers 134-140° for medium-rare or to desired degree of doneness.

Place on cutting board and cover with foil to keep warm. Remove rack from roasting pan. Skim and discard fat from drippings, add bouillon cube, sherry, and water. Heat to boiling over medium-high heat, stirring to loosen brown bits. Remove from heat. Slice tenderloin 1-inch thick and arrange on warmed platter. Garnish with parsley sprigs and serve with reserved sauce. Makes 10 servings.

Colorado Collage

Steak Dinner in a "Pot"

3 medium potatoes,
quartered
1 large onion, chopped
1 (10-ounce) can Italian
green beans, or 1 (10-ounce)
can seasoned French-style
green beans
1 (2-ounce) jar pimiento,
chopped and drained
1 pound boneless round
steak, cut into serving-
size pieces
1/4 cup flour

1/4 cup catsup
1 tablespoon Worcestershire
sauce
1/4 cup green pepper, chopped,
or 2 teaspoons bell pepper
pepper flakes
1 teaspoon instant beef
bouillon
1 teaspoon salt
1/2 teaspoon dried
marjoram leaves
1/4 teaspoon pepper
1/4 cup water

Put potatoes, onion, green beans, and pimiento in slow cooker.
Dredge meat with flour and arrange over vegetables. Combine
catsup, Worcestershire, pepper flakes, bouillon, salt, and marjoram leaves, pepper, and water. Pour over all ingredients. Cover
and cook on low 8-10 hours. Serves 4.

Per serving: 349 calories; 14.1 fat grams.

Quick Crockery

Baked Round Steak

1 tablespoon flour
Dash pepper
1 (1-serving) size round steak
1 tablespoon salad oil
1 medium potato, peeled
1/2 cup chopped onion
and sliced
1/4 teaspoon garlic powder

1/2 cup canned tomatoes
2 teaspoons brown sugar
2 teaspoon Worcestershire
sauce
2 teaspoons lemon juice
1/2 teaspoon prepared
mustard
Dash Tabasco sauce

Mix flour and pepper on a cutting board. Put steak on flour;
turn to coat both sides. Pound on both sides with the back of
a sturdy butcher knife.

In a small skillet, heat oil; brown steak on both sides. Place
potato in a greased 1-quart casserole; top with steak. In same
skillet, mix onion, garlic powder, tomatoes, sugar, Worcestershire
sauce, juice, mustard, and Tabasco. Pour over steak. Cover;
bake at 350° for one hour, or until tender. Serves 1.

Hint: This can easily be multiplied to serve as many as needed.

Easy Recipes for 1, 2 or a Few

Steak Lo Mein

1 pound round steak,
   trimmed
1 teaspoon beef bouillon
3/4 cup water
1/4 cup soy sauce
2 tablespoons cornstarch
2 tablespoons cooking oil
1 clove garlic, minced
2 cups cabbage, shredded
1 cup carrots, sliced and
   partially cooked

1 medium onion, sliced into
   rings
1/2 cup mushrooms, sliced
   fresh
1/2 cup celery, sliced
1/3 cup green onions, sliced
1 package frozen snow peas
1 (8-ounce) can sliced water
   chestnuts, drained
4 ounces thin spaghetti,
   cooked and drained

Cut partially frozen steak into diagonal across grain 1/4-inch strips. Combine bouillon, water, soy sauce, and cornstarch; set aside. In a wok or large skillet heat oil on medium-high. Add meat and garlic; stir-fry until the meat is no longer pink, about 5 minutes. Remove meat to platter. Add cabbage, carrots, onion, mushrooms, celery, and green onions; stir-fry for about 3 minutes. Add pea pods and water chestnuts; stir-fry about 5 minutes. Add meat. Stir bouillon mixture and add to wok. Stir and cook until thickened. Gently toss in spaghetti and heat through. Makes 6 servings.

Grade A Recipes

Carne Asada

You can't beat this for an easy main dish for your next backyard barbecue.

1 cup oil	4 tablespoons vinegar
1/2 cup lemon juice	2 tablespoons salt
2 teaspoons paprika	4 tablespoons sugar
4 tablespoons Worcestershire sauce	1 teaspoon garlic powder
	1 (2-pound) flank steak

Mix marinade ingredients together. Place flank steak in a 9x13-inch dish and pour marinade over. Cover and refrigerate overnight, turning occasionally. Grill meat over hot coals to desired doneness. (Also a good marinade for shish-ka-bob meat.) Serves 4.

Kitchen Keepsakes by Request

Marinated Grilled Flank Steak

Juice of 1 lemon
1/2 cup soy sauce
1/4 cup or more dry red wine
3 tablespoons vegetable oil
2 tablespoons Worcestershire sauce
1 large clove garlic, sliced

Pepper to taste
Chopped green onion or chives (optional)
Chopped dill weed (optional)
Celery seed (optional)
1 (1 1/2-pound) flank steak, trimmed

Mix all ingredients in the pan in which meat is to be marinated. Marinate flank steak, turning occasionally, for 2-12 hours in the refrigerator. Broil meat over hot coals for 5 minutes per side for rare meat. Slice meat on the diagonal across the grain and serve. Makes 3-4 servings.

Colorado Cache Cookbook

Grilled T-Bone 240

2 (16-ounce) T-bone or porterhouse steaks
Salt, to taste
2 tablespoons fresh rosemary, minced

2 tablespoons freshly ground black pepper
1 tablespoon garlic, minced
1/2 cup olive oil
2 tablespoons lemon juice

Prepare charcoal grill. Remove steaks from refrigerator to room temperature 2 hours prior to cooking. Rub steaks thoroughly with salt, rosemary, pepper, garlic, and 2/3 of olive oil. Grill steaks over medium-high heat 3-5 minutes per side until desired level of doneness. Remove steaks to a warm serving plate and tent with foil. Let rest 5 minutes. Carve meat from bone and slice in 1/4-inch slices, reserving all juices. Squeeze lemon juice into reserved meat juices; season with salt and pepper and pour over sliced steak. Serve on warm plates and garnish with Fire Roasted Onions. Serves 4.

FIRE ROASTED ONIONS:
2 sweet onions (Vidalia, Walla-Walla or Maui)

Remaining olive oil from steak
Salt and pepper

Peel and slice onions; toss with olive oil, salt and pepper, and grill along side of steaks for 2-3 minutes each side.
Recipe by Chef Matthew Franklin—240 Union, Lakewood.

Haute Off The Press

Steak on the Stick

2 pounds flank steak   **¹/₂ cup water (if needed)**

Marinate steak 2 hours in container with lid. Add water if marinating longer. Cut meat in strips and put on skewers. Barbeque over grill.

MARINADE:

¹/₂ cup soy sauce
2 tablespoons vinegar
1 tablespoon sesame seed oil
1 large clove garlic
2 green onions, finely chopped

2 tablespoons brown sugar
Dash of Accent
¹/₂ teaspoon prepared mustard

Mix ingredients.

Home Cookin'

Easy Beef Stroganoff

1 pound sirloin steak, cut into small cubes or ¹/₂-inch strips
¹/₂ cup flour
¹/₈ teaspoon garlic powder
3 tablespoons oil
1 cup sliced mushrooms

1 pint beef bouillon
1 can cream of mushroom soup
³/₄ cup sour cream
3-4 cups noodles, cooked and drained
Parsley

Cut steak into cubes or strips. Put ½ cup flour and garlic powder in plastic bag; add meat, and shake to coat meat well. Heat oil in large skillet. Sauté meat and mushrooms over medium head, stirring occasionally. When meat coating is crispy, pour in bouillon and mushroom soup. Mix well. Simmer 20-30 minutes, stirring occasionally. Before serving, stir in sour cream and heat through. Serve over hot noodles. Garnish with parsley. Serves 4.

Kitchen Keepsakes

Marinated London Broil

1 (3-4-pound) London broil-
  cut steak
1 cup soy sauce
1 cup tomato juice

1 cup brown sugar
1 cup peanut oil
6 cloves garlic, minced

Combine well last 5 ingredients and pour over the steak. Marinate 24 hours, the last 2 at room temperature. Grill over medium coals approximately 20 minutes for medium rare. Serves 4-6.

Recipes from Our House

Pork Chops in Apple Juice

4 boneless center cut pork
  loin chops (about 1 pound)
1/4 teaspoon dried whole sage

Salt and pepper to taste
1 cup apple juice
1/4 cup raisins

Preheat oven to 350°. Trim any excess fat from pork chops; brown in a nonstick skillet coated with cooking spray. Arrange in baking dish (single layer if possible). Sprinkle chops with sage, salt and pepper; cover with apple juice. Cover and bake about 1 hour or until meat is tender. Add raisins during last half hour of baking. Yields 4 servings.

Hint: Can be simmered in covered pan on stove if preferred over baking.

Per serving: Cal 276; Fat; 12.8g; Chol 80mg; Sod 214mg.

Simply Colorado

Red Mountain Stuffed Pork Chops

3/4 cup onions, chopped
1/3 cup celery, chopped
1/4 cup butter
1/2 loaf bread, broken into
  bread crumbs
1/2 teaspoon salt
1 tablespoon fresh sage, or
  to taste

1 tablespoon fresh thyme
1 cup chicken broth
5-6 pork chops (have butcher
  cut pockets)
1 can cream of celery soup
1/2 can water
10 small mushrooms
Minced garlic (optional)

Sauté onions and celery in butter until onions are clear. Put bread crumbs in a large bowl and sprinkle with salt, sage, and thyme. Mix in sautéed vegetables and chicken broth. Mix together and stuff into the pork chops. Place stuffed chops into a well greased 12-inch Dutch oven.

Mix the soup, water, mushrooms, and garlic in a bowl and pour over pork; cover with lid. Put the Dutch oven on hot coals and place more coals on the lid. Bake 90 minutes, turning a quarter turn every 20 minutes. (Or bake in conventional oven at 350° for 20-30 minutes.) Yields 4-6 servings.

West of the Rockies

Posole

2 onions, chopped
1 tablespoon oil
1 1/2 pounds pork, cubed
4 tablespoons chile powder
1 tablespoon flour

1 1/2 pounds hominy
1 tablespoon salt
1/2 teaspoon oregano
1 clove garlic, chopped

Fry onions in oil; add pork and blend. Mix chile powder with flour; add to pork mixture. Add hominy, salt, oregano, and garlic. Add hot water as needed. Cook until pork is tender, 2 or 3 hours.

Note: If canned hominy is used, do not add until pork is almost cooked.

Southwestern Foods et cetera

"Way Out West" Spareribs or Short Ribs

**4 pounds spareribs or
  short ribs**
1 onion, chopped
1/2 cup ketchup
1/2 cup water
1/2 cup red wine vinegar
**1/4 cup each: brown sugar
  and soy sauce**
1 cup oil
Salt to taste

**1 teaspoon each: prepared
  mustard, chili powder
  and celery seeds**
**Dash each: Tabasco, paprika,
  cayenne pepper and garlic
  powder**
**2 tablespoons Worcestershire
  sauce**
Juice of 1 lemon

Cut ribs in pieces. Place in deep roasting pan. Mix remaining ingredients and pour over ribs. Bake at 350° for 1½ - 2 hours, covering the last ½ hour. Yield: 6 servings.

Colorado Foods and More. . .

Caribbean Pork Roast

This gives you fabulous flavor with little effort.

1 (2-3-pound) rolled and tied, boneless pork loin roast	1 teaspoon salt
	1/2 teaspoon freshly ground black pepper
1 cup packed brown sugar	1/2 teaspoon ground cloves
2 tablespoons dark rum	1/2 cup chicken broth
1 teaspoon minced garlic	1/4 cup light rum
2 teaspoons ground ginger	1 tablespoon flour
2 whole bay leaves, crumbled	1/4 cup fresh lime juice

Preheat oven to 375°. Place pork in roasting pan. Cook 1 1/2 - 2 hours or until meat thermometer inserted into center registers 160°. Remove from oven, leaving oven on.

In small bowl, combine brown sugar, dark rum, garlic, ginger, bay leaves, salt, pepper, and cloves. Stir to form a paste. Cut string from pork, lay open, and spread with brown sugar mixture. Return to oven and cook about 6 minutes, until pork is glazed. Transfer to platter and cover with foil to keep warm.

Place roasting pan on stove-top or pour drippings into saucepan, scraping up any browned bits. Heat over medium heat. Add chicken broth and light rum and heat to boiling. Sprinkle with flour and whisk to blend. Heat to boiling, whisking constantly. Add lime juice and boil until slightly thickened, whisking constantly, about 2 minutes. Slice pork and serve with sauce. Makes 6-8 servings.

Note: All meats should be allowed to stand 10 minutes after cooking, before being sliced.

Colorado Collage

Steamboat Springs has the only high school marching band that performs on skis.

Pork Fajitas

Fast and fabulous.

1 teaspoon olive oil
1 pound pork tenderloin,
  julienned
$^1/_2$ teaspoon salt
$^1/_4$ teaspoon pepper
1 red bell pepper, thinly
  sliced
1 green bell pepper,
  thinly sliced
1 small onion, thinly
  sliced

1 clove garlic, minced
$^1/_2$ teaspoon ground cumin
2 teaspoons fresh lime juice
8 (6-inch) flour tortillas,
  warmed
$^1/_2$ cup prepared salsa of your
  choice
Garnishes: shredded lettuce,
  chopped tomatoes, avocado
  slices, cilantro, and olives

Heat oil in large skillet over high heat. Add pork; sprinkle with
salt and pepper. Cook, stirring constantly, 2 minutes. Add
peppers, onion, garlic, and cumin. Continue cooking until vegetables are crisp-tender, 3-4 minutes. Stir in lime juice. To
serve, roll 3/4 cup pork mixture in each tortilla with one tablespoon salsa and garnishes, as desired. Makes 4 servings.

Palates

Pork Chops and Potatoes Bake

6 center-cut pork chops,
  3/4 - 1 inch thick
Worcestershire sauce
Salt and pepper to taste
Garlic salt
Flour
Oil
2 fresh pork sausage links,
  sliced and diced
1 onion, chopped
1 red or green (or mixed)
  bell pepper, chopped

3 stalks celery, chopped
1 garlic clove, minced
1/4 cup fresh parsley, minced
Small can sliced mushrooms
2 (14 1/2-ounce) cans beef broth
4 large Colorado potatoes,
  sliced in rounds,
  1/4-inch thick
Salt and pepper to taste
Butter

Rub pork chops with small amount of Worcestershire sauce. Season with salt, pepper, and garlic salt. Coat lightly with flour. Fry in hot oil, quickly, browning on both sides. Remove. Pour out excess oil, leaving one tablespoon. Brown sausages in skillet. Add onion, bell pepper, celery, and garlic. Sauté vegetables, stirring to cook evenly, until tender. Add mushrooms and parsley. Add 1/2 can broth and stir to mix.

In large, flat pan, place sliced potatoes, overlapping, in layer on bottom. Salt and pepper and dot with butter. Top with sausage mixture to cover potatoes. Arrange pork chops on top. Pour one can broth on top. Cover tightly with foil and bake 30 minutes. Uncover, add more broth if necessary, and cook an additional 30 minutes until done. Yield: 6 servings.

Colorado Foods and More. . .

Taste of the Rockies Casserole

1 pound ground beef
1 tablespoon oil
1 tablespoon chili powder
2 cloves garlic, minced
Salt and pepper to taste
1 large onion, chopped
1 green bell pepper,
  chopped
1 can Ro-Tel tomatoes
  with green chilies

1 (14½-ounce) can whole
  tomatoes
1 (15½-ounce) can kidney or
  pinto beans
¾ cup raw rice
1 (14½-ounce) can beef
  bouillon
¼ cup ripe olives, sliced
1 cup Cheddar cheese, grated

Brown meat in oil. Add chili powder, garlic, salt, pepper, onion, and bell pepper. Cook 3 minutes. Add tomatoes with juice, breaking up; then add beans and rice. Turn into greased 2-quart baking dish; pour beef broth over meat and rice mixture and bake, covered, at 350° for 45 minutes. Sprinkle olives and cheese on top, and bake, uncovered, until cheese is melted. Serves 6-8.

Colorado Foods and More. . .

Marinated Beef Strips

⅓ cup soy sauce
¼ cup red wine vinegar
½ cup olive oil
2 tablespoons Worcestershire
  sauce

2 tablespoons mustard
1 clove garlic, minced
1 teaspoon crushed pepper
  corns
2 pounds sirloin steak

Mix all above marinade ingredients and put in gallon Ziploc bag. Slice steak in ½-inch strips and put with marinade; seal. Allow 2 hours or more in marinade. Lay heavy-duty aluminum foil on grill and place meat strips on foil. Grill on low, turning as needed. An alternative method of cooking is to cut in 1-inch cubes and thread on skewers with garden vegetables such as onions, bell peppers, tomatoes, or squash, or use in beef fajitas.

Grade A Recipes

Chris's Favorite Hamburger Casserole

1 pound ground beef
1 medium green pepper, chopped
1 medium onion, chopped
1 cup celery, diced
2 teaspoon chili powder

1 teaspoon salt or to taste
1 (16-ounce) can Franco American spaghetti
1 (16-ounce) can whole kernel corn
1 cup Cheddar cheese, grated

Brown the ground beef in a large skillet. Add the green pepper, onion and celery to meat and cook until tender. Drain off the excess fat and add the chili powder and cook for one minute. Add the remaining ingredients and mix well. Transfer to a large baking pan and bake at 350° for 30 minutes. Makes 4-6 servings.

Great Plains Cooking

Mama Mia Casserole

8 tablespoons diet margarine
1 cup chopped onions
1/2 cup chopped celery
1/2 cup chopped green pepper
6 toes garlic, minced
16 ounces ground veal
1 teaspoon salt
1/2 teaspoon pepper
1 teaspoon Italian seasoning
Pinch of sweet basil

1 tablespoon sugar or 1 teaspoon sweetener
1 (16-ounce) can tomatoes, drained and chopped (reserve juice)
1 (16-ounce) can tomato sauce
Tomato juice and water to equal 2 cups liquid
1 (8-ounce) can mushrooms
16 chopped olives (green or black)
8 ounces uncooked egg noodles
8 ounces mozzarella cheese

Sauté vegetables and veal in margarine until meat is slightly browned and vegetables are soft. Add remaining ingredients, except noodles and cheese, and simmer 15-20 minutes. Spoon small amount of sauce into sprayed 9x13-inch pan. Top with egg noodles, cover with remaining sauce and top with mozzarella cheese. Bake at 350° for 45 minutes. Makes 8 servings.

Fat Mama's Deli

Yum-A-Setta

2 pounds hamburger
1/4 onion, chopped
Salt and pepper to taste
3 tablespoons brown sugar
1 can tomato soup,
  undiluted

1 (16-ounce) package noodles
1 can cream of chicken soup,
  undiluted
8 ounces processed cheese,
  sliced

Brown hamburger with onion, salt, and pepper. Drain grease. Add brown sugar and tomato soup. Mix well. Cook noodles. Drain and add cream of chicken soup. Mix well. In a 9x13-inch casserole, layer noodle mix on bottom, sliced cheese in middle, and hamburger mix on top. Bake at 350° for 30 minutes.

4-H Family Cookbook

Durango Meatballs

1 pound ground pork and
  1 pound ground round,
  ground together
2 cups soft bread crumbs
2 eggs
1/2 cup finely chopped
  onion

2 tablespoons chopped
  parsley
2 teaspoons salt
2 tablespoons butter
1 (10-ounce) jar apricot
  preserves
1/2 cup barbecue sauce

Combine meat, bread crumbs, eggs, onion, and seasonings and mix lightly. Shape into medium-size meatballs and brown in butter. Place in a casserole and pour the apricot preserves and barbecue sauce over the meatballs. Bake at 350° for 30 minutes. Makes 4-5 dozen meatballs.

The Durango Cookbook

Pork Tenderloin a la Crème

A special weekend meal served with a dry white wine, steamed fresh vegetables and crusty French bread.

8 strips bacon
8 sliced pork tenderloin,
  2-inches thick,
  butterflied
1/4 cup brandy or cognac
2 teaspoons dry mustard
Salt and freshly ground
  black pepper to taste

1/4 cup dry white wine
2-3 tablespoons beef bouillon
  granules
2 cups heavy cream
2-3 tablespoons all-purpose
  flour
1/4 pound mushrooms, sliced

Fry bacon until limp. Wrap bacon around outside edge of each butterflied tenderloin, secure with a wooden pick and place in ungreased roasting pan. Using a spoon, drizzle brandy over meat. Sprinkle meat with mustard, salt and pepper. Bake uncovered at 350° for 20-30 minutes. Remove pork. Skim grease from drippings. Add wine and bouillon granules and de-glaze roasting pan over medium heat. Whisk together cream and flour until smooth. Whisk into drippings. Stir and boil until thickened and smooth, about 4 minutes. Return meat to pan, turning to coat both sides. Sprinkle with mushrooms. Bake uncovered at 350° for 15 minutes, or until sauce is thickened. Makes 4-6 servings.

Crème de Colorado

Greek Pitas

4 pita breads
1 pound pork loin or
  beef sirloin, cut into
  1/2-inch cubes
1/8 teaspoon pepper
1 teaspoon oregano

1 cucumber, chopped
1 tomato, chopped
1/2 green pepper, chopped
2 teaspoons olive oil
2 teaspoons red wine vinegar

Cut pita breads down the middle to make 8 half-moon pockets. Sprinkle meat with half of the pepper and oregano. Put meat in roasting pan. In a 300° oven, cook beef for approximately 12 minutes or pork for approximately 17 minutes (pork must be well done). In a bowl, combine all remaining ingredients, except pitas, and toss together. Place meat in pitas and top with vegetable mixture. Serve immediately. Serves 4.

Lowfat, Homestyle Cookbook

Baked Meat and Potato Balls

4 medium potatoes
1 medium onion
2 pounds hamburger
3 large eggs

Salt and pepper
1 can mushroom soup
1/2 cup hot water

Grind potatoes and onion. Mix with hamburger, beaten eggs, salt and pepper. Shape into balls and place in 2-quart baking dish. Mix soup and water and pour over hamburger. Bake 45-60 minutes at 350°.

Goodies and Guess-Whats

A mountain peak over 14,000 feet tall is termed a "14er," and there are only 68 such peaks in the continental US—54 of them are in Colorado. Mount Elbert near Leadville is the highest point in Colorado at 14,433 feet. The approximate mean elevation of 6,800 feet is greater than any other state in the US.

Slovenian Pasties

These meat pies were carried by men working in the silver mines.

DOUGH:

1 cup flour   **Pinch salt**
2 eggs

Mix together and knead. Roll as for noodles. Be sure and flour rolling area very well or dough will stick.

FILLING:

1 1/2 pounds left-over pork,   **Pinch of salt, pepper,**
  beef or hamburger   **marjoram, and rosemary**
1 small onion, finely   **1 egg**
  chopped

Grind the meat. Add onion, salt, pepper, marjoram, and rosemary. Mix together. Add egg to hold meat mixture together.

Divide into about 5 or 6 portions; lay on rolled-out dough. Cut dough around meat portions in triangular shape, fold up like you would a diaper, pinch together. Submerge the pasties into salted water that is barely boiling (do not boil hard as pasties will boil apart) for 20 minutes. Serve hot or cold.

Note: Can use combination of meats.

Aspen Potpourri

Veal Piccata

1 pound thin veal scallopini
2 tablespoons flour
1/2 teaspoon salt
1/4 teaspoon pepper

2 tablespoons margarine or
    butter
1/2 lemon
1/2 cup dry white wine
Parsley

Wipe veal scallopini with damp paper towels. Combine flour, salt, and pepper. Use flour mixture to coat veal well. Heat margarine in a medium skillet until it sizzles. Add half of veal slices, and cook over high heat until well-browned on both sides; remove. Repeat with remaining slices of veal.

Return all veal to skillet. Slice lemon and add, along with dry white wine, to veal. Cook over low heat, covered, for 5 minutes. Arrange veal on serving platter. Garnish with parsley sprigs. Makes 4 servings.

Italian Dishes et cetera

German Cabbage Burgers

1 pound hamburger
1/3 onion, chopped
1/2 teaspoon salt
Pepper

3 cups cabbage, shredded
1 loaf bread dough
Butter, melted

Brown hamburger and onion in skillet. Add salt and pepper; drain grease. Cook cabbage until tender, drain. Roll bread dough 1/4-inch thick and cut into 6-8-inch squares. Combine cabbage and hamburger. Spoon onto dough. Fold over and pinch edges together. Bake in 350° oven for 20-25 minutes or until golden brown. Brush top with butter. Good with your favorite mustard.

More Kitchen Keepsakes

Spicy Bean and Beef Pie

1 pound ground beef
2-3 garlic cloves, minced
1 (11½-ounce) can bean
  with bacon soup,
  undiluted
1 (16-ounce) jar thick and
  chunky salsa, divided
¼ cup cornstarch
1 tablespoon fresh parsley,
  chopped
1 teaspoon paprika
1 teaspoon salt
¼ teaspoon pepper

1 (15-ounce) can black beans,
  rinsed and drained
1 (16-ounce) can kidney beans,
  rinsed and drained
2 cups Cheddar cheese,
  shredded and divided
¾ cup green onions, sliced
  and divided
Pastry for (10-inch) double
  crust pie
1 cup sour cream
1 (2¼-ounce) can ripe olives,
  sliced and drained

In a skillet, cook beef and garlic until beef is browned; drain. In a large bowl, combine soup, one cup salsa, cornstarch, parsley, paprika, salt and pepper; mix well. Fold in beans, 1¼ cups cheese, ½ cup onions, and beef mixture. Line pie plate with bottom pastry and fill with bean mixture. Top with remaining pastry; seal and flute edges. Cut slits in top crust. Bake at 425° for 30-35 minutes or until lightly browned. Let stand for 5 minutes before cutting. Garnish with sour cream, olives and remaining salsa, cheese and onions. Serves 8.

Country Classics II

Mexican Stir-fry

1 pound beef
1 teaspoon salt
1 teaspoon pepper
1 teaspoon oregano
1 cup chopped green
  pepper
1 cup chopped onion

1 cup whole kernel corn,
  partially drained
1 can tomato sauce
1 package taco seasoning mix
1 cup shredded Cheddar
  cheese
6 cups corn chips

Brown beef with seasonings. Add green pepper and onion. Stir-fry until tender. Add corn, tomato sauce, and taco seasoning; stir until well mixed. Add cheese and simmer until melted. Immediately before serving, add chips. Can be served on shredded lettuce and garnished with onion, tomato or taco sauce.

Colorado Boys Ranch Auxiliary Cookbook

Elk Piccata

2 pounds elk steak, cut
  1/2-inch thick, trim
  all fat
Salt, pepper, flour
3 tablespoons butter
2 tablespoons olive oil
3/4 pound fresh mushrooms,
  sliced

2 cloves garlic, minced
1/2 cup dry white wine
3 tablespoons fresh lemon
  juice
3 ounces brandy
4 tablespoons minced parsley
Lemon slices

Sprinkle meat with salt and pepper and pound lightly on both sides. Dust lightly with flour. Heat butter and oil and brown meat on both sides. Remove meat from skillet. Add mushrooms and garlic to pan and cook one minute. Return meat to pan; add wine and lemon juice. Cover and simmer for 25 minutes or until meat is tender. Warm brandy; pour over meat and flame. Remove meat and keep warm on platter. Spoon sauce over meat. Garnish with parsley and lemon slices. Serves 4.

Recipes from Our House

Taco Seasoning Mix

1/4 cup dried minced onion flakes

4 teaspoons cornstarch

4 tablespoons chili powder

3 teaspoons cumin

1 1/2 teaspoons oregano

3 teaspoons garlic powder

2 teaspoons instant beef bouillon

3 teaspoons cayenne pepper

Mix all together; store in an airtight container in refrigerator. Three tablespoons equals one commercial package.

Easy Recipes for 1, 2 or a Few

Garlic and Chili-Rubbed Buffalo Steaks

2 large cloves garlic, chopped

1 teaspoon salt

2 tablespoons chili powder

1 teaspoon ground cumin

3/4 teaspoon sugar

3 1/2 tablespoons Worcestershire sauce

4 (1-inch thick) buffalo rib eye steaks

Combine garlic and salt in a small bowl and mash to a paste. Add chili powder, cumin, and sugar, and mix well. Stir in Worcestershire sauce. Arrange steaks on a plate large enough to hold them in one layer. Rub both sides of steaks with chili paste. Transfer to a zip-lock plastic bag and refrigerate for at least 4 hours and up to 2 days.

Grill steaks on an oiled rack 5 inches over glowing coals, 5 minutes per side for medium rare. Transfer to serving plates and let rest 5 minutes. Makes 4 servings.

Note: Also great on beef steaks and chicken.

Nutritional information per serving: Cal 253.4; Prot 46.9g; Carbo 6.0g; Total Fat 3.9g; Sat Fat 1.0g; Chol 104mg; Dietary Fiber 1.4g; Sod 838mg; Cal from Fat 14.1%; Cal from Carbo 9.8%; Cal from Prot 76.1%.

Shalom on the Range

Colorado Axis Buffalo/Venison with Raspberry Pepper Sauce

This is a sauce that you can be very proud to serve. This main course goes quite nicely with seasonal fresh vegetables and potatoes or rice.

4 (5-ounce) buffalo or venison loins

Clean and de-fat loins. Cook the meat to the state of doneness that you and your guests desire, and serve the sauce in a pouring pitcher, so that each person can add the amount they want, and it is wonderfully delicious! You could probably serve this sauce on cardboard and the cardboard would be gobbled down!

RASPBERRY PEPPER SAUCE:

1 tablespoon olive oil
1 rib celery, diced
1/2 onion, diced
1/2 carrot, diced
1/2 can tomato paste
2 Serrano chilies*
1 tablespoon chopped fresh herbs (sage, rosemary, and thyme)**

1 cup good quality red wine
3 cups veal stock
2 pints fresh raspberries, puréed
8 whole berries for garnish
2 tablespoons picked green peppercorns
Salt and pepper to taste

Sauté vegetables in hot oil until light brown in color. Stir in tomato paste and continue cooking until caramelized. Add wine, mix, cook until syrupy. Add the stock with the raspberries and cook until you have reduced the liquid to 1½ cups.

A quicker version is to cook the sauce as you are getting the vegetables cooked and the table set. If it has not reduced to half the volume, not to worry. It will still be divine. This can be made a day in advance or made and then frozen.

*You may use mild Mexican-style green chilies.

**If using dried herbs, substitute 1 teaspoon.

Raspberry Story

Rocky Mountain Campfire Chili

2 pounds ground beef, elk
  or deer (or mixed)
2 medium yellow onions,
  chopped
3 cloves garlic, minced
Oil
1 (16-ounce) can tomatoes,
  broken up
4 tablespoons tomato paste
4 ounces diced green chilies

2 pickled jalapeño peppers,
  chopped (optional)
3 tablespoons chili powder
1 teaspoon each: salt and
  cumin
1 tablespoon oregano
2 (14$^1/_2$-ounce) cans beef
  broth
5 cups water
1 (15-ounce) can pinto beans

Brown meat with onions and garlic in oil. Add tomatoes, tomato paste, chilies, jalapeños, seasonings, beef broth and water. Bring mixture to a boil. Reduce heat to low and cook 4-5 hours, stirring occasionally. Adjust seasonings, if necessary. Add beans during last 30 minutes of cooking. Serve hot in bowls with an assortment of condiments such as grated cheeses, sliced olives, Pico de Gallo, chopped onions, etc. Yield: 3 quarts.

Colorado Foods and More. . .

Crockett's I25 High Octane Road Kill Chili

6 tablespoons bacon
  drippings
2 large yellow onions, peeled
  and coarsely chopped
  (about 4 cups)
8 medium garlic cloves,
  peeled, and minced
1 tablespoon salt
4 pounds boneless buffalo
  chuck, trimmed and
  cut into $^1/_2$-inch cubes
$^1/_3$ cup mild unseasoned
  chili powder
2 tablespoons ground cumin
2 tablespoons dried oregano
  (preferably imported Hungarian)

1 tablespoon sweet paprika
  (preferably imported
  Hungarian)
1$^1/_2$ teaspoons cayenne
  pepper or to taste
3 cups tomato juice
2$^1/_2$ cups beef stock or
  canned beef broth
1 cup strong black coffee
4 or 5 green chili pods,
  steamed and clear skin
  peeled off (from toasted
  seeds)

In large skillet over medium heat, melt half the bacon drippings. Add the onions and garlic; lower heat slightly, and cook,

CONTINUED

stirring once or twice in a counter-clockwise direction until very tender, about 20 minutes.

Meanwhile, set a 4½ to 5-quart heavy flameproof casserole or Dutch oven over medium heat. Melt the remaining bacon drippings; add the buffalo meat and cook, uncovered, stirring occasionally, until the meat has lost all pink color, about 20 minutes. Scrape the onions and garlic into the casserole with the meat. Stir in chili powder, cumin, oregano, paprika, and cayenne pepper, and cook, stirring in clockwise direction, for 5 minutes. Add the tomato juice, beef stock, and coffee; bring to a boil. Lower the heat and simmer the chili for 1½ hours, stirring occasionally.

Taste, correct the seasoning, and add chopped green chilies that have been steamed and clear skin removed. Simmer for another 30-45 minutes, or until the meat is tender (buffalo will take longer than beef). If the chili becomes too thick before the meat is tender, add ½ cup of water and continue to cook.

Home Cookin'

Trailer Treat

Good to cook over the fire while camping.

1 medium onion, chopped	2 (15-ounce) cans kidney
3 tablespoons oleo	beans
1 pound franks, quartered	1 (16-ounce) can stewed
1 teaspoon salt	tomatoes
1 tablespoon flour	1 (12-ounce) can corn kernels,
1½ teaspoons chili powder	drained

Sauté onions in melted oleo. Add franks. Heat until franks are cooked and onions are lightly browned. Blend together salt, flour, and chili powder. Add mixture to onions and franks. Add beans, tomatoes, and corn. Simmer, covered, about 15 minutes.

Variation: May use 1 (15-ounce) can kidney beans, drained, 1 (15-ounce) can baked beans, 1 (10¾-ounce) can tomato soup, 1 (16-ounce) can tomatoes, and 1 (12-ounce) can corn, drained.

Home Cookin'

Southwestern Grilled Lamb

A dinner combining the fresh taste of herbed lamb with the spicy flavors of the Southwest.

1 (5-pound) leg of lamb, boned and butterflied

MARINADE:

1/2 cup olive oil
1/3 cup fresh orange juice
1 teaspoon freshly grated
orange peel
2 large cloves garlic,
minced
1 1/2 teaspoons minced fresh
thyme or 1/2 teaspoon dried

1 bay leaf, crumbled
1 tablespoon minced fresh
parsley
1/2 teaspoon freshly ground
black pepper
1/2 teaspoon salt
Olive oil

Trim excess fat from lamb. Divide lamb into 2 pieces, separating thicker piece from thin one. In large bowl, combine all marinade ingredients. Place lamb in marinade, turning to coat well. Cover and refrigerate overnight.

Remove lamb from marinade and bring to room temperature. Prepare grill. When coals are white and hot, position grill 3-inches above coals. Brush grill with oil, and brush each piece of lamb with marinade. Sear lamb on grill for one minute each side. Move thinner piece 4-5 inches from heat to prevent charring. Grill, basting frequently with marinade, until internal temperature reaches 135-140° for medium rare, about 20-25 minutes. Slice lamb on diagonal and serve with Jalapeño Mint Sauce.

JALAPEÑO MINT SAUCE:

3 tablespoons water
1/3 cup sugar
1/4 teaspoon unflavored
gelatin
1 teaspoon hot water
1/4 cup shredded fresh mint

2 large fresh jalapeño
peppers, seeded and minced
1/4 teaspoon crushed red
pepper flakes, or to taste
2 drops pure vanilla extract

In small saucepan, combine 3 tablespoons water and sugar. Stir over low heat until sugar dissolves. Soften gelatin in one teaspoon water and add to saucepan. Increase heat and bring to boil. In small bowl, combine mint, jalapeño peppers and red pepper flakes; add to boiling syrup. Let stand until cool, stirring occasionally. Stir in vanilla. Refrigerate 15 minutes or until chilled before serving. Makes 6 servings.

Crème de Colorado

Roasted Leg of Lamb

1 (5-pound) leg of lamb (or shoulder roast)	4 tablespoons olive oil
	1 teaspoon thyme
2 cloves of garlic, slivered	3 pounds potatoes
2-3 lemons	4 medium carrots
1 tablespoon oregano	1 medium onion, pieced
Salt and pepper to taste	1/2 cup wine
3/4 cup water	3 tablespoons cornstarch

With a small knife, cut small slits into the leg and insert garlic pieces. Rub leg with one lemon. Sprinkle liberally oregano, salt and pepper over lamb. Add water, juice from lemons, olive oil, and thyme. Place in preheated 325° oven for one hour. Peel, quarter, and rinse potatoes. Wash and cut carrots. Remove lamb from oven and surround with potatoes, carrots, and onion, basting with juices from pan. Return to oven and cook 1 to 1½ hours or until meat thermometer reads 160° - 170°. Remove lamb, potatoes, carrots and onion from the pan; skim fat from drippings. Mix wine in pan with drippings and bring to a slow boil, adding cornstarch to thicken and make a gravy to serve with the lamb and vegetables.

Christine's Kitchen

Lamb Dijon

1 (5-6-pound) leg of lamb,
  boned and butterflied
1 (8-ounce) jar Dijon
  mustard
1 teaspoon ginger

1 teaspoon dry or 1
  tablespoon fresh
  rosemary
1/2 cup soy sauce
2 tablespoons olive oil
1 clove garlic, minced

Have butcher prepare lamb; remove any excess fat. Combine mustard, ginger, rosemary, soy sauce, garlic, and oil in small saucepan. Heat and whisk until mustard is fairly well blended with other ingredients. Pour mixture over meat. Marinate all day, or at least 2 hours, turning 2 or 3 times.

Broil or barbecue about 6 inches from heat or hot coals 30-40 minutes on each side. Meat should be pink inside after cooking. Serves 8-10.

The Colorado Cookbook

Cakes

Audiences enjoy more than the performances at picturesque
Red Rocks Amphitheatre in Morrison.

Will's Ice Cream Cake

1 package Oreo cookies
1/3 cup butter, melted
1/3 cup slivered toasted
 almonds
2 pints softened coffee ice
 cream

1 pint softened vanilla ice
 cream
2 cups semi-sweet chocolate
 chips
1/4 cup milk or cream
1/4 cup Grand Marnier

Crush cookies and mix 4 cups crumbs with melted butter and toasted almonds. Reserve a few almonds and a small amount of cookie crumbs for topping. Place crumb mixture in a 10-inch springform pan and pat. Bake at 375° for about 15 minutes or until mixture forms a crust. Cool.

Fill the crust with the ice cream, layering the flavors. Sprinkle top with the reserved crumbs and almonds and freeze solid. Make a chocolate sauce by melting the chocolate chips over low heat. Add cream to thin, then stir in liqueur. Serve cake with drizzled chocolate sauce over each slice. Serves 12.

Kitchen Keepsakes by Request

Pumpkin Pudding Cake

Very rich, and so easy!

3 eggs, beaten
1 cup sugar
1 teaspoon cinnamon
1 (32-ounce) can pumpkin
1/2 teaspoon ginger
 (optional)
1/4 teaspoon cloves
1 (14-ounce) can evaporated
 milk

1 (2-layer) white or yellow
 cake mix
1 stick butter, melted
1 cup walnuts or pecans,
 chopped
Whipped cream or ice cream

Mix eggs, sugar, cinnamon, pumpkin, ginger, cloves, and milk. Whisk until blended and pour into a greased or sprayed 9x13-inch pan. Sprinkle one package cake mix over top. Drizzle melted butter over top. Sprinkle with chopped nuts. Bake at 350° for one hour. Serve with whipped cream or ice cream.

Taking Culinary Liberties

Orange Carrot Cake

The best and easiest carrot cake you'll ever make or taste.

3 cups flour, divided	1 (11-ounce) can mandarin
2 cups sugar	oranges, undrained
1 cup shredded coconut	2½ teaspoons baking soda
1¼ cups vegetable oil	2½ teaspoons cinnamon
3 eggs	1 teaspoon salt
2 teaspoons vanilla	2 cups shredded carrots

Blend 1½ cups flour, sugar, coconut, vegetable oil, eggs, vanilla, and mandarin oranges in large mixing bowl on high speed for ½ minute. Add remaining 1½ cups flour, baking soda, cinnamon, and salt. Blend on medium speed 45 seconds. Scrape bowl and stir in carrots. Pour into greased 9x13-inch cake pan (or 2 greased and floured 10-inch round pans). Bake in preheated 350° oven for 45-50 minutes (35-45 minutes for 10-inch pans) until tested done. Cool completely. For round pans, let cool 10 minutes before removing to wire racks to finish cooling. Frost with Orange Cream Cheese Frosting.

ORANGE CREAM CHEESE FROSTING:

3 tablespoons butter or	1 teaspoon orange extract
margarine, softened	2 tablespoons orange juice
1 (8-ounce) package cream	concentrate
cheese, softened	2 cups powdered sugar

Cream butter and cream cheese until smooth. Add the rest of the ingredients and blend until smooth. Frosting will not be as stiff as usual. I prefer it this way to get more cream cheese flavor. You may add more powdered sugar for a stiffer frosting. Frosting will harden with refrigeration. I like to garnish this cake with drained mandarin oranges.

Mystic Mountain Memories

What is a BuskerFest? Buskers are street performers, and some of the top buskers converge on the 16th Street Mall in Denver in June for the International BuskerFest. They juggle, sing, mime, tell jokes, perform magic, swallow swords, and—of course—pass the hat.

Upside Down German Chocolate Cake

1 box German chocolate
cake mix
1 cup coconut
1 cup chopped pecans

1 stick margarine
1 (8-ounce) package cream
cheese
3^1/$_2$ - 4 cups powdered sugar

Mix German chocolate cake mix as directed on box. Sprinkle coconut and pecans on bottom of a greased 9x13-inch pan. Pour batter over coconut and pecans. In saucepan, melt margarine and cream cheese. Then add powdered sugar. Mix. Spread this mixture or drizzle over top of cake. Bake at 350° for 30 minutes or until done.

Doc's Delights

Snicker Cake

1 German chocolate cake mix
1 package caramels
^{1}/$_3$ cup milk

^{1}/$_2$ cup oleo
1 cup chocolate chips
1 cup chopped nuts

Mix cake mix according to directions. Pour ½ of cake batter in a 9x13-inch pan and bake at 350° for 20 minutes. Melt caramels, milk, and oleo together until smooth and creamy. Pour over hot cake and add chocolate chips and nuts. Add the other half of cake batter and bake at 275° for 20 minutes and then 350° for 10 minutes.

Four Square Meals a Day

Fudge Upside Down Cake

3/4 cup sugar
2 tablespoons butter
1/2 cup milk
1 cup flour
2 teaspoons baking powder
1/4 teaspoon salt

2 tablespoons cocoa
1/2 cup chopped walnuts
1/2 cup brown sugar
1/2 cup granulated sugar
1/3 cup cocoa
1 1/2 cups boiling water

Cream together 3/4 cup sugar and butter. Stir in milk. Sift flour, baking powder, salt, and 2 tablespoons cocoa together. Add to creamed mixture and beat until smooth. Stir in walnuts. Spread batter into a 9-inch square pan. In a small bowl, combine brown sugar, 1/2 cup granulated sugar, and 1/3 cup cocoa. Sprinkle over batter. Pour boiling water over top. Bake at 350° for 35-40 minutes. The cake will rise to the top and boiling water will combine with the sugar/cocoa mixture to make a rich chocolate syrup underneath. Serve with ice cream, whipped cream or plain in sherbet glasses or sauce dishes.

What's Cookin' in Melon Country

Chocolate Chip Oatmeal Cake

1 3/4 cups boiling water
1 cup oatmeal
1 cup lightly packed brown
   sugar
1 cup white sugar
1/2 cup margarine
2 large eggs

1 3/4 cups unsifted flour
1 teaspoon soda
1/2 teaspoon salt
1 tablespoon cocoa
3/4 cup nuts, chopped
1 (12-ounce) package
   chocolate chips

Pour boiling water over oatmeal. Let stand for 10 minutes. Add sugars and margarine. Stir until margarine is melted. Beat in eggs. (Recipe is best if mixed by hand). Sift dry ingredients together. Add to above. Mix in 1/2 of nuts and chocolate chips. Pour into a greased and floured 9x13-inch pan. Sprinkle remaining nuts and chocolate chips over top. Bake at 350° for 40 minutes.

Mountain Cooking and Adventure

Chocolate Carrot Cake

2 cups flour
1 1/2 cups sugar
1 cup salad oil
1/2 cup orange juice
1/4 cup cocoa
2 teaspoons baking soda
1 teaspoon salt

1 teaspoon cinnamon
1 teaspoon vanilla
4 eggs
2 cups shredded carrots
1 (4-ounce) package shredded coconut
Orange Glaze

In a large bowl, mix at low speed first 10 ingredients. Mix until well blended, scraping often. Increase speed to high for 2 minutes. Stir in carrots and coconut. Spoon into greased and floured bundt pan. Bake at 350° for 50-55 minutes, or until a toothpick comes out clean. Cool on wire rack about 10-15 minutes and remove from pan. Pour Orange Glaze over cake.

ORANGE GLAZE:

1 cup powdered sugar
2 tablespoons frozen orange juice concentrate (thawed)

1/4 teaspoon grated orange peel (optional)

Combine ingredients; add additional orange juice a few drops at a time until glaze consistency. *Recipe from Ambiance Inn, Carbondale.*

Colorado Bed & Breakfast Cookbook

"Centennial State" Celebration Punch Bowl Cake

1 yellow cake mix
1 large box instant vanilla pudding
1 can cherry pie filling
1 large can crushed pineapple, drained

1 large container Cool Whip
1/4 cup each: chopped pecans, cherries, and shredded coconut

Make cake according to directions. Let cool. Prepare pudding per instructions on box. Into a large punch bowl, layer 1/2 each: crumbled cake, cherry pie filling, crushed pineapple, pudding, and Cool Whip. Repeat. Garnish top with pecans, cherries, and coconut. Cover with plastic wrap and chill. Serve with large spoon. Serves a crowd.

Colorado Foods and More...

Bacardi Rum Cake

1 cup pecans or walnuts,
  chopped
1 (18½-ounce) yellow cake
  mix (without pudding)
1 (3.4-ounce) package Jell-O
  instant vanilla pudding mix

4 eggs
¼ cup cold water
½ cup Wesson oil
½ cup Bacardi light or dark
  rum, 80 proof

Preheat oven to 325°. Grease and flour 10-inch tube or 12-cup bundt pan. Sprinkle nuts over bottom of pan. Mix all cake ingredients together. Pour batter over nuts. Bake about one hour. Cool for approximately 30 minutes and invert onto serving plate. (Make Glaze while cake is cooling.) Prick all over top of cake with a toothpick. Drizzle and smooth Glaze evenly over top and sides, allowing Glaze to soak into cake. Keep spooning the Glaze over cake until all Glaze has been absorbed.

GLAZE:
¼ pound (1 stick) butter
¼ cup water

1 cup sugar
½ cup Bacardi rum

Melt butter in a medium-size saucepan. Stir in water and sugar. Boil for 5 minutes, stirring constantly. Remove from heat and cool slightly. Stir in rum slowly, so it doesn't splatter. While warm, spoon over cake. *Recipe from St. Mary's Glacier Bed and Breakfast, Idaho Springs.*

Colorado Bed & Breakfast Cookbook

Chocolate Fudge Torte Without Eggs

This cake is adapted from the winning recipe in a recent contest. This version captures all the delicious decadence of the original—without the offending ingredients!

FILLING:

1/4 cup milk

1/2 cup dairy-free chocolate chips

In small saucepan, combine milk and chocolate over low heat and stir until smooth. (Or melt in microwave, stirring until smooth.) Set aside.

CAKE:

1/2 cup brown rice or bean flour
1/4 cup potato starch
1/4 cup tapioca flour
1/2 cup unsweetened cocoa
1/2 teaspoon xanthan gum
3/4 teaspoon baking soda
1/2 teaspoon baking powder
3/4 teaspoon salt
2 teaspoons ground cinnamon
1 cup brown sugar

1 teaspoon Egg Replacer
1/3 cup cooking oil
2 teaspoons gluten-free vanilla
1(16-ounce) can pears, drained
1/3 cup hot strongly brewed coffee
1/2 cup chopped nuts (macadamia or pecans), optional
2 teaspoons water

Preheat oven to 325°. Spray 8-inch non-stick springform pan with cooking spray. Set aside. In large bowl, mix flours, cocoa, xanthan gum, baking soda, baking powder, salt, cinnamon, brown sugar, and Egg Replacer together with oil and vanilla until thoroughly mixed. Mixture will be dry and crumbly. Set aside 1/2 cup of the mixture. In blender or food processor, purée drained pears.

In large bowl, thoroughly mix dry cake mixture, puréed pears, and hot coffee with electric mixer. Spread batter in prepared pan. Spoon filling onto top of batter. Stir nuts and 2 tea-spoons water into remaining 1/2 cup dry cake mixture and sprinkle over filling. Bake for 50 minutes or until top of cake center springs back when touched lightly. Cool in pan on wire rack for 10 minutes. Remove from pan. Let cool completely. Serves 12.

Per serving: Cal 295; Fat 13g; 37% Fat Cal; Prot 4g; Carbo 47g; Chol 1mg; Sod 244mg; Fiber 4g. Exchanges: Carbo 3; Fat 2³/4.

Special Diet Solutions

Coffeecake Exceptional

³/4 cup butter or margarine
1 ¹/2 cups sugar
3 eggs
1 ¹/2 teaspoons vanilla
3 cups flour

1 ¹/2 teaspoon baking powder
1 ¹/2 teaspoons soda
¹/4 teaspoon salt
1 ¹/2 cups sour cream
Filling

Heat oven to 350°. Grease tube or Bundt pan or 2 loaf pans. In a large mixer bowl, combine butter, sugar, eggs, and vanilla. Beat on medium speed 2 minutes. Mix in flour, baking powder, soda, and salt alternately with sour cream. For tube or Bundt pan, spread ¹/3 of batter in pan and sprinkle with ¹/3 of filling; repeat twice. For loaf pans, spread ¹/4 of batter in each pan and sprinkle with ¹/4 of filling; repeat. Bake about 60 minutes or until wooden pick inserted in center comes out clean. Ice with a glaze while slightly warm, if desired.

FILLING:
¹/2 cup packed brown sugar
1 ¹/2 teaspoons cinnamon

¹/2 cup finely chopped nuts

Mix well.

Four Square Meals a Day

Spuddin' Spice Cake with Quick Caramel Frosting

1³/4 cups sugar
1 cup Colorado potatoes, cold, mashed, unseasoned
³/4 cup shortening
¹/2 teaspoon salt
1¹/2 teaspoons cinnamon
1 teaspoon nutmeg
3 eggs, unbeaten
1 teaspoon soda combined with 1 cup buttermilk
2 cups all-purpose flour

Cream sugar, potatoes, shortening, salt and spices for 4 minutes. Add eggs and beat until thoroughly blended. Add buttermilk mixture alternately with flour, starting and ending with flour. Pour into 2 greased and floured 8-inch pans or one 9x13-inch pan. Bake at 350° for 30-35 minutes or until cake tester inserted in middle comes out clean.

QUICK CARAMEL FROSTING:
¹/4 cup butter
³/4 cup brown sugar, firmly packed
3 tablespoons milk
2 cups powdered sugar, sifted

Melt butter in pan; stir in brown sugar. Cook over low heat 2 minutes. Add milk. Bring to full boil. Cool to lukewarm without stirring. Add powdered sugar. Beat until smooth and of spreading consistency. Frost cooled cake. Makes 12 servings.

Per serving: Cal 494; Prot 4.8g; carbo 79g; Fat 18g; Chol 64mg; Sod 243mg; Dietary Fiber .79g.

Colorado Potato Favorite Recipes

White Chocolate Raspberry Cheesecake Santacafe

2 pints raspberries

CRUST:
2 cups graham cracker crumbs
1 cup slivered blanched almonds
¹/4 cup clarified butter in its liquid (unchilled) form

CONTINUED

In food processor, blend together the graham cracker crumbs and the almonds until the almonds are ground fine; add the butter and combine the mixture well. Press the mixture onto the bottom and 2/3 of the way up the side of a 10-inch springform pan.

FILLING:

8 ounces fine quality white chocolate (Callebaut)	4 large whole eggs
	2 large egg yolks
4 (8-ounce) packages cream cheese, softened	2 tablespoons all-purpose flour
1/2 cup plus 2 tablespoons sugar	1 teaspoon vanilla
	2 pints raspberries

In a metal bowl set over a pan of barely simmering water, melt the chocolate, stirring until it is smooth, and remove the bowl from the heat. In a large bowl with an electric mixer, beat the cream cheese until it is light and fluffy. Add the sugar and beat in the whole eggs and the egg yolks, one at a time, beating well after each addition. Beat in the flour and the vanilla and add the melted chocolate in a slow stream, beating until the filling is combined well.

Scatter the raspberries over the bottom of the crust; pour the filling over them and bake the cheesecake in the middle of a preheated 250° oven for one hour or until the top is firm to the touch. Let the cheesecake cool in the pan on a rack; chill it, covered loosely overnight and remove the side of the pan..

RASPBERRY SAUCE:

2 (10-ounce) packages frozen raspberries in syrup, thawed	1/4 cup sugar
	3 tablespoons Grand Marnier liqueur

Use syrup from only one package of raspberries, draining the other. Combine all ingredients in food processor or blender; strain purée to remove seeds. Chill until ready to use. Drizzle over plate; place cheesecake on top. This sauce freezes beautifully and looks elegant with the cheesecake.

Recipes from Our House

Turtle Cheesecake

CRUST:

**1 cup chocolate wafer
crumbs**

**4 tablespoons butter or
margarine, melted**

Combine crumbs and butter. Press onto bottom of 9-inch springform pan.

FILLING:

**4 (8-ounce) packages cream
cheese, softened**
1 1/2 cups sugar

1 teaspoon vanilla
4 eggs

Beat cream cheese and sugar until light and fluffy. Add vanilla; then beat in eggs, one at a time. Pour into crust. Bake at 300° for 1 hour 40 minutes. Turn off heat; let cake cool in oven, with door ajar, for one hour. Remove from oven.

TOPPING:

20 caramels
3 tablespoons milk

1 cup pecans, chopped

In small saucepan over low heat, melt caramels with milk. Stir until smooth. Pour over cake. Sprinkle with chopped pecans. Chill.

Cheesecakes et cetera

Kahlúa Mousse Cheesecake

CRUST:

**1 cup chocolate wafer
crumbs**

**1/4 cup butter or margarine,
melted**

Combine crumbs and butter. Press onto bottom of 9-inch springform pan. Chill.

FILLING:

1 envelope unflavored gelatin
1/2 cup cold water
**3 (8-ounce) packages cream
cheese, softened**
1 cup sugar
1 can evaporated milk

1 teaspoon lemon juice
1/3 cup Kahlúa
1 teaspoon vanilla extract
**3/4 cup heavy or whipping
cream, whipped**

CONTINUED

In small saucepan, sprinkle gelatin over cold water; let stand one minute. Stir over low heat until completely dissolved; set aside.

In large bowl, beat cream cheese and sugar until fluffy. Gradually add evaporated milk and lemon juice. Beat till mixture is very fluffy. Gradually beat in gelatine mixture, kahlua, and vanilla until thoroughly blended. Fold in whipped cream. Pour into crust. Chill 8 hours or overnight.

Cheesecakes et cetera

Fudge Truffle Cheesecake

CRUST:

1½ cups vanilla wafer
  crumbs
½ cup powdered sugar

¼ cup cocoa
⅓ cup margarine, melted

Combine all crust ingredients and press into bottom and 2 inches up the sides of a 9-inch springform pan; chill.

FILLING:

3 (8-ounce) packages cream
  cheese, softened
1 (14-ounce) can sweetened
  condensed milk

2 cups semi-sweet chocolate
  chips, melted
3 eggs
2 teaspoons vanilla

Beat cream cheese in a large mixing bowl until fluffy. Gradually add milk; beat until smooth. Add melted chips, eggs, and vanilla; mix well. Pour into crust. Bake at 300° for 65 minutes. (Center will still jiggle slightly.) Cool for 15 minutes. Carefully run a knife between crust and sides of pan. Cool for 3 hours at room temperature; remove sides of pan. Chill overnight. May garnish with chocolate curls or whipped cream.

Country Classics II

Strawberry Glazed Cheesecake

CRUST:

1 cup graham cracker crumbs   **¹/4 cup melted butter**
2 tablespoons sugar

Combine crust ingredients. Mix well with pastry blender. Press evenly over bottom and sides of 9-inch pie pan. Bake at 350° for 5 minutes.

FILLING:

1 package cream cheese   **1 teaspoon vanilla**
2 tablespoons milk or   **¹/4 teaspoon salt**
   half-and-half   **¹/4 cup sugar**
1 teaspoon lemon juice   **2 eggs**

Beat cream cheese, milk, lemon juice, vanilla, salt, and sugar until smooth and creamy. Add eggs, one at a time, beating well after each addition. Pour into crust. Bake at 350° until filling is firm, 20-25 minutes.

TOPPING:

1 package frozen strawberries,   **1 tablespoon cornstarch**
   defrosted   **1 pint fresh strawberries,**
¹/4 cup sugar   **cleaned and halved**

Whiz defrosted strawberries and juice in blender until smooth or put strawberries through sieve. Combine sugar and cornstarch in saucepan. Stir in strawberry mixture. Cook over low heat, stirring constantly, until thick and clear. Cool slightly. Arrange strawberry halves on cheesecake. Spoon glace over strawberries. Chill. Serves 8.

What's Cookin' in Melon Country

Colorado Facts: The US Mint in Denver makes more than 5 billions coins each year. Rocky Ford is known as the "Melon Capital of the World" for its cantaloupes. The world's largest hot springs pool is in Glenwood Springs. Colorado leads all states in production of silver and is second in gold. And the skiing is said to be the best in the nation.

German Chocolate Cheesecake

Another delicious choice for cheesecake fanatics!

CRUST:

1 package German chocolate
  cake mix
1/2 cup shredded coconut

1/3 cup butter or margarine,
  softened
1 egg

FILLING:

16 ounces cream cheese
2 eggs

3/4 cup sugar
2 teaspoons vanilla

TOPPING:

2 cups sour cream
1 teaspoon vanilla

1/4 cup sugar

Mix crust ingredients until crumbly. Press into ungreased 9x13-inch pan. Beat filling ingredients together until smooth and fluffy. Spread over crust. Bake at 350° for 25-30 minutes. Cool. Combine topping ingredients and spread over cooled filling. Refrigerate for several hours before serving. Serves 8-10.

Kitchen Keepsakes by Request

Pumpkin Cheesecake

CRUST:

2 cups crushed cinnamon graham crackers
1/4 cup sugar

1/2 teaspoon cinnamon
1/2 cup melted butter

Mix all ingredients. Press mixture into bottom and about 3/4-inch up the sides of a buttered 9-inch springform pan. Chill for one hour.

FILLING:

3 (8-ounce) packages cream cheese
3/4 cup sugar
3/4 cup brown sugar
5 eggs
1/4 cup whipping cream

1 pound plain, solid pack, canned pumpkin
1 teaspoon cinnamon
1/2 teaspoon ground cloves
1/2 teaspoon nutmeg

Cream first 3 ingredients. Add eggs, one at a time, beating well after each addition. Add all remaining ingredients and beat 3-5 minutes at medium speed, scraping sides of bowl. Pour filling into chilled crust. Place pan on an edged baking sheet (cake will drip) and bake at 350° for 1 1/2 - 1 3/4 hours. Cool on rack until cake settles. Cover lightly and refrigerate for 6 hours.

Steamboat Entertains

Angel Food Cake

Never fails, even in the classroom.

1 1/2 cups egg whites
1/4 teaspoon salt
1 teaspoon cream of tartar
1 cup sifted granulated sugar

1 cup powdered sugar
1 cup sifted cake flour
1 teaspoon vanilla
1/2 teaspoon almond extract

Set oven at 425° and put 10-inch angel food pan in oven to preheat. Beat egg whites, salt, and cream of tartar until stiff. Fold in granulated sugar 2 tablespoons at a time until all is used. Sift together the powdered sugar and cake flour 5 times. Fold it into the egg white mixture 2 tablespoons at a time. Add flavoring. Put in the tube pan and bake 23 minutes. Cool inverted.

Goodies and Guess-Whats

Not-Just-For-Passover
Chocolate Torte

1 pound semi-sweet
  chocolate chips
1/2 cup margarine or butter
5 large eggs, separated
1 tablespoon vanilla

1/4 cup plus 2 tablespoons
  sugar, divided
Cocoa
1 cup whipping cream
Raspberries

Preheat oven to 250°. Melt chocolate and margarine in a 2-quart saucepan over low heat. Beat egg yolks with vanilla in a large bowl. Slowly beat chocolate mixture into yolks until blended. Beat egg whites in another bowl with mixer at high speed, until soft peaks form. Gradually add 1/4 cup sugar and continue beating until stiff peaks form. Fold into chocolate mixture a third at a time.

Generously grease a 9-inch springform pan and line bottom with a circle cut from parchment or waxed paper. Generously grease paper and dust with cocoa. Spread batter evenly in pan and bake until toothpick inserted in center comes out almost clean, 1 hour to 1 hour and 15 minutes. Cool in pan, then remove side of pan. Remove torte from bottom of pan and discard paper. Place on serving dish and cut into 12 wedges. Beat whipping cream with remaining sugar until stiff. Top each torte slice with whipped cream and raspberries. Makes 12 servings.

Shalom on the Range

7-Up Pound Cake

$^1/_2$ cup shortening
1 cup margarine
2$^1/_2$ cups sugar
5 eggs

3 cups flour
8 ounces 7-Up
1 teaspoon vanilla
1 teaspoon butter flavoring

Cream shortening, margarine, and sugar together. Add eggs. Alternate flour, 7-Up, and flavors while adding into cream mixture and blending. Bake in a greased bundt pan at 325° for one hour and 30 minutes.

Home Cookin'

Cookies and Candies

Council Tree Pow Wow. Delta, Colorado.

Coconut Chews

3/4 cup shortening
  (half butter or
  margarine), softened
3/4 cup powdered sugar
1 1/2 cups all-purpose flour
2 eggs

2 tablespoons flour
1/2 teaspoon baking powder
1/2 teaspoon salt
1/2 teaspoon vanilla
1/2 cup walnuts, chopped
1/2 cup flaked coconut

Heat oven to 350°. Cream shortening and powdered sugar. Blend in 1½ cups flour. Press evenly in bottom of ungreased 13x9x2-inch baking pan. Bake 12-15 minutes. Mix remaining ingredients; spread over hot baked layer and bake 20 minutes longer. While warm, spread with icing. Cool. Cut into bars. Makes 32 cookies.

ORANGE-LEMON ICING:

1 1/2 cups powdered sugar
2 tablespoons butter or
  margarine, melted

3 tablespoons orange juice
3 teaspoon lemon juice

Mix until smooth and of spreading consistency.

Cookie Exchange

Coconut Joys

1/2 cup butter or margarine
1 cup powdered sugar

3 cup coconut
2 squares unsweetened
  chocolate, melted

Melt butter in saucepan. Remove from heat. Add powdered sugar and coconut. Mix well. Shape into balls. Make indent in center of each and place on cookie sheet. Fill centers with melted chocolate. Chill until firm. Store in refrigerator. Makes 3 dozen.

Colorado Cookie Collection

The Leadville Boom Days Celebration features a 21-mile burro race. "Jackass jockeys" are not allowed to ride the burros, but may push, pull, or carry them.

Danish Apple Bars

CRUST:

2¹/₂ cups flour
¹/₂ teaspoon baking powder
1 teaspoon salt
1 tablespoon sugar

1 cup shortening
Milk
1 egg, separated
¹/₂ teaspoon vanilla

FILLING:

1 cup cornflakes, crushed
4-5 apples, peeled and
  sliced

1 cup sugar
1 teaspoon cinnamon
Egg white

GLAZE:

1 cup powdered sugar
1 teaspoon hot water

¹/₂ teaspoon vanilla

Mix dry ingredients for crust. Cut in shortening as for pie crust. Mix egg yolk, plus milk, to equal ²/₃ cup liquid; add vanilla. Combine with dry ingredients. Divide dough in half. Roll out to fit a 12x15-inch pan. Over top of dough, sprinkle cornflakes and a layer of apples. Sprinkle with sugar and cinnamon. Roll out rest of dough and put on top; moisten edges and seal well. Beat egg white, brush on top. Bake at 400° for 10 minutes. Reduce heat to 350° and bake 35-40 minutes. Mix Glaze ingredients. Drizzle over the top of warm bars. Makes 12-15.

Country Classics

Pumpkin Bars

Delicious, easy, and ingredients usually on hand.

4 eggs	2 teaspoons cinnamon
2 cups pumpkin	1/2 teaspoon salt
1 cup oil	1 teaspoon soda
2 cups sugar	1/2 cup nuts and/or raisins,
2 cups flour	if desired

Mix. Cover jellyroll pan with foil. Spread batter. Bake at 350° for 20 minutes. Frost.

ICING:

1 (3-ounce) package cream cheese, softened	3/4 stick margarine
	2 tablespoons milk
1 teaspoon vanilla	1 2/3 cups powdered sugar

Beat together and spread over bars.

Colorado Cookie Exchange

Cranberry Bars

1 1/2 cups flour	1/4 teaspoon baking soda
1 1/2 cups oats	1/4 cup margarine, melted
3/4 cup brown sugar, packed	1 (16-ounce) can whole cranberry sauce
1 teaspoon lemon peel, shredded	1/4 cup pecans, chopped

In a large bowl, combine flour, oats, brown sugar, lemon peel, and soda. Add margarine and mix thoroughly. Reserve one cup mixture for topping. Pat remaining mixture into ungreased 12x7 1/4x2-inch pan. Bake at 350° for 20 minutes. Carefully spread cranberry sauce over baked crust. Stir nuts into remaining oat mixture. Sprinkle over cranberry layer and lightly pat into sauce. Bake at 350° for 25-30 minutes until top is golden. Cool on wire rack and cut into bars.

Cookie Exchange

Karin's Fruit Bars

A special friend gave this recipe to Cyndi; she used to bring them to the doctor's office where we all worked. We would gain 10 pounds on those days because we ate so many!

2¹/₃ cups sugar	4 teaspoons soda
1 cup plus 3 tablespoons	3 teaspoons vanilla
shortening	3 teaspoons cinnamon
3 eggs	1¹/₂ pounds dates
¹/₂ cup honey	1 pound raisins
2 tablespoons water	2 cups walnuts
5 cups flour	1 egg
¹/₂ teaspoon salt	2 tablespoons milk

Mix all ingredients together, except last egg and the milk; dough will be very stiff. Chill dough for easier handling. Spread into 3 long rolls about ³/₄-inch thick onto one or two cookie sheets. Beat one egg and 2 tablespoons milk together and brush on unbaked rolls. Bake at 325-350° for 18-20 minutes. Watch closely because the honey in the dough burns easily. Cut while warm—just as good cold. Makes lots. They freeze well.

Cookie Exchange

Cherry Mash Bars

2 cups sugar	6 ounces chocolate chips
²/₃ cup evaporated milk	1 (4-ounce) Hershey's bar
¹/₂ cup butter	¹/₂ cup peanut butter
Dash of salt	2 cups salted peanuts,
15 big marshmallows	crushed
6 ounces cherry chips	1 teaspoon vanilla

Cook first 5 ingredients together until the marshmallows are melted. Remove from heat, add cherry chips and stir until smooth. Pour into a buttered 9x13-inch pan. Refrigerate. Melt chocolate chips and broken-up Hershey's in top of double boiler. Add peanut butter, peanuts, and vanilla. Spread over top of cooled and set cherry mixture. Store, covered, in refrigerator.

Colorado Cookie Collection

Cookies and Cream Wedges

CRUST:

**2 cups finely crushed
Oreos (24 cookies)**

¹/₃ cup melted butter

FILLING:

**2 (8-ounce) packages cream
cheese**
²/₃ cup sugar
1 tablespoon vanilla

**1 cup cream, whipped
(okay to use packaged)**
**2 ounces semi-sweet chocolate
(use chocolate chips and
pulverize)**

Press Oreo crumbs mixed with butter into bottom of springform pan. Beat cream cheese until fluffy. Add sugar and vanilla. Fold in whipped cream and grated chocolate. Pour over crust. Freeze 2 hours. Serve. *Recipe from Leadville Country Inn, Leadville.*

Pure Gold—Colorado Treasures

Black Bean Brownies

Yes! There is no flour in this recipe!

¹/₂ cup margarine
2 cups sugar
6 tablespoons cocoa
**1 tablespoon instant coffee
powder**

4 eggs
1 cup black bean purée
**¹/₂ cup walnuts, chopped
(optional)**

Beat margarine, sugar, cocoa, and coffee. Add eggs, one at a time. Beat in bean purée. Stir in nuts. Pour into 9x13-inch greased pan. Bake at 350° for 45 minutes for moist, fudgy brownies. If you like drier brownies, bake 5-10 minutes longer. Cool completely in pan. Cut into 1½ x 2-inch bars.

Per serving (¹/₁₆ recipe): Calories 212, Prot 3.8g; Sugars 24.18g, Fiber 1.75g, Sat. Fat 1.95g, Poly. Fat 3.48mg, Choles. 50.6mg, Sod 84.37mg, Potas. 114.25mg.

More Than Soup Bean Cookbook

Colorado has 14 million tourists each year who spend $5.6 billion in the state.

Speedy Little Devils

1 stick margarine, melted
1 Duncan Hines Deluxe II
   Devils Food cake mix
3/4 cup creamy peanut butter
1 (7 1/2-ounce) jar marshmallow creme

Combine melted margarine and dry cake mix. Reserve 1½ cups of this topping for top crust. Pat remaining crumb mixture into ungreased 13x9x2-inch pan. Top that layer with combined peanut butter and marshmallow creme and spread evenly. Crumble remaining mixture over that. Bake 20 minutes at 350°. Cool. Cut into 3 dozen bars.

Colorado Cookie Collection

Pumpkin Cheesecake Bars

CRUST:
1 (16-ounce) package pound
   cake mix
1 egg
2 tablespoons butter or
   margarine
2 teaspoons pumpkin pie
   spice

In large bowl combine cake mix, egg, butter, and spice until crumbly. Press onto bottom of 15x10-inch jellyroll pan. Set aside.

FILLING:
1 (8-ounce) package cream
   cheese
1 (14-ounce) can sweetened
   condensed milk
2 eggs
1 (16-ounce) can pumpkin
2 teaspoons pumpkin pie
   spice
1/2 teaspoon salt
1 cup chopped nuts

In large bowl beat cheese until fluffy. Gradually beat in sweetened condensed milk. Add eggs, pumpkin, spice, and salt. Mix well. Pour over crust; sprinkle nuts on top. Bake at 350° 30-35 minutes or until set. Cool. Chill; cut into bars. Store in refrigerator.

Cheesecake et cetera

Krisi's Brownies with Hot Fudge Sauce from the Pine Creek Cookhouse

BROWNIES:

1 stick plus 3 table-
  spoons butter
2 ounces semi-sweet
  chocolate
4 ounces unsweetened
  chocolate
1 cup brown sugar,
  tightly packed

1 cup granulated sugar
1 1/2 teaspoon vanilla
1 1/2 cups flour
1 teaspoon salt
2 teaspoons baking powder
4 eggs
1/2 cup chopped nuts
  (your choice)

Preheat oven to 350°. Use a 9x13-inch pan. In a heavy medium-sized saucepan, melt butter and chocolates over low heat, stirring occasionally. When all are melted, remove from heat and stir in sugars and vanilla. Add flour, salt, and baking powder and mix well. Then add the eggs, stirring briefly after each addition. Sprinkle top with chopped nuts. Bake 25-30 minutes, more for a double batch. Toothpick should come out dry. (Recipe directions for high altitude cooking.)

HOT FUDGE SAUCE:

5 tablespoons butter
1/4 cup cocoa powder
2 squares unsweetened
  chocolate
3/4 cup granulated sugar

2/3 cup whipping cream or
  evaporated milk
Pinch salt
1 teaspoon vanilla

In a small saucepan, melt butter. Remove from heat, add cocoa, whisk until smooth. Stir in chocolate, sugar, and evaporated milk or whipping cream. Bring to boil over medium heat, stirring constantly. Remove from heat. Stir in salt, cool, and stir in vanilla. Serve brownies with Hot Fudge Sauce and whipped cream! Makes 24.

Lighter Tastes of Aspen

Colorado, the eighth largest state in the union, is known as the Centennial State because it joined the Union on the 100th anniversary of the Declaration of Independence.

Best-Ever Thumb Print Cookies

1 cup butter	2 egg whites, slightly beaten
1/2 cup brown sugar	Finely chopped nuts
2 egg yolks	Butter Cream Frosting
1 teaspoon vanilla	Crabapple jelly or
2 cups flour	maraschino cherries
1/2 teaspoon salt	

Cream butter and brown sugar. Add yolks and vanilla, mix well. Stir in flour and salt. Roll into 1-inch balls. Dip each ball into egg whites then roll in chopped nuts. Place on ungreased cookie sheet. Bake 5 minutes at 375°. Make thumb print in center of each cookie. Bake 8 minutes longer. At Christmas, these are pretty filled with green Butter Cream Frosting and topped with a spoonful of crabapple jelly or a maraschino cherry.

BUTTER CREAM FROSTING:

1/3 cup butter	1 1/2 teaspoons vanilla
3 cups powdered sugar	2-3 tablespoons milk

Cream butter and sugar, stir in vanilla and add enough milk to make frosting smooth and spreading consistency. Makes 30-36 cookies.

Kitchen Keepsakes

Pinto Cookies

1 cup brown sugar	1 teaspoon baking powder
1/2 cup shortening	2 1/4 cups flour
2 eggs	1/2 teaspoon cinnamon
3/4 cup cooked pintos, mashed	1/2 teaspoon cloves
3/4 cup applesauce	1/2 cup nuts, chopped
1 teaspoon baking soda	1/2 cup raisins

Cream sugar, shortening, and eggs. Add pintos and applesauce; beat till fluffy. Add dry ingredients; beat till smooth. Stir in nuts and raisins. Drop by teaspoon onto greased cookie sheet. Bake at 375° for 15-20 minutes or till golden brown. Cool on rack. Yield: About 36 cookies.

Variation: Substitute chocolate chips for raisins.

Per cookie: Calories 106, Prot. 1.9g, Sugars 8.19g, Fiber 1g, Sat. Fat 1.14 g, Poly. Fat 1.23mg, Choles. 12.8mg, Sod. 6.1mg, Potas. 75.25mg.

More Than Soup Bean Cookbook

Chocolate Chunk/White Chocolate Chip Cookies

3/4 cup brown sugar
3/4 cup butter or margarine
2 eggs
1 teaspoon vanilla
2 1/2 cups flour

1 teaspoon baking soda
6 ounces chocolate chunks
5 ounces Hershey's vanilla
   chips
1/4 cup chopped walnuts

Preheat oven to 375° - 400°. Soften brown sugar and butter in microwave for one minute on HIGH. Add eggs and vanilla. Mix well. Add flour and baking soda to sugar/egg mixture. When well mixed, add chocolate chunks, vanilla chips, and walnuts. Place by well-rounded teaspoonfuls on ungreased in-sulated cookie sheet. Bake for 10-12 minutes or until slightly brown on top. Makes approximately 2 dozen cookies. *Recipe from Holden House, Colorado Springs.*

Colorado Columbine Delicacies

Chocolate Brownies

These brownies are very dense, more like fudge than cake. Serve them plain or with a dusting of powdered sugar. Or, for a really decadent brownie, top with melted bittersweet chocolate.

1/2 cup brown rice flour
2 tablespoons tapioca flour
1/2 cup cocoa (not Dutch)
1/2 teaspoon baking powder
1/2 teaspoon salt

6 tablespoons canola oil
1 1/2 cups brown sugar, packed
2 large eggs
1 teaspoon vanilla extract
1/2 cup chopped walnuts

Preheat oven to 350°. Spray 8-inch square pan with cooking spray. Stir together the flours, cocoa, baking powder, and salt. In large mixing bowl, beat the oil and brown sugar with electric mixture on medium speed until well combined. Blend in eggs and vanilla. With mixer on low speed, add dry ingredients. Mix until just blended (a few lumps may remain). Stir in nuts.

Spread batter in prepared pan and bake for 35 minutes or until a toothpick inserted in center comes out almost clean. Cool brownies before cutting. Serves 16 (very small pieces).

Per serving: Cal 135 (39% from fat); Fat 6g; Prot 3g; Carb 19g; Sod 92mg; Chol 27mg. Brown rice substitute (not for celiacs): ½ cup amaranth flour.

Wheat-Free Recipes and Menus

Grandma's Crackle Tops

2³/4 cups flour
2 teaspoons baking soda
¹/2 teaspoon salt
2 teaspoons pumpkin pie
  spice
³/4 cup butter or margarine

³/4 cup sugar
¹/2 cup molasses
1 egg
1 teaspoon vanilla
Granulated sugar

Sift flour, baking soda, salt, and pumpkin pie spice onto waxed paper. Beat butter and ³/4 cup sugar until light and fluffy in large bowl with electric mixer on high speed. Beat in molasses and egg until smooth. Stir in vanilla. Blend in flour mixture to make a soft dough. Cover bowl with plastic wrap and refrigerate 4 hours. Sprinkle granulated sugar on waxed paper. Roll dough into 1-inch balls and roll in sugar. Place balls 3 inches apart on ungreased cookie sheets. Flatten with bottom of glass dipped in sugar. Sprinkle cookies with few drops water. (This gives the crackle tops.) Bake at 375° for 10 minutes or until cookies are firm, but not hard. Store in metal tin with tight cover. Makes 5 dozen.

Colorado Cookie Collection

Mock Toffee

Soda crackers
2 sticks margarine

1 cup brown sugar
1 (12-ounce) package
   chocolate chips

Line cookie sheet with foil. Lay soda crackers on foil. Mix margarine and sugar in saucepan. Bring to full rolling boil. Pour boiling mixture over crackers. Bake 10 minutes in 350° oven. Remove from oven and pour chocolate chips on top while still hot. As they melt, spread them around. Place cookie sheet in refrigerator until cold. Break crackers into pieces and store in closed container in refrigerator.

Colorado Cookie Collection

V.V.C.'s (Vicki's Volleyball Cookies)

2¼ cups flour
1 teaspoon soda
1 cup margarine, softened
¼ cup sugar
¾ cup brown sugar
1 teaspoon vanilla

1 small package instant
   vanilla pudding
2 eggs
1 (12-ounce) package
   chocolate chips

Mix flour and soda. Beat butter, sugars, vanilla, and ppuddinguntil creamy. Beat in eggs. Add flour mixture. Drop on slightly greased cookie sheets. Bake at 375° for 8-10 minutes.

Cookie Exchange

Cottage Cheese Cookies

1 cup shortening
1 cup sugar
¾ cup brown sugar
1 cup cottage cheese
2¾ cups flour

1 teaspoon baking powder
½ teaspoon salt
½ teaspoon soda
½ cup nuts, chopped

Combine ingredients. Chill overnight. Roll into small balls and roll in powdered sugar. Bake on greased cookie sheets at 350° for 11 minutes.

Colorado Cookie Collection

Raggedy Ann Cookies

1 cup butter or margarine	¹/₂ teaspoon baking powder
1 cup packed brown sugar	¹/₂ teaspoon salt
1 egg	¹/₂ teaspoon cinnamon
1 teaspoon maple flavoring	1 cup shredded coconut
2¹/₄ cups flour	1 cup finely chopped nuts (optional)

Cream butter, brown sugar, egg, and flavoring until fluffy. Add flour, baking powder, salt, and cinnamon. Mix well. Stir in coconut and nuts, if desired. Drop by teaspoonsful 2 inches apart on greased cookie sheet. Butter bottom of a glass, dip into granulated sugar, and press cookie flat. Bake at 350° 10-12 minutes. Cool on rack. Yields 5 dozen.

The Colorado Cookbook

Split Second Cookies

2 cups flour	³/₄ cup butter, softened
²/₃ cup sugar	1 egg
Pinch of salt	1 teaspoon vanilla
¹/₂ teaspoon baking powder	Red jelly or jam

Sift together flour, sugar, salt, and baking powder. Cut in butter, unbeaten egg and vanilla. Form into dough. Place on lightly floured board. Divide into 4 parts. Shape into rolls 13 inches long, ³/₄-inch thick. Put on ungreased cookie sheets, 4 inches apart and 3 inches from edge. Make a depression with handle of knife about ¹/₃-inch deep lengthwise and down the center of each. Fill with red jelly or jam (about ¹/₄ cup in all). Bake at 350°, 15-20 minutes, until golden brown. While warm, slice diagonally. Makes about 4 dozen.

Cookie Exchange

Dad's Favorite Cookies

This is our Dad's favorite cookie! Also unusual with the cooked raisins—boy, are they good!

1 cup raisins
1 cup water
1 cup shortening
1 cup sugar
1 egg
6 tablespoons raisin juice, cooled
2 cups flour

1 teaspoon soda
1 teaspoon cinnamon
1/2 teaspoon nutmeg
1/2 teaspoon salt
1/4 teaspoon cloves
2 cups oats, old fashioned
1 1/2 cups chocolate chips

In saucepan add raisins and water. Bring to boil; cool. Meanwhile, mix shortening, sugar, and egg together. Add cooled raisin juice. Add dry ingredients. Mix in chocolate chips and drained raisins. Bake at 350° for 8-10 minutes or until golden brown. Makes 3-4 dozen.

Country Classics

Porter House Oatmeal Cranberry Cookies

Reach for one of these delicious cookies whenever you need a pick-me-up!

1 cup butter (2 sticks), softened	2 cups oatmeal (old fashioned or quick)
1 cup brown sugar, firmly packed	1 1/2 cups dried cranberries
2 eggs	1 1/2 cups white chocolate chips
2 cups flour	1/2 cup chopped walnuts, optional
1 1/2 teaspoons baking soda	

Beat together the butter and brown sugar. Add eggs and mix until combined. Stir in the flour, baking soda, and oatmeal. Add the cranberries, chips, and nuts. Use a cookie scoop for evenly-sized cookies, or drop by rounded tablespoon onto lightly greased baking sheet. Bake in preheated oven at 375° for 10-12 minutes. Let stand for about 2 minutes; remove to wire rack to cool completely. Makes about 7-8 dozen cookies. *Recipe from The Porter House Bed and Breakfast, Windsor.*

Colorado Bed & Breakfast Cookbook

Oatmeal Carrot Cookies

3/4 cup margarine	1/4 teaspoon ground cloves
3/4 cup brown sugar	1 teaspoon vanilla
1/2 cup sugar	1 3/4 cups flour
1 egg	2 cups rolled oats
1 teaspoon baking powder	1 cup finely shredded carrots
1/2 teaspoon cinnamon	1/2 cup raisins
1/4 teaspoon baking soda	

In a mixing bowl beat margarine with an electric mixer on medium to high speed for 30 seconds or until softened. Add brown sugar, sugar, egg, baking powder, cinnamon, baking soda, cloves, vanilla, and half of flour. Beat until combined, scraping sides of bowl occasionally. Beat in remaining flour. Stir in oats, carrots, and raisins. Drop by rounded teaspoon 2 inches apart onto an ungreased cookie sheet. Bake at 375° for 10-12 minutes, or until edges are golden.

4-H Family Cookbook

Kristen's Mocha Chip Cookies

These are wonderful! Keep some in the freezer. Heated in the micro-wave for a few seconds, they taste like they were freshly baked.

2¹/2 cups semi-sweet chocolate chips, divided	4 tablespoons instant coffee granules
1 cup butter, softened	2 teaspoons vanilla
1 cup brown sugar	3 cups flour
1 cup granulated sugar	1¹/2 teaspoons baking soda
2 eggs	¹/2 teaspoon salt
4 teaspoons hot water	Powdered sugar

Melt one cup of the chocolate chips over low heat and set aside. In a large bowl, cream together butter, brown sugar, and granulated sugar. Add the eggs and mix until smooth. Stir coffee granules into hot water until dissolved, and stir it into the butter mixture, along with the vanilla. Mix in melted chocolate.

In small bowl, combine flour, baking soda, and salt. Gradually stir this into the butter mixture. Blend in remaining 1½ cups chocolate chips. Refrigerate dough until stiff. Preheat oven to 350°. Form chilled dough into small balls, and roll in powdered sugar. Place on ungreased cookie sheet and bake for about 8-10 minutes. Remove from oven when surface appears "cracked" and dough has spread somewhat, but not yet flat.

Especially yummy and chewy when served warm. Makes about 8 dozen. *Recipe from The Boulder Victoria Historic Inn, Boulder.*

Colorado Bed & Breakfast Cookbook

Good and Delicious Cookies

1 cup brown sugar
1 cup granulated sugar
1 cup margarine
1 cup oil
1 egg
3 teaspoons vanilla
1 teaspoon salt
1 teaspoon soda

1 teaspoon cream of tartar
1 cup rolled oats
1 cup coconut
3¹/2 cups flour
1 cup rice krispies cereal
1 (12-ounce) package
chocolate chips

Mix by order of ingredients. Drop by teaspoonfuls onto baking sheet. Bake at 350° for 12-15 minutes. Makes 6 dozen cookies.

Colorado Cookie Collection

Forgotten Kisses

2 egg whites
Pinch of salt
Pinch of cream of tartar
²/3 cup sugar

Green food coloring (or red)
1 package chocolate mint
chips (or regular chips
and mint extract)

Heat oven to 350°. Beat whites until frothy. Add salt and tartar. Keep beating, gradually adding sugar. Fold in food coloring and chips. Drop onto ungreased baking sheets. Turn oven off and leave cookies in oven several hours or overnight. Makes about 24 cookies.

Variations:

SANTA'S KISSES

2 egg whites
¹/4 teaspoon cream of
tartar
¹/2 cup sugar

¹/3 teaspoon salt
¹/2 teaspoon vanilla
1 (3¹/4-ounce) can flaked
coconut

Preheat oven to 350°. Beat egg whites; while beating, gradually add cream of tarter and sugar. When stiff, add salt and vanilla. Fold in coconut. Drop onto brown paper on a cookie sheet. Bake 20 minutes at 325°. Peel off paper when cool.

WITCHES KISSES:

Fold in 1 (6-ounce) package chocolate chips, melted with coconut. Can be decorated with candy corn or other Halloween candy.

Colorado Cookie Collection

Frosted Cremes

2 cups water	2 eggs
1 cup raisins	3 cups flour
1 teaspoon soda	1 teaspoon cinnamon
1 cup brown sugar	1/2 teaspoon cloves
1 cup white sugar	1/2 teaspoon salt
1/4 cup shortening	

Cook the raisins in water for 5 minutes; drain raisin water into one cup measure and add enough water to make one cup. Add soda to raisin, water (it will foam, so hold over a bowl.)

Mix the sugars and shortening. Add the eggs and soda water. Sift together the dry ingredients and add to the mixture. Add the raisins and stir well. Bake in a greased and floured jellyroll pan at 350° for 15-20 minutes. Frost with glaze while warm.

GLAZE:

3 tablespoons milk or water	1 teaspoon vanilla
1 1/2 cups powdered sugar, sifted	

Add the milk or water to powdered sugar and vanilla. Stir until mixture is smooth, and just slightly thick. Spread over the cake.

Great Plains Cooking

Bugs in a Rug

1 (8-ounce) package reduced-fat cream cheese, softened	1/4 cup raisins
1/3 cup sifted powdered sugar	6 slices whole-wheat or white bread, crusts removed, or 6 (6-inch) flour tortillas
1/2 teaspoon cinnamon	
1/2 teaspoon vanilla extract	

Combine first 4 ingredients, stirring until mixture is smooth; stir in raisins. Spread about 3 tablespoons mixture evenly on each slice of bread or tortilla; roll up. Wrap each roll separately in plastic wrap, twisting ends to seal. Refrigerate one hour or until firm. Yield: 6 servings.

Sharing Our Best

Orange Fudge

2 cups sugar
1 (5⅓-ounce) can
  evaporated milk (²/₃ cup)
10 large marshmallows (or
  100 miniature)

1 cup chopped walnuts
¹/₂ cup butter or margarine,
  cut into small pieces
Grated peel or 2 oranges

In saucepan, combine sugar, evaporated milk, and marshmallows. Bring to boil over medium heat, stirring to dissolve the sugar. Boil for 6 minutes, stirring constantly. Remove from heat and add remaining ingredients. Beat well until fudge thickens, about 5 minutes. Pour into a buttered 8-inch-square baking pan. Chill until firm and cut into squares.

Mystic Mountain Memories

Creamy Potato Fudge

3 (1-ounce) squares
  unsweetened chocolate
3 tablespoons butter
¹/₃ cup Colorado potatoes,
  mashed, unseasoned

¹/₈ teaspoon salt
1 teaspoon vanilla
1 pound powdered sugar,
  sifted
¹/₂ cup nuts, chopped

Melt chocolate and butter in top of double boiler. Remove from heat. Add potatoes, salt, and vanilla. Mix well. Blend in sugar and mix thoroughly. Add nuts and knead until smooth. Press into buttered 8-inch square pan. Cool in refrigerator before cutting. Makes 1¼ pounds.

Per serving: Cal 147; Prot .91g; Carbo 25g; Fat 5.9g; Chol 4.6mg; Sod 32mg; Dietary Fiber .83g.

Colorado Potato Favorite Recipes

Marcy's Peanut Butter Balls

1 cup chopped dates
1 cup chopped pecans
1 cup coconut
3/4 cup peanut butter
1 cup powdered sugar

1 egg, beaten
1 teaspoon vanilla extract
1 (12-ounce) package
  chocolate chips
1 sheet parafin

Combine all ingredients and shape into balls. Chill for one hour or overnight. Melt chocolate chips and paraffin, using a double boiler. Coat peanut butter balls. Place over wax paper to dry.

Note: You can also use Candiquick, yogurt Candiquick or chocolate flavored candy coating instead of chocolate chips.

Home Cookin'

Puppy Chow for People

1/2 pound oleo
12 ounces milk chocolate
  chips
3/4 cup peanut butter

1 large box Crispix cereal
1 pound salted peanuts
1 1/2 cups powdered sugar

Melt oleo, chocolate chips, and peanut butter. Place Crispix cereal and peanuts in a paper bag. Pour melted mixture over cereal and shake well. Pour powdered sugar in bag and shake well again.

Grade A Recipes

Cracker Jacks

8 or 9 quarts popped popcorn
2 cups brown sugar
1 cup margarine or butter
1/2 teaspoon salt

1/2 cup white corn syrup
1/2 teaspoon baking soda
1 teaspoon vanilla
Peanuts, optional, to taste

Pop popcorn and shake to remove old maids. Place in large roaster pan. Cook brown sugar, margarine, salt, and corn syrup until it comes to a rolling boil, then boil 5 minutes. Remove from heat; add baking soda and vanilla. Pour immediately over popped corn. Add peanuts; stir well to coat popcorn. Bake one hour at 250°; stir several times while baking.

Doc's Delights

Molasses Taffy

1 cup unsulphured molasses	1/4 teaspoon salt
1/2 cup water	5 tablespoons butter
1 1/2 cups dark brown sugar	1/8 teaspoon baking soda
1 1/2 tablespoons cider	Confectioners' sugar
vinegar	

Place the molasses, water, brown sugar, vinegar, salt, and butter in a heavy saucepan. Bring to a boil, stirring until sugar dissolves. Boil without stirring until the mixture registers 250-280° on a candy thermometer or forms a hard ball when a little is dropped into cold water. Stir in the baking soda and pour onto a buttered marble slab or heat-proof platter. When taffy is cool enough to handle, pull it with both hands to a spread of about 18 inches. Fold the taffy back on itself and continue pulling, twisting slightly until ridges of twists retain their shape (about 15 minutes). Form into a long rope on a surface sprinkled with confectioners' sugar. Cut into bite-sized pieces. Yields about one pound.

Eating Up The Santa Fe Trail

Cinnamon Walnuts

1 cup sugar
1/4 teaspoon salt
1/8 teaspoon cream of tartar
1/2 teaspoon cinnamon

1/4 cup boiling water
1/2 teaspoon vanilla extract
1 1/2 cups walnut halves

Combine sugar, salt, cream of tartar and cinnamon in heavy saucepan. Add boiling water; mix well. Bring to rolling boil, stirring constantly. Reduce heat. Cook to 240 - 248° on candy thermometer (236° at high altitude), firm ball stage. Remove from heat.

Add vanilla and walnuts, stirring until walnuts are coated and syrup begins to turn sugary. Spoon onto wax paper or greased baking sheet, separating walnuts. Cool. Store in airtight containers. Yields 24 servings.

Per serving: Cal 73: T Fat 4g; 46% Cal from Fat; Prot 1g; Carbo 10g; Fiber <1g: Chol 0mg; Sod 23mg.

The Flavor of Colorado

Pies and Other Desserts

Many happy couples enjoy winter vacations in the romantic Colorado Rockies.

Triple Chocolate Brownie Pie

2 eggs
1 cup sugar
1/2 cup butter or margarine,
   melted
1/2 cup all-purpose flour
1/3 cup Hershey's cocoa
1/4 teaspoon salt

1/2 cup Hershey's semi-sweet
   chocolate chips
1/2 cup chopped nuts
1 teaspoon vanilla extract
Vanilla ice cream
Hershey's Chocolate Shoppe
   Topping

Heat oven to 350°. Grease 8-inch pie plate. In small mixer bowl, beat eggs; blend in sugar and butter. In separate bowl, stir together flour, cocoa, and salt; add to egg mixture, beating until blended. Stir in chocolate chips, nuts, and vanilla. Spread batter into prepared pie plate. Bake 35 minutes or until set (pie will not test done in center). Cool completely; cut into wedges. Serve with ice cream; top with your favorite Hershey's Chocolate Shoppe Topping. Makes 6-8 servings.

Note: A 9-inch pie plate may be used; bake at 350° for 30 minutes.

The Durango Cookbook

Pecan Pie Surprise Bars

1 package Pillsbury plus
   yellow or butter cake mix
1/3 cup margarine or butter,
   softened
1 egg
1/2 cup brown sugar, packed
   firmly

1 1/2 cups dark corn syrup
1 teaspoon vanilla
3 eggs
1 cup pecans, chopped

Heat oven to 350°. Grease 13x9-inch pan. Reserve 2/3 cup of dry cake mix for filling. In large bowl, combine remaining dry cake mix, margarine, and one egg at low speed until well blended. Press in bottom of greased pan. Bake at 350° for 15-20 minutes or until light golden brown. In large bowl, combine reserved 2/3 cup dry cake mix, brown sugar, corn syrup, vanilla, and 3 eggs at low speed until moistened. Beat one minute at medium speed or until well blended. Pour filling mixture over warm base. Sprinkle with pecans. Bake an additional 30-35 minutes or until filling is set. Cool completely. Cut into bars. Store in refrigerator. Makes 36 bars.

What's Cookin' in Melon Country

Cherry Brandy Pie

This takes very little time to prepare and it stays in the freezer until needed.

1½ cups chocolate wafers,
  finely crushed (30)
6 tablespoons margarine,
  melted
1 (7-ounce) jar marshmallow
  creme

⅓ cup cherry brandy
2 tablespoons maraschino
  cherries, chopped
2 cups whipping cream

Combine the crushed wafers and margarine. Press mixture firmly onto the bottom and up sides of a 9-inch pie plate. Combine marshmallow creme and brandy; beat smooth with rotary mixer. Fold in chopped cherries. Beat whipping cream to soft peaks; fold into marshmallow mixture. Turn into crust. Freeze overnight. Serve directly from freezer.

Great Plains Cooking

Coconut Pie

This pie makes its own crust.

4 eggs
1¾ cups sugar
½ cup flour
2 cups milk

¼ cup melted butter
1½ cups coconut
1 teaspoon vanilla

Combine all the ingredients, in order, in a blender. Mix until smooth. Pour the mixture into a greased 10-inch pie pan. Bake for 45 minutes at 350°, until a tester inserted into the middle comes out clean. *Recipe from The Leadville Country Inn, Leadville.*

Distinctly Delicious

Rollin' Pin Strawberry Pie

This was the favorite pie at the Rollin' Pin Bakery and Restaurant. It is unlike any strawberry pie you will eat!

3 egg whites
1/2 teaspoon baking powder
3/4 cup sugar
10 soda crackers,
　crushed fine

1/2 cup pecans, chopped
2-3 pints fresh strawberries,
　sliced
Frozen whipped topping,
　thawed

Spray a 9-inch pie pan with non-stick cooking spray. Beat egg whites and baking powder until stiff. Add sugar and continue beating until very stiff. Fold in crackers and pecans. Pour into pie pan. Bake at 300° for 50 minutes. Remove from oven; with fork, press crust down. Cool completely. Fill with strawberries. (Add no sugar to strawberries.) Press strawberries down to compact them. Cover with whipped topping. Chill at least 2 hours. Serves 6-8.

Country Classics

Coconut Banana Cream Pie

PIE CRUST:
1 1/3 cups coconut
2/3 cup rolled oats

3 tablespoons margarine,
　melted

Put all ingredients into a 9-inch pie pan; mix well. Press into bottom and sides of pan. Bake at 300° for 15 minutes, or until golden.

FILLING:
3 cups milk
1/3 cup cornstarch
3 eggs, separated
3/4 cup sugar, divided

2 tablespoons margarine
1 1/2 teaspoons vanilla
2 large bananas

In large saucepan, mix milk, cornstarch, yolks, 1/2 cup sugar and margarine. Cook over medium heat, stirring constantly until it boils and thickens. Boil one minute. Stir in vanilla. Slice bananas into pie shell. Pour custard on top. Beat egg whites until stiff peaks form. Gradually stir in 1/4 cup sugar. Spread meringue over filling, being sure to seal edges. Bake in preheated 400° oven 10 minutes, or until meringue is golden. Cool on wire rack. Makes 8 servings.

Easy Recipes for 1, 2 or a Few

Strawberry Super Pie

CRUST:

3/4 cup (11/2 sticks) unsalted butter, melted
11/2 cups all-purpose flour

1 tablespoon confectioners' sugar
3/4 cup chopped pecans

Preheat oven to 375°. Mix melted butter with flour, confectioners' sugar, and pecans. Press into a buttered 10-inch pie plate. Bake for 25 minutes or until light brown. Allow to cool completely.

TOPPING:

2 pounds strawberries, divided
1/2 cup water

1 cup sugar
3 tablespoons cornstarch

Mash enough strawberries to make one cup. Cut the tops off the rest of the strawberries and set aside. Place mashed berries in a saucepan and add water. Mix sugar and cornstarch into crushed berry mixture and bring to a boil on top of stove, stirring. Boil about one minute or until clear and thickened. Set aside to cool.

FILLING:

11/4 cups whipping cream
1/4 pound cream cheese, softened

3/4 teaspoon vanilla extract
1/2 cup confectioners' sugar

Whip cream until stiff. In another bowl, beat cream cheese with vanilla and confectioners' sugar. Carefully fold whipped cream into cream cheese mixture. Spread in cooled crust and refrigerate.

When crushed berry mixture is cool, pie can be assembled. Stand whole strawberries (or halved, if you prefer, cut-side down) on top of the cream filling. When entire filling is covered with whole berries, carefully spoon cooled crushed berry mixture over all. Cream filling should not be seen between the whole berries. Once the crevices have been filled, do not overload the pie with the crushed berry mixture, as it will just drip over the sides. Yields 8-10 servings.

Note: Any leftover crushed berry mixture is delectable on toast or English muffins.

West of the Rockies

Grandma Cook's Peaches and Cream Pie

1 (9-inch) pie crust, unbaked
5 cups fresh peaches,
  sliced
3/4 cup sugar (or more, if
  peaches not ripe
  and sweet)

4 tablespoons flour
1/4 teaspoon salt
1/2 teaspoon cinnamon
1 cup cream

Place peaches in unbaked pie crust. Mix together sugar, flour, salt, cinnamon, and cream. Pour over peaches. Bake in 400° oven for 40 minutes.

More Kitchen Keepsakes

Dixie's Buttermilk Pie

1 (9-inch) unbaked pie shell
1 1/2 cups sugar
3 tablespoons flour
2 eggs, well beaten

1/2 cup butter, melted
1 cup buttermilk
2 teaspoons vanilla
1 teaspoon lemon extract

Combine sugar and flour; stir in eggs. Add melted butter and buttermilk; mix well. Stir in vanilla and lemon extract. Pour into chilled pie shell and bake at 425° for 10 minutes. Reduce heat to 350° and bake 35 additional minutes. Serves 8.

Kitchen Keepsakes

Juicy Fruit Cobbler

1/2 cup butter
3/4 cup flour
2 teaspoons baking
  powder
1/4 teaspoon salt
1/2 cup sugar
1 cup milk

4 cups fresh fruit alone or
  in combination (peaches,
  strawberries, blueberries,
  raspberries, plums,
  or rhubarb)
1/2 - 3/4 cup sugar
Juice and zest of 1 lemon
Cinnamon to taste

Melt butter in 13x9-inch pan in 350° oven. Remove from oven.
Sift together dry ingredients. Add milk and stir until just mixed.
Pour mixture into melted butter. DO NOT STIR. Toss fruit
with remaining ingredients. Place on top of milk mixture. DO
NOT STIR. Bake at 350° for 40 minutes until top is golden.
Serves 8.

Steamboat Entertains

Sour Cream Apple Pie

Although this pie contains no sour cream, it tastes as if it does.

3 tablespoons flour
1/4 cup sugar
1/8 teaspoon salt
1 cup whipping cream
1 egg, well beaten
1 teaspoon vanilla extract

1 teaspoon lemon juice
2 cups chopped peeled apples
1 unbaked 9-inch pie shell
1 cup flour
1/2 cup packed brown sugar
1/2 cup butter

Mix 3 tablespoons flour, sugar, and salt in medium bowl. Combine whipping cream, egg, vanilla, and lemon juice in mixer bowl;
mix well. Add flour mixture gradually, stirring until smooth.
Stir in apples. Spoon into pie shell. Mix one cup flour and
brown sugar in small bowl. Cut in butter until crumbly.
Sprinkle over pie. Bake at 425° for 15 minutes. Reduce temperature to 350°. Bake 30 minutes longer. Cool. Serves six.

Per serving: Cal 712; Prot 6.5g; Carbo 81.1g; T Fat 41.3g; Chol 141.0mg; Potas
190.0mg; Sod 395.0mg.

Beyond Oats

Boulder has the distinction of having its water supply from what is said to be
the only city-owned glacier anywhere—The Arapahoe is the source of water for
the city.

Apple Pecan Poorboy Pie

CRUST:

3 cups flour	**²/₃ cup solid shortening**
4 tablespoons powdered sugar	**2 egg yolks blended with 8 tablespoons water**
1 teaspoon salt	

TOPPING:

¹/₄ cup butter, softened	**²/₃ cup brown sugar**
³/₄ cup pecans	

FILLING:

³/₄ cup raisins, soaked in ¹/₄ cup bourbon	**2 tablespoons flour**
10 cups Granny Smith apples, peeled and sliced	**¹/₂ cup sugar**
2 tablespoons lemon juice	**¹/₂ teaspoon cinnamon**
	¹/₂ teaspoon nutmeg

Mix dry ingredients for crust. Cut shortening into dry ingredients and slowly add egg yolk and water mixture. Dough will be crumbly. Roll out into 12-inch circles.

Line 8-inch round cake pans with parchment paper. Press butter into pans and top with pecan pieces and then brown sugar. Line pan with pie crust over bottom and up sides. Fill with apple-raisin filling. Bake at 425° for 15 minutes then reduce heat to 350° for 25 minutes. Cool 5 minutes. Invert cake pan onto serving plate, remove paper and cool completely. Makes 2 pies. *Recipe by Bob Starekow—Silverheels Southwest Grill, Silverthorne, Colorado.*

Haute Off The Press

Pike's Peak Spiked Apple Crisp

5 cups peeled and sliced apples (Pippin, Jonathan or Winesap)	³/₄ cup granulated sugar
	¹/₄ cup light brown sugar, packed
¹/₂ teaspoon cinnamon sugar	³/₄ cup sifted flour
1 teaspoon grated lemon rind	¹/₄ teaspoon salt
	¹/₂ cup butter or margarine
1 teaspoon grated orange rind	Cream, whipped cream or ice cream for topping
1 jigger Grand Marnier	
1 jigger Amaretto de Saronno	

Arrange apple slices in greased 2-quart round casserole. Sprinkle cinnamon, lemon and orange rinds and both liqueurs on top of apples. In a separate bowl, mix sugars, flour, salt, and butter with a pastry blender until crumbly. Spread mixture over top of apples. Bake uncovered at 350° until apples are tender and top is lightly browned, approximately one hour. Serve warm with cream, whipped cream or with vanilla or cinnamon ice cream. Makes 8 servings.

Colorado Cache Cookbook

Mrs. Z's Strawberry Delite

CRUST:

3 egg whites	1 teaspoon baking powder
1 cup sugar	¹/₂ cup chopped pecans or walnuts
1 teaspoon vanilla	
18 crushed soda crackers	

Beat egg whites until stiff; gradually add sugar, then the vanilla. Fold in dry ingredients. Spread in 9-inch pie pan. Bake at 350° for 30 minutes.

FILLING:

2 cups Cool Whip	1 box frozen strawberries, drained

Combine Cool Whip and strawberries. Spread over cool crust. Refrigerate 4 hours or more before serving.

More Kitchen Keepsakes

Cherry Delight

2¹/₂ cups crushed graham
  crackers
²/₃ cup melted margarine or
  butter
¹/₂ cup sugar
12 ounces cream cheese at
  room temperature

1 (9-ounce) container
  whipped topping
¹/₂ cup chopped walnuts
2 cups powdered sugar
1 can cherry pie filling

Mix graham cracker crumbs, margarine, and sugar. Press into large baking dish to form crust. (Chill, or bake a few minutes in oven to set crust, then cool). Combine cream cheese, whipped topping, walnuts, and powdered sugar. Pour into crumb crust. Chill. Spread pie filling over top.

For strawberry delight, mix one large package strawberry gelatin with 2 cups boiling water. Add 2 small boxes frozen strawberries. Set aside to congeal slightly. Instead of cherry pie filling, pour strawberry mixture over cream cheese layer to make top layer. Chill thoroughly.

Note: Six double honey grahams equals one cup crumbs.

More Goodies and Guess-Whats

Dottie's Pumpkin Pleaser Dessert

1 (30-ounce) can pumpkin
  pie mix
1 (13-ounce) can evaporated
  milk
4 eggs, lightly beaten

1 box yellow cake mix
¹/₂ cup butter or margarine,
  melted
¹/₂ - 1 cup chopped nuts

Combine pumpkin, milk, and eggs. Mix well and pour into greased and floured 9x13-inch baking pan. Sprinkle cake mix evenly over pumpkin, then drizzle butter evenly over cake mix. Sprinkle on nuts. Bake 50-60 minutes at 350°. Chill overnight. Serves 16-20.

Note: This cake does not freeze well.

The Colorado Cookbook

Chocolate Divine Dessert

Paradise found!

1/2 cup slivered almonds
12 ounces semi-sweet
   chocolate chips
3 tablespoons sugar
3 large egg yolks,
   beaten

3 large egg whites, stiffly
   beaten
2 cups heavy cream, whipped
1 teaspoon pure vanilla
   extract
1 (8-ounce) angel food cake

Place almonds on ungreased cookie sheet and bake at 350° until light golden brown. Watch carefully so almonds do not burn! Cool and set aside.

In top of double boiler over hot water, melt chocolate chips with sugar. Cool. Mix in beaten egg yolks. Gradually fold in stiffly beaten egg whites. Fold in whipped cream and vanilla. Tear up angel food cake into 1/2-inch pieces. Put half of cake pieces on bottom of buttered 10-inch springform pan. Cover with half of chocolate mixture. Layer remaining cake and chocolate. Refrigerate at least 24 hours. Remove springform rim. Top with toasted almonds. May be made up to 3 days in advance. Makes 10-12 servings.

Crème de Colorado

Cannoli

CANNOLI SHELLS:

3 cups sifted all-purpose
   flour
1 tablespoon sugar
1/4 teaspoon cinnamon
3/4 cup port wine

Salad oil or shortening for
   deep-frying
1 egg yolk, slightly beaten
Chopped pistachio nuts
   (optional)
Confectioners' sugar

Sift flour with sugar and cinnamon onto a board. Make a well in center and fill with port. With a fork, gradually blend flour into port. When dough is stiff enough, knead about 15 minutes, or until dough is smooth and stiff. (If too moist and sticky, knead in a little more sifted flour.) Refrigerate dough, covered, for about 2 hours.

In deep-fat fryer, electric skillet or heavy saucepan, slowly heat oil (3 or 4 inches deep) to 400° on deep-frying thermometer. Meanwhile, on lightly floured surface, roll 1/3 of dough to paper thinness, making a 16-inch round. Cut into 8 (5-inch) circles. Wrap a circle loosely around a 6-inch-long cannoli form or dowel, one inch in diameter; seal with egg yolk.

Gently drop dough-covered forms, two at a time, into hot oil and fry one minute or until browned on all sides. (Turn, if necessary.) With tongs or slotted utensil, lift out of oil, drain on paper towels. Carefully remove forms. Continue until all dough is used. Just before serving, with teaspoon or small spatula, fill shells with ricotta mixture. Garnish ends with chopped pistachios; sprinkle tops with confectioners' sugar.

FILLING:

3 pound ricotta cheese
1 1/2 cups confectioners' sugar
1/4 cup semi-sweet chocolate
   pieces or grated sweet
   chocolate

2 tablespoons citron, chopped
10 candied cherries, finely
   chopped
1/4 teaspoon cinnamon

In a large bowl, with portable electric mixer, beat ricotta cheese one minute. Add confectioners' sugar, beat until light and creamy—about one minute. Add chocolate, citron, cherries, cinnamon; beat at low speed until well blended. Refrigerate, covered, until well chilled—at least 2 hours. Yields 24.

CONTINUED

Note: Cannoli shells can be made a day or two ahead and stored, covered, at room temperature, then filled about one hour before serving.

Italian Dishes et cetera

Caramel Dumplings

SYRUP:

1 cup sugar	2 tablespoons butter
2½ cups boiling water	1 teaspoon vanilla

Caramelize ½ cup sugar until golden brown in a heavy pan. Add boiling water. Stir until lumps are dissolved. Add rest of sugar, butter, and vanilla. Pour into a 9-inch baking pan.

BATTER:

½ cup sugar, divided	1 teaspoon salt
2 tablespoons butter	1 teaspoon baking powder
1½ cups flour	½ cup milk

Mix sugar with butter. Then mix in flour, salt, baking powder and milk. Mix well. Drop by tablespoons into hot syrup. Bake in 425° oven for 20 minutes.

Colorado Boys Ranch Auxiliary Cookbook

Strawberry Tiramisu

Guaranteed rave reviews from guests.

3/4 pound (1 1/2 cups) Mascarpone cheese, room temperature	**1 1/2 cups heavy cream**
3 tablespoons powdered sugar	**1 pint strawberries, rinsed and hulled**
3 tablespoons orange-flavored liqueur, divided	**1/4 cup granulated sugar**
	1/4 cup orange juice
	24 sponge ladyfingers

In medium bowl, whisk Mascarpone cheese, powdered sugar, and one tablespoon of the orange liqueur until well blended. In large chilled bowl with electric mixer at medium speed, beat heavy cream until soft peaks form; gently fold whipped cream into Mascarpone mixture until blended. In blender or food processor, blend together remaining liqueur, strawberries, sugar, and orange juice to a smooth purée. Pour strawberry mixture into shallow bowl.

Dip 12 ladyfingers in strawberry mixture to coat; arrange in a 9-inch square glass dish, side-by-side, in 2 rows touching. Spread 1/2 of the strawberry mixture evenly over rows. Spread 1/2 of the cream mixture on top. Repeat with remaining ladyfingers; arrange over cream layer. Spread with remaining strawberry mixture. Spread with remaining cream, smoothing top with spatula. Cover and refrigerate at least 8 hours or overnight.

To serve, cut into 9 squares. Place on dessert plates and dust each with cocoa powder and top with a sliced fanned strawberry.

Note: If Mascarpone cheese is unavailable, purée in blender or food processor 2 tablespoons of the heavy cream with 1 1/4 cups ricotta cheese, 3 tablespoons softened cream cheese, and one teaspoon fresh lemon juice until smooth.

Recipes from Our House

Tira Misu

1 (500-gram) tub mascarpone*
1 cup heavy cream
1/4 cup sugar
1/2 tablespoon vanilla extract
1 1/2 packages lady fingers**

1/2 - 1 cup espresso
1/4 cup dark rum
1/2 cup chopped bittersweet
  chocolate

Combine the first 4 ingredients in a mixing bowl; whip by hand or with an electric mixer on high until stiff. Do not over-mix or it will become grainy. Place a layer of lady fingers in the bottom of the pan. Sprinkle with half the espresso and half the rum. Spread half the marscarpone mixture evenly over the lady fingers. Cover with chopped chocolate.

Place a second layer of lady fingers and sprinkle the remaining espresso and rum. Spread the remaining mascarpone mixture, cover and refrigerate overnight. Dust the top with cocoa powder or shaven chocolate. Cut and carefully remove with a small spatula. Serves 8.

*Mascarpone is Italian cream cheese found in specialty stores.
**Enough lady fingers to cover a 6x10x4-inch pan twice.

Lighter Tastes of Aspen

Chocolate Disgust

1 (9x13-inch) devil's food
   cake
Kahlua liqueur
1 large carton Cool Whip

2 (6-ounce) packages vanilla
   pudding
Heath or Skor candy bars

Cut cake into bite-size cubes. Put half of cake cubes in a large bowl. Sprinkle with Kahlua. Spread half of pudding over cake. Top with half of Cool Whip, then sprinkle with half of crushed candy bars. Repeat layers. Chill. Looks nice in a clear bowl.

Taking Culinary Liberties

Cream Puff Dessert

1 stick oleo
1 cup water
1 cup flour
4 eggs
1 large box instant
   vanilla pudding

3 cups milk
1 (8-ounce) package cream
   cheese
1 (8-ounce) carton Cool Whip
Hershey's syrup

Boil together the oleo and water; add flour. Mix well. Cool slightly. Stir in eggs, one at a time. Mix well and spread into a 9x13-inch greased pan. Bake at 400° for 30 minutes; cool. To pudding add milk and softened cream cheese. Mix together with a wire whip so lumps disappear. Pour into cream puff crust. Spread Cool Whip on top of pudding. Drizzle Hershey's syrup on top for color. Refrigerate. Keeps well for days.

Grade A Recipes

Toffee Crunch Trifle

Dynamite dessert looks and tastes spectacular, but is easy to make.

1 (18-ounce) chocolate cake
  mix
Eggs, oil and water (as
  directed on cake mix)
1/2 cup Kahlua
1 (16-ounce) jar chocolate or
  fudge sauce

3 Skor or Heath candy bars,
  broken into bite-size
  pieces
1 (12-ounce) carton frozen
  whipped topping, thawed

Prepare cake according to package directions, baking in a 9x13-inch pan. Cool. Poke holes all over top of cake with a large fork. Pour Kahlua slowly over cake, allowing it to soak in. Cover tightly with plastic wrap; refrigerate at least 3 hours or overnight.

Assemble the day you want to serve (trifle gets watery assembled too far ahead) in a 3-quart trifle or straight sided, see-through bowl. Layer ingredients beginning with about a 1-inch layer of cake, 1/4 fudge sauce, 1 candy bar, and 1/4 whipped topping. Repeat layers 2 more times, reserving the last candy bar and 1/4 of fudge sauce to decorate top of trifle. Drizzle fudge sauce over top layer of whipped topping and sprinkle with candy pieces. Refrigerate until ready to serve. Makes 10-12 servings.

Note: A 3-quart trifle dish (about 7 inches in diameter and 5 inches deep) will only use about half of cake. Freeze remaining cake in a plastic bag for later use. If you have a larger container or make 2 trifles at the same time, double the fudge sauce, candy, and whipped topping.

Palates

One popular version of how Telluride got its name is that many desperadoes who hid out in this inapproachable box canyon (including Butch Cassidy) had a code phrase for the place: "To Hell You Ride."

Spanish Bread Pudding

1 1/2 cups brown sugar
2 1/2 cups water
2 tablespoons grated orange peel
1 cup Cheddar cheese

1/3 cup nuts, walnut or pecan
1 cup raisins
9 slices toasted bread, cut in halves or smaller

Combine sugar, water, and orange peel. Bring to boil over low heat. Combine cheese, nuts, raisins in bowl. Place alternate layers of bread and raisins and cheese mixture in a greased 2-quart casserole until filled. Pour syrup mixture over top. Bake in moderate oven (350°) 30 minutes.

What's Cookin' in Melon Country

Amaretto Bread Pudding

1 loaf French bread
1 quart half-and-half or milk
2 tablespoons butter
3 eggs

1 1/2 cups sugar
2 tablespoons almond extract
3/4 cup golden raisins
3/4 cup sliced almonds

Break up bread and cover with half-and-half. Cover and let stand one hour. Preheat oven to 325°. Grease 9x13x2-inch dish with the butter. Beat eggs, sugar, and almond extract. Stir into bread mixture. Gently fold in raisins and almonds. Spread evenly in dish. Place on middle rack and bake 50 minutes. Remove and cool.

AMARETTO SAUCE:

8 tablespoons unsalted butter
1 cup powdered sugar

1 egg, beaten
4 tablespoons amaretto liqueur

Using double boiler, stir together butter and sugar until very hot. Remove from heat. Whisk the egg well into butter and sugar mixture. Add liqueur. To serve, cut pudding into 12-15 pieces. Spoon sauce over and serve immediately.

The bread pudding freezes well. The sauce will keep in the refrigerator for several weeks.

Recipes from Our House

Glorified Rice

A great way to use up rice from the night before.

1 cup cold rice
1/2 cup sugar
1 1/2 cups crushed pineapple, drained
1/2 teaspoon vanilla

1 cup whipping cream, whipped
8 large marshmallows, cut-up
1/4 cup chopped maraschino cherries

Mix all ingredients and chill thoroughly. Makers 6-8 servings.

Note: Here's an idea you can go wild with. Use any flavor yogurt and fruit, fresh or canned, nuts, honey, cinnamon, peanut butter, etc. Use whatever sounds good to you; see how easy it is to be creative.

Mystic Mountain Memories

Cocoa Syrup

A favorite recipe.

1 cup cocoa
2 cups sugar
1/2 teaspoon salt
1 tablespoon flour

1 cup white or gold syrup
2 tablespoons vanilla
1 cup water

Sift together cocoa, sugar, salt, and flour. Mix in syrup, vanilla, and water; boil for 5 minutes.

Goodies and Guess-Whats

Peaches with Sour Cream and Strawberries

8 ripe peaches
Brandy
Lemon juice
2 cups sour cream
1 pint hulled strawberries

Superfine granulated sugar
2 tablespoons Grand Marnier,
 rum, or brandy
Macaroon crumbs

Skin peaches; halve and pit them. Sprinkle with brandy and lemon juice. Chill well. Fold sour cream into strawberries, add sugar (not too much) and Grand Marnier.

To serve, arrange peach halves in large bowl, or in individual champagne glasses. Spoon strawberry cream mixture over top and sprinkle with finely crushed macaroon crumbs. Serves 8.

The Colorado Cookbook

Cherry Fruit Swirl

1 1/2 cups sugar
1/2 cup margarine or butter
1/2 cup shortening
4 eggs
1 teaspoon almond extract

1 teaspoon vanilla extract
1 1/2 teaspoons baking powder
3 cups flour
1 cup cherry pie filling

GLAZE:
1 cup powdered sugar
1-2 tablespoons milk

Few drops almond extract

Preheat oven to 325°. Blend sugar, butter, shortening, eggs, extracts, and baking powder in bowl. Beat at high speed 3 minutes. Stir in flour and spread 2/3 of the batter in 18x10-inch jellyroll pan. Spread or drop the pie filling over the batter. Drop remaining 1/3 batter over filling. Swirl slightly on top. Bake about 45 minutes. After cooling, but while still warm, drizzle Glaze over top.

Grade A Recipes

The highest valley in the world is the San Taos Valley in Monte Vista.

Pizza Fruit Platter

CRUST:

1 package (1 layer) yellow cake mix	2 tablespoons butter, melted
2 tablespoons water	2 tablespoons brown sugar
1 egg	1/2 cup nuts, chopped

Combine the cake mix, water, egg, butter, and brown sugar. Fold in the nuts and pour batter on heavily greased and floured 12-inch pizza pan. Bake at 375° for 15 minutes and let cool.

SAUCE:

12 ounces cream cheese	1 teaspoon vanilla
1/2 cup sugar	

Mix the cream cheese, sugar, and vanilla together. Spread over crust.

TOPPINGS:

1 pint fresh strawberries, cut in half	2 bananas, sliced
1 (20-ounce) can pineapple tidbits	1/2 cup apricot preserves
Medium bunch of green grapes	2 tablespoons water

Arrange fruit in circular pattern over cheese mixture. Heat apricot preserves with 2 tablespoons water until the preserves melt. Remove from heat and let cool. Brush apricot glaze on fruit. Cut into wedges and refrigerate until ready to serve. Use whatever fresh fruit is in season. Kiwi is especially attractive and tasty.

Great Plains Cooking

Fudge Striped Cookie Salad

2 packages instant vanilla
  coconut cream pudding
1 1/2 cups half-and-half
1 (10-ounce) carton
  whipped topping

1 (11-ounce) can mandarin
  oranges
1 (8-ounce) can pineapple
  tidbits
1 package fudge-striped
  cookies

Beat pudding and half-and-half. Fold in whipped topping. Add well drained fruit. Break cookies into small pieces. Fold half of the cookies into the mixture. Put the rest on top. Cool for 4 hours.

Grade A Recipes

Catalog of Contributing Cookbooks

Sunlight threads the trees and lights the leaves in beautiful Cache La Poudre River Canyon near Fort Collins.

CATALOG
of
CONTRIBUTING COOKBOOKS

All recipes in this book have been selected from the Colorado cookbooks shown on the following pages. Individuals who wish to obtain a copy of any particular book may do so by sending a check or money order to the address listed by each cookbook (not Quail Ridge Press). Please note the postage and handling charges that are required. State residents add tax only when requested. Prices and addresses are subject to change, and books may sell out and become unavailable. Retailers are invited to call or write to same address for discount information.

ASPEN POTPOURRI

by Mary Eshbaugh Hayes
P. O. Box 497
Aspen, CO 81612   970-925-7127

Aspen Potpourri includes 260 photographs of Aspen people and their recipes. There are also many scenes of Aspen, including Victorian houses and architectural details. Thirty years in the making . . . the photographs were taken in the 60s, 70s, and 80s by Mary Eshbaugh Hayes, longtime reporter, photographer and editor of *The Aspen Times*.

$ 18.95   Retail price
$ .57   Tax for Colorado residents
$ 4.00   Postage and handling
Make check payable to *Aspen Potpourri*
ISBN 0-9641960-0-X

THE BEST OF FRIENDS

Fort Morgan Museum
P. O. Box 184   E-mail: ftmormus@ftmorganmus.org
Fort Morgan, CO 80701   970-867-6331/Fax 970-542-3008

Over 200 pages of recipes contributed by members of the Friends of the Museum. This wide variety of recipes is enhanced by drawings and information about historic homes and buildings in the community. This book is in its third printing; the recipes are just as good today as when it was first published.

$ 5.00   Retail price
$ .30   Tax for Colorado residents
$ 1.00   Postage and handling
Make check payable to Fort Morgan Museum

BEYOND OATS:
A Horse Lover's Cookbook

Arabian Horse Trust
12000 Zuni Street
Westminster, CO 80234   303-450-4710

The term "horse lover" includes everyone who has ever stopped to admire a beautiful horse and marveled at the grace and symmetry of God's beautiful creation. Our book contains delicious recipes from an interesting mix of people who are involved in some way with horses. The proceeds support the heritage, education and research programs of the Arabian Horse Trust.

$ 10.00   Retail price Visa/MC accepted
$ 3.00   Postage and handling
Make check payable to Arabian Horse Trust
ISBN 0-87197-257-3

CHEESECAKES ET CETERA

by Shirley Michaels
2560 Begonia Court
Loveland, CO 80537 970-203-1870

Cheesecakes et cetera is a collection of 50 cheesecake recipes, including baked and unbaked cakes, mini-cakes, and bars. The book also contains a variety of crusts that can be mixed and matched with the recipes, as well as some helpful hints and some humorous poetry to read while the cheesecakes bake.

$ 6.50   Retail price
$ 2.50   Postage and handling
Make check payable to Shirley Michaels

CHRISTINE'S KITCHEN

by Christine and Regas Halandras
P. O. Box 677
Meeker, CO 81641 970-878-3394

Christine's Kitchen—an especially nice cookbook. *Christine's Kitchen* is unique and offers an ethnic insight and authenticity that is hard to find. Many of the 65+ recipes are family favorites passed down generation after generation in traditional Greek style.

$ 9.90   Retail price
$ .30   Tax for Colorado residents
$ 1.60   Postage and handling
Make check payable to *Christine's Kitchen*

COLORADO BED & BREAKFAST COOKBOOK

Carol Faino and Doreen Hazledine
Peppermint Press
P. O. Box 370235
Denver, CO 80237-0235 800-758-0803

The *Colorado Bed & Breakfast Cookbook* highlights 142 recipes from 85 B&B's and country inns. These select recipes, often with make-ahead tips, range from the simple to the gourmet. This unique, 310-page hardcover book, with a hidden spiral binding, also serves as a travel guide to romantic destinations.

$ 18.95   Retail price
$ 1.38   Tax for Colorado residents
$ 3.00   Postage and handling
Make check payable to Peppermint Press
ISBN 0-9653751-8-8

COLORADO BOYS RANCH AUXILIARY COOKBOOK

Colorado Boys Ranch
28071 State Hwy 109
La Junta, CO 81050 719-384-5981

Colorado Boys Ranch Auxiliary Cookbook, a sequel to the first book produced in 1981, is a tribute to hardy pioneers who established the city of La Junta. This edition has 268 pages which include 410 recipes, unique hints and miscellaneous information. The proceeds help support youth projects at Colorado Boys Ranch.

$10.00 Retail Price
 $2.25 Postage and handling
Make check payable to Colorado Boys Ranch

COLORADO CACHE COOKBOOK

The Junior League of Denver, Inc.
6300 East Yale Avenue   www.jld.org
Denver, CO 80222   800-552-9244

Colorado Cache . . . offers a treasure trove of recipes that reflects our state's casual style of living, rich heritage, and natural bounty. Each of the 15 sections features recipes that are upscale, yet uncomplicated; inspiring, yet reliable; and in the tradition of great American cooking!

$15.95 Retail price
   $.48 Tax for Colorado residents
  $4.95 Postage and handling; $2.00 each additional book
Make check payable to The Junior League of Denver, Inc.
ISBN 1-9603946-5-6

COLORADO COLLAGE

The Junior League of Denver, Inc.
6300 East Yale Avenue   www.jld.org
Denver, CO 80222   800-552-9244

The best-selling authors of *Colorado Cache* and *Crème de Colorado* have created another culinary masterpiece. *Colorado Collage* is a wonderful collection of more than 500 triple-tested recipes, plus breathtaking landscape and tantalizing food photography. A wide variety of recipes with an emphasis on fresh ingredients. You'll find yourself craving seconds.

$24.95 Retail price
   $.79 Tax for Colorado residents
  $4.95 for first book, $2.00 each additional, postage and handling
Make check payable to The Junior League of Denver, Inc.
ISBN 0-9603946-4-8

COLORADO COLUMBINE DELICACIES

Winters Publishing
P. O. Box 501   TMWinters@juno.com
Greensburg, IN 47240   800-457-3230

This 112-page cookbook/directory features 115 tempting recipes from 43 Colorado B&B inns. Everything from Apple Dessert Pancakes to Walnut Streusel Coffee Cake, Bacon and Swiss Quiche to Wild Rice Egg Casserole. Complete information about each participating inn is included to help plan your stay. Special lay-flat binding.

$10.95 Retail
 $2.00 Postage and handling
Make check payable to Winters Publishing
ISBN 1-883651-02-6

THE COLORADO COOKBOOK

Friends of the Libraries/University of Colorado at Boulder
Boulder, CO

A versatile and imaginative collection of 662 recipes in step-by-step format. Nutritional analysis of each recipe and hints for healthier cooking. Contains 18 new art book quality full-color photographs of Colorado's beauty. A winner for all culinary skills and lifestyles. 417 pages. This book is currently out of print.

COLORADO COOKIE COLLECTION

Cyndi Duncan and Georgie Patrick
C & G Publishing, Inc
P. O. Box 5199   www.cgpub.com
Greeley, CO 80634   970-356-9622 or 800-925-3177

Colorado Cookie Collection is a best seller and a popular collector
for tourists. Features a detailed explanation of how to have a
cookie exchange. Easy to use recipes from which to choose
your favorites. 5½ x 8 ½, wire-o, 216 pages, 300 recipes of
nothing but cookies.

$14.95 Retail price
  $.45 Tax for Colorado residents
$2.00 Postage and handling
Make check payable to C & G Publishing, Inc.
ISBN 0-9626335-0-X

COLORADO FOODS AND MORE . . .

Judy Barbour
P. O. Box 2588
Bay City, TX 77404-2588   979-241-8958

Colorado Foods and More . . . is a result of extensive research of
the history of Colorado and its foods for all to enjoy. Two
books in one, the book highlights the colorful history and
many points of interest and contains outstanding recipes of
foods reflective of the bounty of the state. Beautiful green
cover with gold aspen leaves.

$6.95 Retail price
$1.50 Postage and handling
Make check payable to Judy Barbour
ISBN 0-9611746-2-5

COLORADO POTATO FAVORITE RECIPES

Colorado Potato Administrative Committee
P. O. Box 25   E-Mail mateer@pagosasprings.net
Hilliard, OH 43026   800-242-4643/Fax 614-889-2587

Sixty-four page full-color cookbook featuring over 100 delicious Colorado potato recipes from award-winning chefs
and many cherished farm kitchen recipes handed down
from generation to generation including appetizers, soups,
salads, breads, main dishes and desserts.

$ 12.95 Retail price Visa/MC accepted
$ 3.50 Postage and handling
Make check payable to Colorado Potato Cookbook

COOKIE EXCHANGE

Cyndi Duncan & Georgie Patrick
C & G Publishing, Inc.
P. O. Box 5199   www.cgpub.com
Greeley, CO 80634   970-356-9622 or 800-925-3177

Cookie Exchange includes quick instructions about how to hold
your own cookie exchange. Features a low-fat section. Easy to
use recipes from easy to complicated. *Cookie Exchange* is a
quality cookbook, fun to have 200 recipes in one cookbook.
5½ x 8½ wire-o binding, 160 pages.

$12.95 Retail price
  $.39 Tax for Colorado residents
$2.00 Postage and handling
Make check payable to C & G Publishing, Inc.
ISBN 0-9626335-0-X

COOKING WITH COLORADO'S GREATEST CHEFS

Marilynn A. Booth
Westcliffe Publishers
2650 S. Zuni Street
Englewood, CO 80110   800-523-3692

People from around the world travel to Colorado to ski, hike, climb, raft, or to simply enjoy the scenery, and therefore it has attracted the finest chefs. These recipes are the signature dishes of more than forty award-winning restaurants, each signed personally by the chef. This beautiful book includes stunning nature photography by renowned Colorado photographer, John Fielder.

$14.98 Retail price
 $4.50 Postage and handling
Make check payable to Westcliffe Publishers
ISBN 1-56579-127-4

COUNTRY CLASSICS

Ginger Mitchell and Patsy Tompkins
25401 County Road 27.4
Karval, CO 80823   719-446-5232 or 590-7818

Country Classics is a collection of our family's favorite recipes—some have been passed down from great-grandmothers and great aunts. They are good home-cooking and use common ingredients you keep in the pantry.

$ 14.95   Retail price
$ .45   Tax for Colorado residents
$ 2.95   Postage and handling
Make check payable to *Country Classics Cookbooks*
ISBN 0-9646160-0-9

COUNTRY CLASSICS II

Ginger Mitchell and Patsy Tompkins
25401 County Road 27.4
Karval, CO 80823   719-446-5232 or 590-7818

Country Classics II is a continuation of good home-cooking recipes. They are simple, easy-to-follow recipes that can be made after a day at work. No matter how many times we do "fast food," everyone loves to sit down to a home cooked meal!

$ 14.95   Retail price
$ .45   Tax for Colorado residents
$ 2.95   Postage and handling
Make check payable to *Country Classics* Cookbooks
ISBN 0-9646160-1-7

CRÈME DE COLORADO COOKBOOK

The Junior League of Denver, Inc.
6300 East Yale Avenue   www.jld.org
Denver, CO 80222   800-552-9244

Crème de Colorado features "Colorado Wild," a game section . . . because game and game birds are indigenous to our region and always a welcome treat; a Mexican section . . . because we owe a debt of gratitude to Southwest seasonings, style and influence in Colorado cooking; and a chocolate section . . . because we all have our weaknesses. Excellent for entertaining.

$19.95 Retail price
 $.60 Tax for Colorado residents
 $4.95 Postage and handling; $2.00 for each additional book
Make check payable to The Junior League of Denver, Inc.
ISBN 0-9603946-2-1

DISTINCTLY DELICIOUS

by David J. Richardson & Javana M. Richardson
StarsEnd Creations
8547 E. Arapahoe Road #J224   info@Starsend.com
Greenwood Village, CO 80112   303-694-1664/Fax 303-694-4098

A collection of more than 260 recipes gathered from the
kitchens of the most distinctive Bed and Breakfast Inns in
Colorado. The book includes information about the inns, as
well as coupons good for discounts on stays at any of the participating inns. Reissued as *Best of the Historic West.*

$21.95 Retail price
  $.68 Tax for Colorado residents
 $3.50 Postage and handling
Make check payable to StarsEnd Creations
ISBN 1-889120-14-6

Keefe Memorial Hospital

DOC'S DELIGHTS

Keefe Memorial Hospital
P. O. Box 578
Cheyenne Wells, CO 80810   719-767-5661

If you love old fashioned country cooking, this is the book
for you! Our cookbook contains many of Dr. Keefe's special
recipes as well as tried and true selections from members of
our staff, many of whom come from three and four generation farm/ranch families. A must for recipe collectors.

$ 10.00   Retail price
$ .30   Tax for Colorado residents
$ 5.00   Postage and handling
Make check payable to Keefe Memorial Hospital

THE DURANGO COOKBOOK

by Jan Fleming
P. O. Box 325
Durango, CO 81302   970-247-3438

Recipes collected from Durango residents. Recipes include
appetizers, soups, salads, vegetables, main dishes and desserts. Also features unique game recipes and southwestern
dishes. Original water color cover. Spiral bound, 60 pages.

$ 14.95   Retail price
$ 1.00   Tax for Colorado residents
$ 3.50   Postage and handling
Make check payable to Jan Fleming

EASY RECIPES FOR 1, 2 OR A FEW

Anna Aughenbaugh
Starlite Publications
2209 Purdue Road
Fort Collins, CO 80525   970-493-7969

The reduced fat and sugar content make this book fit today's
busy, health-conscious lifestyle. Novice cooks and empty
nesters will enjoy the wide variety of recipes. Easy-to-follow
instructions and nutritional analysis. 232 pages, 266 recipes,
plus pages of menus and substitutions lists.

$12.95 Retail price
  $.39 Tax for Colorado residents
 $2.00 Postage and handling
Make check payable to Starlite Publications
ISBN 0-9625869-1-9

EATING UP THE SANTA FE TRAIL

Sam'l P. Arnold
University Press of Colorado
P. O. Box 849
Niwot, CO 80544   800-268-6044

Written by Sam Arnold, famous chef and owner of the popular Fort Restaurant in Morrison, *Eating Up the Santa Fe Trail* works for today's kitchens as well as for the buckskinner's campfire. This unique blend of culinary and western history has the delicacies and oddities of the Old West and is a must for the professional chef, buckskinner, historian, and gastronome.

$ 14.95   Retail price
$ 3.00   Postage and handling
Make check payable to The University Press of Colorado
ISBN 0-87081-187-8

FAT MAMA'S DELI

Helen Cadaro Rayers
Charlene Ann Rayers
771 Santa Fe Drive, Suite 200
Denver, CO 80204   303-454-8077

Helen, a New Orleans native, shares her personal collection of recipes in this cookbook organized in her memory. A percentage of the proceeds will be given to the American Cancer Society in her honor. Her love for food and cooking is evident throughout this 126-page collection of recipes that is sure to please!

$15.00   Retail price
  $.45   Tax for Colorado residents
 $3.00   Postage and handling
Make check payable to Charlene Rayers

THE FLAVOR OF COLORADO

Colorado State Grange
A Appletree Publication
404 South 3rd Avenue
Superior, CO 80027

Colorado State Grange is an agricultural fraternity organized in 1874, nationally known as the oldest farm organization—130 years. Grange is a place for families, massive community service work of rural and urban life. Grange potluck meals have a widely known reputation. Spiral bound, 6 x 9. 300 recipes. 190 pages.

$ 11.95   Retail price
$ 5.00   Postage and handling
Make check payable to A Appletree Publication
ISBN 0-87197-336-7

4-H FAMILY COOKBOOK

Morgan County Extension Center
P. O. Box 517
Fort Morgan, CO 80701   970-867-2493/Fax 970-867-8607

This book was put together by our county 4-H members. The cookbook has 135 pages and 297 delicious recipes. It has a daily guide for food choices, altitude adjustments, etc., plus pictures and poems from 4-H members and leaders. It's just good home cooking.

$ 6.00   Retail price
$ .39   Tax for Colorado residents
$ 4.00   Postage and handling
Make check payable to Morgan County Extension Fund

FOUR SQUARE MEALS A DAY

Women's Ministries
1807 S. 11th Street
Lamar, CO 81052   719-336-9579

This 110-page cookbook is dedicated to all cooks. In our homes today, as always, life is centered around the kitchen. It is with this thought in mind that these recipes have been compiled. Some of the recipes are treasured family keep-sakes and some are new; however, they all reflect the love of good cooking!

$ 10.00   Retail price
$ 2.95   Postage and handling
Make check payable to Women's Ministries

FROM AN ADOBE OVEN . . .
TO A MICROWAVE RANGE

Junior League of Pueblo
501 N. Main Suite 310
Pueblo, CO 81003   719-542-0491

A Pueblo favorite for many years, *From an Adobe Oven* was first published in 1972. This cookbook combines Southwest flavor with traditional favorites. The cookbook has over 600 recipes from appetizers to desserts. 414 pages.

$10.75 Retail price
  $.48 Tax for Colorado residents
$3.95 Postage and handling
Make check payable to Junior League of Pueblo

GOOD MORNING, GOLDIE!

Goldie Veitch
P. O. Box 2135
Meeker, CO 81641   970-878-0733

Good Morning, Goldie! is a collection of breakfast recipes that she developed for use at the lodge where she is chef for the morning and noon meals. It was important to her to present beautiful tasty dishes using fresh ingredients and flair. At the same time she wanted recipes that could be fixed at home for family and friends.

$12.00 Retail price
  $.27 Tax for Colorado residents
$3.00 Postage and handling
Make check payable to Good Morning, Goldie!

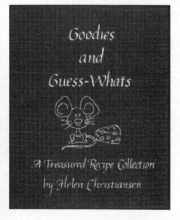

GOODIES AND GUESS-WHATS

Helen Christiansen
46881 State Hwy 116
Walsh, CO 81090   719-498-4231

Goodies and Guess-Whats is a delightful collection of 519 recipes printed on 228 pages in a 3-ring plastic binder. Additional recipes can be easily added. The author is a retired home econ-omist and teacher. The recipes are quite simple and many were used in the classroom.

$11.50 Retail price
  $1.50 Postage and handling
Make check payable to Helen Christiansen
ISBN 0-9621419-2-5

GRADE A RECIPES

Idalia Playground and Park Committee
P. O. Box 21
Idalia, CO 80735   970-354-7500/Fax 970-354-757.

This cookbook was put together by a group of concerned
parents trying to raise money for a new playground and
park to better their community. The cookbook was the firs
big fund raiser we did. The whole community gave us thei
treasured recipes for the cookbook. The cookbook has 34
pages and 897 recipes.

$ 12.00   Retail price
$ 3.00   Postage and handling
Make check payable to Idalia Visions/Playground and Park

GREAT AMERICAN BEER COOKBOOK

by Candy Schermerhorn
Brewers Publications
736 Pearl Street
Boulder, CO 80302   303-447-081

All 217 recipes in this book use beer to enhance flavor poten
tial, giving food an added culinary dimension.   Candy
Schermerhorn features mouth-watering recipes that are chi
(Lobster and Brie Soup with Weisshier), exotic (Apple and
Ham Pie with Curry Sauce using Indiab pale ale), down-home
(Potent Portered Beef Ribs), and sinful (Chocolate Stout Cake)

$24.95 Retail price
 $1.85 Tax Boulder residents
 $1.04 Tax Colorado residents
 $3.00 Postage and handling
Make check payable to Brewers Publications
ISBN 0-937381-38-1

GREAT PLAINS COOKING

P.E.O. Chapter AA, c/o Linda Carson
857 Lincoln Street
Wray, CO 80758   970-332-5957 Fax 970-332-483.

Nested in the valley of the Northfork of the Republican Rive
and surrounded by bluffs and sandhills lies the small community of Wray. The tranquil setting provides the perfect back
drop for Chapter AA's *Great Plains Cooking*. We hope you wil
enjoy a bit of the flavor from our little corner of the West. 39(
pages. Over 900 recipes.

$12.00 Retail price
 $2.00 Postage and handling
Make check payable to P.E.O. Chapter AA

HAUTE OFF THE PRESS

Pat Miller and Bob Starekow
TDF Publishing
P. O. Box 1609   E-mail rbs414@colorado.ne
Dillon, CO 80435   970/262-8462/Fax 970/468-4778

A collection from chefs of 34 fine restaurants in Colorado
and beyond; 100 recipes in English and Spanish, including
a glossary in Spanish and English. Contributing chefs such
as Zerla Martinez (NYC), Stephen Pyles "Star Canyon"
(Dallas), Jimmy Schmidt (Detroit) and many more. Al
copies are autographed.

$ 16.95   Retail price   Visa, MC accepted
$ 1.25   Tax for Colorado residents
$ 3.00   Postage and handling
Make check payable to *Haute Off the Press* (Special discount for Quail Ridge
Press customers— 45% off retail price); send check for $11.00.
ISBN 0-918481-11-2

HOME COOKIN'

NPS Denver Employees' Association
12795 W. Alameda Parkway
Denver, CO 80225-0287   303-969-2370

Home Cookin' is filled with 500 of our best family-tested recipes. These are home cooked recipes from the folks that work for the National Park Service in Denver. We offer many exciting and diverse recipes that were created or collected from our folks' travels throughout different cultural areas.

$ 8.00   Retail price
$ 1.75   Postage and handling
Make check payable to NPS Denver Employees' Assn.

HOME COOKIN' CREATIONS

First Baptist Church
1250 Pioneer Road
Delta, CO 81416   970-874-3847

Members and friends of First Baptist Church have collected their favorite recipes. Included are 126 pages of all those wonderful recipes you get at Pot Luck Suppers, Showers, Barbecues and other bring-a-dish activities the church has.

$ 8.00   Retail price
$ 2.00   Postage and handling
Make check payable to First Baptist Church

HOW TO FEED A VEGETARIAN

by Suzanne D'Avalon
Placidly Amid the Noise
P. O. Box 16914
Colorado Springs, CO 80935-6914   719-550-0562

At last, an easy-to-use vegetarian cookbook written for people who aren't! (Or aren't yet . . . .) Non-vegetarians and vegetarian wannabe's will learn about buying weird food, substituting for animal products, and even how to be friends with tofu. All ingredients are available in supermarkets. Proven recipes have even the meat-eaters asking for seconds.

$ 12.95   Retail price
$ .52   Tax for Colorado residents
$ 1.95   Postage and handling
Make check payable to Placidly Amid the Noise
ISBN 0-9650941-0-3

ITALIAN DISHES ET CETERA

by Shirley Michaels
2560 Begonia Court
Loveland, CO 80537   970-203-1870

Italian Dishes et cetera is a compilation of favorite family recipes, currently being mastered by the fifth generation of Italian-American children and grandchildren. The book also contains some amusing little tales to be enjoyed with a glass of chianti and some homemade biscotti.

$ 6.50   Retail price
$ 2.50   Postage and handling
Make check payable to Shirley Michaels

KITCHEN KEEPSAKES

Bonnie Welch and Deanna White
39265 Kiowa-Bennett Road
Kiowa, CO 80117   303-688-6538

Charming country illustrations catch the eye . . . delicious
down-home, tested recipes tempt the palate! Now in its 9th
printing, *Kitchen Keepsakes* offers "homey and highly usable"
recipes for family and guests. Concise directions, menu sug-
gestions, and helpful hints round out this cookbook, making it
truly a keepsake for every kitchen. 256 pages. Comb binding.
Hardback.

$14.95 Retail price
 $2.00 Postage and handling
Make check payable to *Kitchen Keepsakes*
ISBN 0-9612258-0-7

KITCHEN KEEPSAKES BY REQUEST

Bonnie Welch and Deanna White
39265 Kiowa-Bennett Road
Kiowa, CO 80117   303-688-6538

After sales of *Kitchen Keepsakes* and *More Kitchen Keepsakes*
topped 100,000, requests for a third cookbook prompted the
authors to request the favorite recipes of their readers. The
result . . . *Kitchen Keepsakes by Request*, an all-new collection of
over 450 kitchen-tested, home-style recipes from America's
best home cooks! 256 pages. Comb binding. Hard back.

$14.95 Retail price
 $2.00 Postage and handling
Make checks payable to *Kitchen Keepsakes*
ISBN 0-9612258-2-3

LIGHTER TASTES OF ASPEN

Jill Sheeley
P. O. Box 845
Aspen, CO 81612   970-925-6025

This book features best recipes from Aspen and Snowmass'
best restaurants. Each restaurant has a description proceed-
ing the recipes. Includes hints on how to cut the fat and
how to convert recipes to low altitudes.

$ 19.95   Retail price
$ 1.64   Tax for Colorado residents
$ 3.00   Postage and handling
Make check payable to Jill Sheeley
ISBN 0-9609108-2-4

LOWFAT, HOMESTYLE COOKBOOK

by Christina Korenkiewicz
Brook Forest Publishing
P. O. Box 1224
Conifer, CO 80433-1224

Over 100 great-tasting homestyle recipes with less fat and
calories! Most of the recipes are easy to prepare, and the
book has a lay-flat binding. Fat grams and calories are
computed for each recipe. Enjoy pizza, pot roast, lasagna,
potato salad, brownies, peach cobbler, and many more wonderful homestyle favorites.

$ 10.00   Retail price (postage included)
$ .48   Tax for Colorado residents
Make check payable to Brook Forest Publishing
ISBN 0-9643017-0-9

MORE GOODIES & GUESS-WHATS

by Helen Christiansen
46881 State Hwy 116
Walsh, CO 81090   719-498-4231

This 192-page, easy-to-cook-from book is a continuation of
my first book, *Goodies & Guess-Whats.* The 315 recipes are
in a convenient 3-ring plastic binder. The ingredients for
most recipes are found in most kitchens so one doesn't need
to go shopping to use the recipes.

$ 11.50   Retail price
$ 1.50   Postage and handling
Make check payable to Helen Christiansen
ISBN 0-9621419-1-7

MORE KITCHEN KEEPSAKES

Bonnie Welch and Deanna White
39265 Kiowa-Bennett Road
Kiowa, CO 80117   303-688-6538

Featuring the same down-home goodness, but a new down-
home look, *More Kitchen Keepsakes* is a continuation of the
highly successful *Kitchen Keepsakes* cookbook. This collection
of 500 easy-to-prepare recipes prove cooking doesn't have to
be complicated to be delicious. Hats off to home cooking! It is
still the best! 282 pages. Comb binding. Hard back

$14.95 Retail price
 $2.00 Postage and handling
Make check payable to Kitchen Keepsakes
ISBN 0-9612258-1-5

MORE THAN SOUP BEAN COOKBOOK

Anna Aughenbaugh
2209 Purdue Road
Fort Collins, CO 80525   970-493-7969

Great, tasty ways to get more fiber and protein into your diet.
Each recipe includes a nutritional analysis. 125 pages, 110
recipes showcasing beans in easy-to-do desserts, salads, main
dishes; plus cooking tips.

$7.95 Retail price
 $.24 Tax for Colorado residents
$2.00 Postage and handling
Make check payable to Starlite Publications
ISBN 0-9625869-2-7

MOUNTAIN COOKING AND ADVENTURE

Montrose Chamber of Commerce
Montrose, CO

The Montrose County Chamber of Commerce and its members are proud of our area, where fertile farmlands grow sweet
fruits and vegetables, where our ranches produce fine meat
and dairy products, and where our mountains, lakes, rivers
and streams offer fish and game that make for delicious eating.
These recipes attest deliciously to this great bounty. This book
is currently out of print.

MYSTIC MOUNTAIN MEMORIES

Josie & Jerry Minerich/C & G Publishing, Inc.
Greeley, CO

Jerry encouraged his mother Josie, to write her recipes into this cookbook, then he added his own special recipes. Jerry is a baker—and creates other recipes as well. Some of his most famous recipes are featured in restaurants around Denver. Great cookbook for a beginning cook, cookbook collector, or reader. This book is currently out of print.

NOTHIN' BUT MUFFINS

Cyndi Duncan & Georgie Patrick/C & G Publishing, Inc.
P. O. Box 5199   www.cgpub.com
Greeley, CO 80634   970-356-9622 or 800-925-3177

This cookbook is used by bed and breakfast hosts around the United States. Easy-to-use recipes of whole grain, vegetable, fruit, and other delectable choices. It is a recipient of the prestigious Benjamin Franklin Award for design. $5\frac{1}{2}$ x $8\frac{1}{2}$, wire-o, special wrap-around cover, 89 great muffin recipes.

$12.95 Retail price
  $.39 Tax for Colorado residents
 $2.00 Postage and handling
Make check payable to C & G Publishing, Inc.
ISBN 0-9626335-1-8

101 WAYS TO MAKE RAMEN NOODLES

Toni Patrick/C & G Publishing, Inc.
P. O. Box 5199   www.cgpub.com
Greeley, CO 80634   970-356-9622 or 800-925-3177

Toni Patrick was a college student at the time of writing this creative little cookbook. The recipes are good for breakfast, lunch, dinner and even desserts. It's a great gift for the college student, and is popular with backpackers, RVers and anyone who loves Ramen Noodles. $5\frac{1}{2}$ x 7, wire-o bound.

 $9.95 Retail price
  $.30 Tax for Colorado residents
 $2.00 Postage and handling
Make check payable to C & G Publishing, Inc.
ISBN 0-9626335-2-6

PALATES

Museum Shop
Colorado Springs Fine Arts Center
30 West Dale Street
Colorado Springs, CO 80903

A delectable collection of 300 recipes showcasing the culinary creativity of Colorado Springs' chefs and talented cooks. From regional specialties to party dishes, these easy to prepare recipes will become favorites. Enhanced with photographs of the Fine Arts Center's collection, this beautiful hardcover book will delight food and art lovers.

$15.95 Retail price
 $1.11 Tax for Colorado residents
 $3.00 Postage and handling
Make check payable to MVA

PURE GOLD—COLORADO TREASURES

Winters Publishing
P. O. Box 501
Greensburg, IN 47240

tmwinters@juno.com
800-457-3230

This 96-page cookbook/directory features over 100 delicious time-tested recipes from 54 of Colorado's finest B&B inns. Everything from Apple Pan Dowdy to Spanish Corn Quiche. Informative travel guide includes listing and line drawings for over 50 B&B inns throughout the state.

$9.95 Retail price
$2.00 Postage and handling
Make check payable to Winters Publishing
ISBN 0-9625329-3-2

QUICK CROCKERY COOKING

Cyndi Duncan and Georgie Patrick/C & G Publishing, Inc.
P. O. Box 5199
Greeley, CO 80634

www.cgpub.com
970-356-9622 or 800-925-3177

One hundred-fifty easy to use recipes designed for busy people. No special shopping for ingredients, quick preparation—end results delicious dishes, ready to supplement with complimentary side dish. Recipes from drinks, appetizers, soups, main dishes and side dishes. 7½ x 7, perfect bound. 168 pages.

$14.95 Retail price
$.45 Tax for Colorado residents
$2.00 Postage and handling
Make check payable to C & G Publishing, Inc.
ISBN 0-9626335-5-0

RASPBERRY STORY

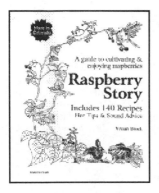

by Vivian Brock
1000 E Stanford Avenue
Englewood, CO 80110

303-789-2116

A book for every raspberry lover. Over 140 kitchen-tested raspberry recipes (all using fat-reduced cooking techniques) will tempt the palate. PLUS the raspberry's historical significance, herbal and homeopathic characteristics, and important information on the ancient and modern medicinal properties of raspberries.

$ 10.95 Retail price
$ .81 Tax for Colorado residents
$ 2.75 Postage and handling
Make check payable to Vivian Brock. Visa and MasterCard accepted
ISBN 0-9657668-4-5

RECIPES FROM OUR HOUSE

Assistance League of Denver
Denver, CO

Recipes From Our House is a compilation of recipes submitted by over 300 members of the Assistance League of Denver, a philanthropic organization addressing issues and needs within the community. The 6 x 9-inch, spiral-bound, paperback book features over 500 recipes using fresh ingredients in easy, yet sophisticated combinations. This book is currently out of print.

SHALOM ON THE RANGE

Friends of Shalom Park
14800 East Bellview Drive
Aurora, CO 80015-2258   303-680-5000

Shalom on the Range: A Roundup of Recipes and Jewish Traditions from Colorado Kitchens is a collection of contemporary, traditional and creative recipes with a Colorado attitude, all suitable for preparation in a kosher home. Short anecdotes convey the warmth of our Jewish culture and the importance of family, tradition and food. Over 359 double kitchen-tested recipes in 298 pages.

$24.95 Retail price
 $1.60 Tax for Colorado residents
 $5.50 Postage and handling
Make check payable to Shalom Park
ISBN 0-9656849-0-3

SHARING OUR BEST

St. Mary Magdalene Episcopal Church
c/o Pam Spinelli
4775 Cambridge Street
Boulder, CO 80301   303-530-1421

Sharing Our Best contains 187 recipes from members of the church. They include East Indian, diabetic, gourmet and many of those delicious recipes from covered-dish dinners! The proceeds go toward outreach projects in our community.

$ 7.00   Retail price
$ .28   Tax for Colorado residents
$ 1.50   Postage and handling
Make check payable to Episcopal Churchwomen

SHARING OUR BEST:
Muleshoe Ranch Cookbook

La Vaughn Linnens
15504 Road 32
Mancos, CO 81328

John and Mary Roscoe headed west in 1861 and finally settled in Montezuma County. They would be astonished to learn that six generations have stayed on this ranch, but not surprised at their interest in food. These 200 favorite recipes attest to the family's continual love and sharing of good food.

$ 10.00   Retail price
$ 2.50   Postage and handling
Make check payable to LaVaughn Linnens

SIMPLY COLORADO

Colorado Dietetic Association
4945 Meade Street
Denver, CO 80221-1031   720-855-8652

Simply Colorado contains Colorado cuisine which is not only wholesome and nutritious but flavorful and easy to prepare. Each recipe is designed to fit into a healthful eating style. While preserving flavor and convenience, these recipes have been adapted to be lower in fat, cholesterol and sodium, and higher in fiber than traditional dishes.

$14.95 Retail price
 $.57 Tax for Colorado residents
$3.00 Postage and handling
Make check payable to Simply Colorado, Inc.
ISBN 0-9626337-1-2

SOUTHWEST FOODS ET CETERA

by Shirley Michaels
2560 Begonia Court
Loveland, CO 80537　　　　　　　　　　970-203-1870

Inspired by many delightful visits to the Taos/Santa Fe area, *Southwest Foods et cetera* contains recipes for 50 basic dishes of the Southwest. The book also contains drawings of many traditional designs found in the pottery, weavings, and paintings of the area, along with explanations of their symbolism.

$ 6.50　Retail price
$ 2.50　Postage and handling
Make check payable to Shirley Michaels

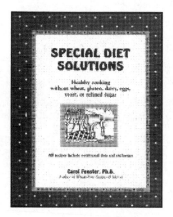

SPECIAL DIET SOLUTIONS

by Carol Fenster, Ph.D./Savory Palate, Inc.
8174 S. Holly #404　　　　　　E-Mail: savorypala@aol.com
Littleton, CO 80122-4004　　　　800-741-5418/Fax 303-741-0339

A cookbook for those who must avoid wheat, gluten, dairy, eggs, yeast, or refined sugar. Ideal for those with Celiac disease, food allergies or intolerances, diabetes, or other special diet needs. Includes nutrient data, diabetic food exchanges for each recipe. 150 recipes, 200 pages.

$15.95　Retail price　　Discover, Visa, MC accepted
　$.61　Tax for Colorado residents
$3.50　Postage and handling
Make check payable to Savory Palate, Inc.
ISBN 1-889374-00-8

STEAMBOAT ENTERTAINS COOKBOOK

2155 Resort Drive, Suite 207
Steamboat Springs, CO 80487　　　　　　970-879-7115

With over 750 winning recipes from "Ski Town, USA," *Steamboat Entertains* benefits the Steamboat Springs Winter Sports Club which offers competitive ski training programs to local youth and future Olympians. The book offers not only delicious and imaginative recipes, but also tidbits of local history and whimsical artwork.

$19.95　Retail price
　$.60　Tax for Colorado residents
$5.95　Postage and handling
Make check payable to *Steamboat Entertains Cookbook*
ISBN 0-9631010-2-1

TAKING CULINARY LIBERTIES

Liberty High School Library/Media Center
8720 Scarborough Drive　　　　　E-mail: lalbara@d20.co.edu
Colorado Springs, CO 80920　　　719-282-1000x262/Fax 719-282-1006

Help Liberty High School's Library/Media Center grow in resources by purchasing the wonderful, incredible, *Taking Culinary Liberties* cookbook. The cookbook contains over 1,000 recipes submitted by staff, students and community members with many casseroles for quick family dinners and scrumptious desserts to take to potluck dinners.

$10.00　Retail price
　$.64　Tax for Colorado residents
$2.00　Postage and handling
Make check payable to Liberty High School

WEST OF THE ROCKIES

Junior Service League of Grand Junction
P. O. Box 3221
Grand Junction, CO 81502   970-243-7790

West of the Rockies offers 360 pages of tested recipes from campfire to candlelight! Experience the flavor of the West in 439 recipes from "Clean Livin" (light and healthy recipes), "On the Wild Side" (Colorado game recipes), "Rio Grandé" (sizzlin' southwestern fare), and "Campfire Café" (western grub with an outdoor flair).

$17.95 Retail price
 $.53 Tax for Colorado residents
 $3.95 Postage and handling
Make check payable to West of the Rockies
ISBN 0-9641314-0-4

WHAT'S COOKIN' IN MELON COUNTRY

Rocky Ford Chamber of Commerce
105 North Main
Rocky Ford, CO 81067   719-254-7483

Rocky Ford is located on US Highway 50 in the Arkansas Valley near the Mountain Branch of the Santa Fe Trail. Because of its rich crops, Rocky Ford is known as the "Melon Capitol of the World." Utilizing the skills of the area's many talented cooks, this book is comprised of approximately 700 recipes in 232 pages.

$ 15.95   Retail price
$ 3.00   Postage and handling
Make check payable to Rocky Ford Chamber of Commerce

WHEAT-FREE RECIPES & MENUS

by Carol Fenster, Ph.D.
Savory Palate, Inc.
8174 S Holly #404   E-Mail: savorypala@aol.com
Littleton, CO 80122-4004   800-741-5418/Fax 303-741-0339

A cookbook for those who must avoid wheat, gluten, and dairy. Ideal for those with Celiac disease, food allergies or intolerances, or other special diet needs. Each recipe has nutrient data. 275 recipes, 300 pages.

$19.99 Retail price   (Discover, Visa, MC accepted)
 $.76 Tax for Colorado residents
 $3.50 Postage and handling
Make check payable to Savory Palate, Inc.
ISBN 1-889374-05-9

Index

The Colorado setting sun casts long shadows on one of its many beautiful slopes.

INDEX

Special Discount Offers!

The Best Club *Enjoy the grand flavors of America all at once!*

- You receive the entire 35-volume BEST OF THE BEST STATE COOKBOOK SERIES.
- The cost is only $445.00—a 25% discount off the retail price of $593.25.
- The UPS shipping cost is only $10.00 for addresses anywhere in the United States.
- You receive advance notice of each new edition to the series and have the first opportunity to purchase copies at a 25% discount with no obligation.

The Best of the Month Club
Experience the taste of our nation, one state at a time!

- You receive a different BEST cookbook each month or, if you prefer, every other month.
- You enjoy a 20% discount off the price of each book ($16.95 discounted to $13.56).
- You automatically become a member of the BEST CLUB once you receive all available volumes, which entitles you to a 25% discount on future volumes.
- No minimum purchase required; cancel at anytime.
- Members say: "My BEST books are my very favorite cookbooks."
  "I usually buy more than one copy—they have a way of disappearing."
  "Most of my other cookbooks are on the shelf—my BEST books stay on the kitchen counter."

Join today! 1-800-343-1583

Speak directly to one of our friendly customer service representatives, or visit our website at **www.quailridge.com** to order online.

Recipe Hall of Fame Collection

The extensive recipe database of Quail Ridge Press' acclaimed BEST OF THE BEST STATE COOKBOOK SERIES is the inspiration behind the RECIPE HALL OF FAME COLLECTION. These Hall-of-Fame recipes have achieved extra distinction for consistently producing superb dishes. *The Recipe Hall of Fame Cookbook* features over 400 choice dishes for a variety of meals. The *Recipe Hall of Fame Dessert Cookbook* consists entirely of extraordinary desserts. The *Recipe Hall of Fame Quick & Easy Cookbook* contains over 500 recipes that require minimum effort but produce maximum enjoyment. Appetizers to desserts, quick dishes to masterpiece presentations, the RECIPE HALL OF FAME COLLECTION has it all.

All books: Paperbound • 7x10 • Illustrations • Index
The Recipe Hall of Fame Cookbook • 304 pages • $19.95
Recipe Hall of Fame Dessert Cookbook • 240 pages • $16.95
Recipe Hall of Fame Quick & Easy Cookbook • 304 pages • $19.95

NOTE: All three HALL OF FAME cookbooks can be ordered as a set for $39.90 (plus $4.00 shipping), a 30% discount off the total list price of $56.85. Over 1,300 HALL OF FAME recipes for about 3¢ each—an incredible value!

Preserving America's Food Heritage

Best of the Best State Cookbook Series

Best of the Best from
ALABAMA
288 pages, $16.95

Best of the Best from
ARIZONA
288 pages, $16.95

Best of the Best from
ARKANSAS
288 pages, $16.95

Best of the Best from
CALIFORNIA
384 pages, $16.95

Best of the Best from
COLORADO
288 pages, $16.95

Best of the Best from
FLORIDA
288 pages, $16.95

Best of the Best from
GEORGIA
336 pages, $16.95

Best of the Best from the
GREAT PLAINS
288 pages, $16.95

Best of the Best from
ILLINOIS
288 pages, $16.95

Best of the Best from
INDIANA
288 pages, $16.95

Best of the Best from
IOWA
288 pages, $16.95

Best of the Best from
KENTUCKY
288 pages, $16.95

Best of the Best from
LOUISIANA
288 pages, $16.95

Best of the Best from
LOUISIANA II
288 pages, $16.95

Best of the Best from
MICHIGAN
288 pages, $16.95

Best of the Best from the
MID-ATLANTIC
288 pages, $16.95

Best of the Best from
MINNESOTA
288 pages, $16.95

Best of the Best from
MISSISSIPPI
288 pages, $16.95

Best of the Best from
MISSOURI
304 pages, $16.95

Best of the Best from
NEW ENGLAND
368 pages, $16.95

Best of the Best from
NEW MEXICO
288 pages, $16.95

Best of the Best from
NEW YORK
288 pages, $16.95

Best of the Best from
NO. CAROLINA
288 pages, $16.95

Best of the Best from
OHIO
352 pages, $16.95

Best of the Best from
OKLAHOMA
288 pages, $16.95

Best of the Best from
OREGON
288 pages, $16.95

Best of the Best from
PENNSYLVANIA
320 pages, $16.95

Best of the Best from
SO. CAROLINA
288 pages, $16.95

Best of the Best from
TENNESSEE
288 pages, $16.95

Best of the Best from
TEXAS
352 pages, $16.95

Best of the Best from
TEXAS II
352 pages, $16.95

Best of the Best from
VIRGINIA
320 pages, $16.95

Best of the Best from
WASHINGTON
288 pages, $16.95

Best of the Best from
WEST VIRGINIA
288 pages, $16.95

Best of the Best from
WISCONSIN
288 pages, $16.95

Cookbooks listed above have been completed as of December 31, 2002. All cookbooks are ringbound except California, which is paperbound.
Note: Great Plains consists of North Dakota, South Dakota, Nebraska, and Kansas; Mid-Atlantic includes Maryland, Delaware, New Jersey,
and Washington, D.C.; New England is comprised of Rhode Island, Connecticut, Massachusetts, Vermont, New Hampshire, and Maine.

Special discount offers available!
(See previous page for details.)

To order by credit card, call toll-free **1-800-343-1583** or visit our website at **www.quailridge.com**
to order online. Use the form below to send check or money order.

Ⓠ Order form

Use this form for sending check or money order to:
QUAIL RIDGE PRESS • P. O. Box 123 • Brandon, MS 39043

❏ Check enclosed

Charge to: ❏ Visa ❏ MC ❏ AmEx ❏ Disc

Card #_____

Expiration Date _____

Signature _____

Name _____

Address _____

City/State/Zip_____

Phone # _____

Email Address _____

Qty.	Title of Book (State) or Set	Total

Subtotal _____

7% Tax for MS residents _____

Postage ($4.00 any number of books) + 4.00

Total _____